THE HEAD'S HANDBOOK

A GUIDE FOR ASPIRING, NEW, AND EXPERIENCED HEADS OF SCHOOL

Gene Batiste and Jay Riven, Editors

The opinions expressed in this book are not necessarily those of the publisher, NAIS.

ISBN: 1-893021-89-0

Printed in the United States of America.

The National Association of Independent Schools represents approximately 1,643 independent private schools in the United States and other countries. All are accredited, non-discriminatory, nonprofit organizations governed by independent boards of trustees. NAIS's mission is to serve and strengthen member schools and associations by "articulating and promoting high standards of education quality and ethical behavior; to work to preserve their independence to serve the free society from which that independence derives; to advocate broad access for students by affirming the principles of diversity, choice, and opportunity." To find out more information, go to the NAIS website at *www.nais.org*. To receive a listing of NAIS books, call (800) 793-6701 or (240) 646-7052.

Editors: Susan Hunt, Nancy Raley
Designer: Fletcher Design, Inc./Washington, DC

FROM GENE BATISTE:

To four extraordinary independent school leaders — Reveta Bowers (The Center for Early Education, California), Liza Lee (Columbus School for Girls, Ohio), Doreen Oleson (St. Mark's School, California), and Marcia Prewitt Spiller (The Children's School, Georgia) — who exemplify the very best in doing well and doing important and necessary good as heads of independent schools.

FROM JAY RIVEN:

To Gordon Bondurant, my first head of school when I was a student at Montgomery Bell Academy in Nashville, Tennessee. He was my first professional role model and continues to inspire me even in his retirement.

and

To Mike Murphy, my first head of school who took a chance on hiring me (twice) at Pace Academy in Atlanta, Georgia. There is not a harder working, more ethical and empathetic head of school in the field of education.

CONTENTS

FOREWORD

JAY RIVEN AND GENE BATISTE's *The Head's Handbook: A Guide for Aspiring, New, and Experienced Heads of School* provides, at long last, a how-to guide for the various stages of school leadership: preparing for a headship, executing it, and leaving it. For all those contemplating becoming an independent school head, or in the job now, or considering retiring, or who have already left, this is a book that will be a rich and fulfilling read, each section a different "chapter" in the life of headship: examining the pathway to school leadership; reveling in the existential joys of being a head charged with "meaning-making" for a school; knowing when and how to leave the headship; and reflecting back on the life's work of being a school head. While the *Handbook* presents trends gleaned by NAIS research on school leadership, it largely informs by sharing the stories of the dozens of heads featured in the book, either as authors of chapters or providers of "perspectives" (in the book's plentiful sidebars).

Themes addressed in *The Head's Handbook*:

- One thing I had to learn that in a million years I never thought I'd need to know

- Some things I learned along the way
- The imminent retirement of Boomer heads presenting both a challenge and an opportunity for the industry
- Planning and preparing to interview for headships
- When to withdraw from a search, even when you are the leading contender
- Head and heart commitment to an enterprise that offers the opportunity to create meaning for yourself and others
- Knowing when to leave by being "the first to hear the footsteps"
- Retiring from headship: the "nowhere zone" between two "somewheres"
- Ten hats a school head wears
- The *Headmasters' Wives' Cookbook*: expectations of the head's family
- Leadership in crisis: dealing with the fear factor
- Messaging to parents from the very beginning
- The head as academic leader, "standing forward but stepping back"
- The change imperative: articulating the difference between "growth" and "change"
- What about the students? Sage advice on how to communicate to students, and to parents and boards about students
- The board of trustees: how to find your board chair's "favorite radio frequency"
- The head's executive assistant: meeting planner, traffic cop, weather forecaster, and more
- Entering a new school as head: "walking into the middle of a movie"

All these themes and more invite readers to reflect about the meaning and practice of headship. If you need a respite from the maelstrom of the daily work at school, take cover (literally) in this book. The blend of profoundly moving and inspirational stories with sensible and time-proven tips on leading schools is the perfect field guide for school leaders.

Patrick F. Bassett
NAIS President

PART I

WHY BE A HEAD OF SCHOOL?

NEW VISION FOR HEADSHIPS

Marcia Prewitt Spiller

IF YOU LOOK at independent schools today, you will not see a very diverse group of heads. While today's heads are a slightly more inclusive group than in the past, they are still not fully representative of multiple ethnicities and gender. The good news, however, is that they are all ages and have varied backgrounds and training. The word is out that being the head of an independent school is both challenging and rewarding work. The position is attracting a wide range of people who are intrigued by the possibilities of making positive changes in our schools.

For many, becoming a head of school has provided the unique opportunity to guide, manage, and direct the education of hundreds of students. It allows big thinkers and visionaries to plan strategically and to see their visions implemented.

When you ask people why they have become heads, they will tell you that they love the work; they have the ability to influence everything that happens at their schools; and the work is never boring — no two days are the same. Here is a sampling of what heads say about their work:

> "I love the people. Everyone at school is committed to the same goals."
>
> "This job gives me the joy of accomplishment. Every day I leave my school thinking how much we have accomplished in a day. It is an incredible feeling."
>
> "Before becoming a head, I did not know I could handle people relying on me as much as they do. While it can sometimes be a little overwhelming, I am pleased that I am learning to balance everyone's expectations in a way that has me feeling successful."
>
> "Learning to delegate and empower others has made me a better leader. I think that has been the key to my survival (and my enjoyment!).
>
> "While I sometimes feel I can never get it all done, I am never discouraged because I can see the progress we are making."
>
> "Everyone thinks I know all the answers and they give me the utmost respect as the leader of the school."
>
> "It is meaningful, moral, and honest work. I can actually see the results of hard work on a daily, weekly, and monthly basis."
>
> "There is nothing more exciting than seeing the student graduate whom everyone in the school had to support to make it happen."

But what exactly is the job of the head? When I recently asked one of my students what he thought my job was, he hesitated for a moment and then thoughtfully responded, "I think your job is to save children's lives!" Maybe this was a dramatic characterization of the job, but, as heads, we *do* get the opportunity to influence hundreds of people in so many ways. And it is not always about the students.

The head of today's independent school must lead in multiple ways. This person is not only the tone setter but also the person who establishes priorities as they relate to finance, physical plant, diversity, fund-raising, marketing, and future planning. In most cases, once a person becomes a head, that person gets to do things he or she has not done before. This can be particularly gratifying. Fairly early in my career, I discovered that I was actually a good fund-raiser. This was great for my professional growth and for my leadership role. I discovered that being good at fund-raising helped me make good choices of others to lead in that effort. Learning a new skill was exciting as I helped others develop the same skill.

Ensuring that teachers and staff have opportunities to develop and grow is a role of the head that has evolved through the years. While some time ago, it was perfectly acceptable for heads to be more like managers, we now know that good schools for students also have to be good schools for teachers and staff, requiring heads to be programmatic leaders for adults as well. Opportunities for professional development have to occupy a place of importance in the school's philosophy and the school's budget. Having teachers who are also learners is a trademark of today's excellent schools.

Heads get the opportunity to experience the success of their work. It is not just the students who are being educated but faculty, parents, and trustees as well. The head of school is positioned to facilitate communication and introduce new initiatives. It is probably for these reasons that headships are attracting more "nontraditional" people to the job — that is, people who have come from a career field outside the independent school sector, such as higher education, the military and military academies, or public schools, rather than following the traditional path from classroom teacher to assistant division head to division head or, more often, upper school head to assistant head to headship.

Today's heads are not all trained educators. Several have come to the field from professions such as law, business, psychology, and sociology. Comer Yates left his law practice 13 years ago to assume the leadership of the Atlanta Speech School (GA) and has never looked back. Always nursing a yearning for education while pursuing a career in law, Yates finally made the leap when he agreed to become a candidate during the school's search for new leadership. He says that he sees his headship role as one of supporting the staff and facilitating their success, not managing them.

Pinney Allen, also a trained lawyer, surprised many in the legal community when she left her firm to become head of the Atlanta Girls' School (GA). Believing that she had had a very full and rewarding life, she wanted to give back. She wanted to have a profession that gave her the ability to reach out and touch the future. Heading the Atlanta Girls' School gave her the opportunity to make a difference in girls' lives.

Another unusual trajectory to school leadership was that of Elizabeth Duffy. With an M.B.A., Duffy came to her position as head of the Lawrenceville School (NJ) after successfully leading several nonprofits and foundations. This was a historic appointment because the independent school world has

PERSPECTIVE

LEARNING ON THE JOB: THE BEST PREPARATION FOR AN ASPIRING HEAD OF SCHOOL

Clair Ward, Head of School
Valley School of Ligonier
LIGONIER, PENNSYLVANIA

Once I was appointed to my first headship, I found myself wondering whether I had collected enough graduate courses, attended enough professional workshops, and read enough authors to know the job. I had worked hard during the interview process to convince schools (and myself) that I was ready. Now I can tell you frankly that what I call on each and every day is my experience. The graduate degree gave me credibility, and the workshops were necessary to learn best practice. But my best education, my soundest preparation, came from the experiences that were carefully planned for me by gifted mentors.

The most obvious form of mentoring includes relationships with those who are already doing the job you aspire to do. In my case, I enjoyed the mentorship of two highly skilled female heads. These women saw the value of allowing me, as associate head of school, to practice being a leader without the ultimate accountability of leadership. They positioned me as a co-leader in the school community. I managed school initiatives both large and small; I communicated with all school constituent groups on important matters; I worked closely with faculty during evaluation and curriculum improvement. Mistakes were permitted, and my mentors provided support and encouragement, especially in those moments of disappointment. The leaders built confidence by trusting me to lead with them. In moments of failure, they restored my confidence by highlighting their own shortcomings in the work. In this apprenticeship, I evaluated my leadership priorities and passions and learned to root each action and decision in both my own ethics and the school's mission.

Both women felt that a crucial part of my training included working closely with, and therefore learning from, all parts of the school community. I can recall all the ways in which I learned from trustees, consultants, teachers, and children. The preparation that aspiring heads need most but rarely get is the opportunity to work closely with the board of trustees. Meetings of the full board are one thing, but the board work that gets done at the committee level is crucial to understanding how the school operates. I worked closely with trustees and committee chairs during financial planning, strategic planning, facilities management, fund-raising, and diversity not always acknowledged or accepted that schools did not have to be headed by trained educators. Because Duffy always valued education, she was instrumental in promoting educational partnerships in her nonprofit work with urban school districts as well as with colleges and universities. She believes that her management experience made her an attractive candidate for headship. Her transition from foundation work to Lawrenceville was seamless because she knew what it was like to be in charge. She is thoroughly enjoying the day-to-day connection with young people and the ability to make things happen in an educational setting as historic as Lawrenceville.

initiatives. In addition, I worked with the school's organizational psychologist on the human side of the institution. Learning to see the school community as a series of systems that shape human behavior helped develop me as a more compassionate leader — someone more likely to *understand* people than to personalize their actions.

I am passionate about K-8 schools, but my entire teaching career was in middle school. So I knew early on that I was going to have to spend time learning about early elementary children and early elementary curriculum if I wanted to be an educational leader for a school. This brings me to name my final mentors: teachers and children. I joined weekly planning/curriculum meetings with each grade-level team in the school. I listened and watched as visionary educators debated the nuances of instruction geared specifically toward the children in their rooms that year. I visited the classrooms and spoke with children about their work and learned the developmental milestones of each age. I participated in parent conferences and listened carefully as teachers delineated progress or gently alerted parents to a growing concern. I attended workshops with teachers as they mastered new techniques or debated the value of old ones. Spending time with teachers and children was the only way for me to balance my middle school experience with that of the youngest learners and their teachers in the K-8 setting.

I am fairly sure that if you were to poll all new heads, each might name something unique about the best path to headship in an independent school. To some extent, this is a very personal journey, a journey naturally tied to the leadership style that emerges from the core of who you are as a person. As for this new head in her third year, there was no better preparation than experience on the job. I will remain forever grateful for every head, trustee, teacher, and child who took my education seriously enough to spend that time with me. My advice to aspiring heads is to secure administrative positions under exceptional leaders who are excited by — not threatened by — your aspirations. Allow them to position you to build relationships with, and ultimately learn from, all members of the school community. Do not overlook any opportunity to practice both the vision and the humility you will need to be a successful head of school. ■

Both women and men are serving as heads today. However, the statistics of women in headships have remained stagnant, without significant growth in the numbers. Historically, women have made up a third of the heads of school and that remains true today. Public schools have made greater progress in demonstrating that women can successfully manage schools. Many female heads, much like their male counterparts, report high satisfaction with their jobs and express the joys associated with the responsibility. It should also be noted that today several schools are headed by males and females who self-identify as gay or lesbian — another example of the slow but steady evolution of inclusivity in the independent school world.

There is slight growth in encouraging younger educators to become heads of school. Some are single; others are married. Many have young children and are adapting their work schedules to be more family-friendly. Many heads no longer work the traditional 14-hour days. They have figured out how to be successful at their jobs while respecting and valuing their families at the same time. If heads live on campus or at least close to their schools, they often divide their days to manage their workday and enjoy some family time, even if there is an evening activity that requires their presence.

Wanda Holland Greene was pregnant with her second child when she was appointed head of The Hamlin School (CA). Already the mother of a three-year-old, she and her husband moved their young family from the Boston area to San Francisco to begin her tenure as head of school. Holland Greene believes that she does not have to sacrifice her life for her job nor does she have to sacrifice her job for her life. She says, "Being a head of school, a wife, and a mother means choosing a life characterized by imbalance and exhaustion. However, I wouldn't have it any other way. What a blessing it is to have work that is simultaneously tiring and deeply satisfying! What I strive for on a daily basis is joy and health. I ask myself, 'Am I happy and strong?' 'Is my family thriving?' Answering yes to those questions helps keep me on track." Holland Greene serves as a role model for the girls at her school and others as she demonstrates on a daily basis that women can be in charge, have families, be happy, and claim success.

As we move forward, heads will called upon to deal with the issues of

21st-century independent schools. Schools will be facing questions such as these:

- **How do we remain affordable?** Heads will have to lead the discussions and make the decisions about tuition increases, faculty compensation, and financial aid that will impact financial viability.
- **Is our mission sustainable?** Heads will have to ensure that their schools remain mission-driven and that mission statements guide the current and future direction of their schools.
- **Are we prepared for the diversity of the future?** If it is true that our country will become a majority of people of color, are independent schools ready for that change, and how will it be embraced? In what other ways will schools build and sustain themselves as intentionally diverse, inclusive, and equitable?
- **Is our curriculum preparing students for their next step?** Heads will have to lead the continued development and assessment of their school's curriculum to determine whether it is giving students the appropriate academic rigor and life skills preparation they will need to be the leaders of a very different future.
- **How do we include and acknowledge the influence of technology in our programs?** With the onset of social networking and the day-to-day dependence on technology, schools will have to manage and predict how to balance technology needs in an ever-changing environment.
- **How is our school supporting the environment?** With the increasing need to be green and earth-friendly, schools will have to determine whether this emphasis will change their mission, values, and operations.
- **How do we remain competitive?** Marketing and branding independent schools of the future will be crucial to an individual school's success as consumers continue to be more savvy.
- **Will enough parents continue to view independent education as a must?** As independent schools continue to compete with public and charter schools, not to mention the growing virtual schooling movement, will parents still commit to tuition payments?

Independent schools will have to continue to be bold and decisive in their decisions to assess their needs. In an increasing number of cases, bold decisions will include making nontraditional choices for leadership. In our 21st-century schools, there will be no cookie-cutter pattern of headships. It will be the leaders who can find solutions to the questions listed above who will not just survive but will thrive in our schools. Our schools will benefit from being led by a wide variety of leaders who bring new and different passions and skills to their headships. Creative thinkers and dreamers who dare will be the emerging leaders. The face of headship is slowly changing and will continue to change. That is a good thing.

PROFILE OF TODAY'S HEADS OF SCHOOL

Amada Torres

OVERWHELMINGLY, heads of independent schools are Caucasian, male, and in their 50s. Historically, there has been little change with respect to the typical profile of a head, but new demographic trends in school leadership and attitudes toward headship expressed by school administrators stress the need and importance of creating a strong pipeline in our schools.

A large part of the task ahead for NAIS and independent schools is to develop the skills of talented administrators, middle managers, and teachers, and to encourage them to pursue a career path toward headship. We need to empower a new cadre of leaders to move up the school leadership ladder and, at the same time, we need to create a more diverse pool of candidates that will include more women, people of color, and those from other underrepresented groups.

The next sections analyze different demographic information including gender, ethnicity, age, career path, and tenure, and provide some thoughts on what can be done to encourage more administrators and promising individuals to consider aspiring to independent school headship.

PROFILE OF INDEPENDENT SCHOOL HEADS

Gender

While women fill a majority of the administrative positions (62 percent[1]), women have historically made up only a third of heads. Figure 1 shows the gender gap since 1981. During the eighties, close to 70 percent of heads were male. The only exception was 1983, when 39 percent of the 846 schools reporting data for that year were headed by a woman.

Throughout the nineties, the gender gap decreased a little bit, and the percentage of female heads increased to around 40 percent. During that decade, the highest number of female heads was reached in 1999 with 458 school heads who were women, representing 45 percent of the total number of heads of the schools reporting data for that year.

Between 2000 and 2009, the percentage of men and women heads has remained mostly constant at around 65 percent and 35 percent, respectively, and slightly above the numbers recorded during the eighties. The results of a recent leadership study conducted by NAIS suggest that this differential could be exacerbated in the future given the fact that among current heads of school, more women (43 percent) are planning to retire or change jobs in the next five years than men (35 percent).[2]

In the same study, when heads were asked to rank different factors that could explain why there were fewer female heads, 28 percent of female heads indicated that having few women in assistant/associate/division head positions in independent schools was one of the top factors. Twenty percent of female heads also considered having few women in the pipeline in other positions a top factor. In addition, the perception that women were passed over in the hiring and promotion process in favor of candidates who fit the

Figure 1: Percentage of Male vs. Female Heads at NAIS Schools, 1981–2009

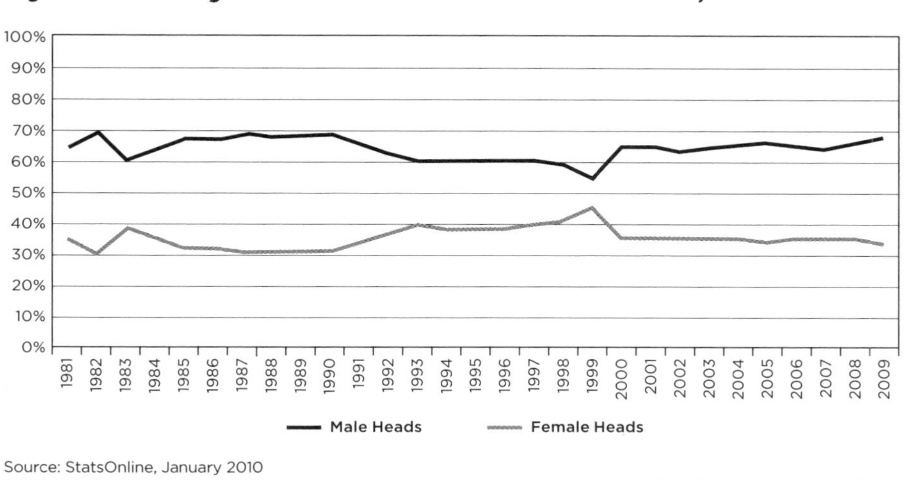

Source: StatsOnline, January 2010

traditional male profile was considered as somewhat of a factor by 37 percent of women heads.

Another study commissioned by NAIS[3] on school administrators who completed the NAIS Fellowship for Aspiring School Heads seems to corroborate these perceptions, but the study also found other factors rooted both in women's backgrounds and in their own decisions about the job search that shed some light on explaining why fewer women than men from the Fellowship have become heads of schools.

First of all, women in the Fellowship, in spite of their many years of experience, were less likely than men to have risen to the rank of assistant head — an important precursor in getting the job as a head in some school searches. Second, in comparison to the men, women seemed to have less confidence in their networking, interviewing skills, the reputation of schools where they have worked, and their ability to fit into a school's culture.

Women were also more likely than men to say that while becoming a head of school was a goal, their desired timeframe was within the next five years or longer than that. Thus, as a group, the women were less likely than men to pursue headships tenaciously, forgoing such efforts as registering with multiple search firms and applying for multiple positions.

Finally, women also expressed more doubts about undertaking the position as a head of school and sacrificing their home or personal life. Staying in their local area seemed to be an important factor because of children and working spouses.

Ethnicity/Race[4]

Figure 2 shows a clear and consistent increase in the number of heads of color at independent schools. However, they continue to represent the smallest number of the total. During the eighties, heads of color represented, on average, 0.8 percent of the total, with the peak year being 1988 when 13 heads were people of color or an ethnic minority (1.5 percent).

From 1990 to 1999, heads of color represented between one percent and 2.4 percent of the total (1.8 percent on average). The peak year was 1998 when 25 heads of all heads answering the diversity question identified themselves as people of color or from an ethnic minority (2.4 percent). Finally, from 2000 to 2009, there has been a consistent increase in the number of heads of color (with the exception of the year 2002). In particular, during 2008 and 2009, we saw a bit of a spike, with heads of color and those identifying themselves as an ethnic minority representing 4.3 percent and 4.8 percent, respectively, of the total pool (1,247 heads in 2008, 1,219 in 2009).

When these figures are analyzed by gender, it is evident that the gender gap has historically favored female heads of color/ethnic underrepresentation. As Figure 3 shows, between 1984 and 2001, the percentage of female heads of color and ethnic minorities has varied between 56 percent and 100

Figure 2: Percentage of Heads of Color/Ethnic Minorities at NAIS Schools, 1984–2009

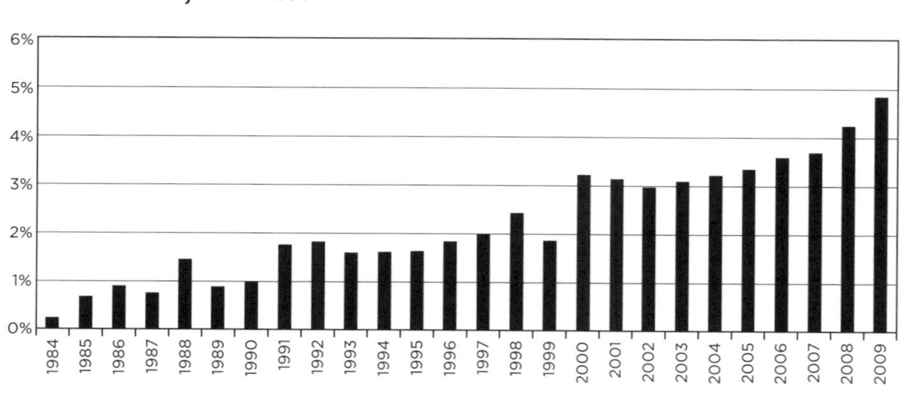

Source: StatsOnline, January 2010

Figure 3: Percentage of Male vs. Female Heads of Color/Ethnic Minorities at NAIS Schools, 1984–2009

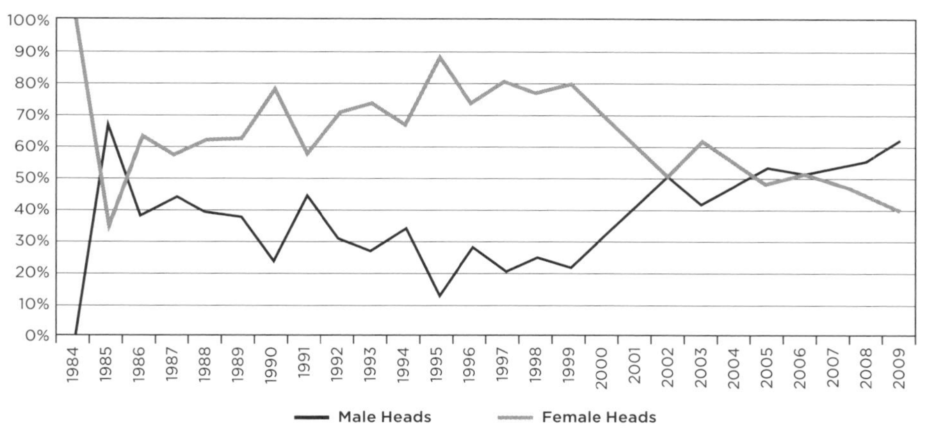

Source: StatsOnline, January 2010

percent (with the exception of 1985 when male heads of color and ethnic minorities outnumbered their female counterparts). But since 2005, male heads of color and ethnic minorities have represented 50 percent or more of all heads of color and those of ethnic underrepresentation. In 2009, 61 percent of heads of color were male or of an ethnic minority.

Figure 4 shows heads of color by ethnicity and race. Historically, the majority of heads of color have been African American. Since 2000, they

Figure 4: Heads of Color by Ethnicity/Race at NAIS Schools, 2009

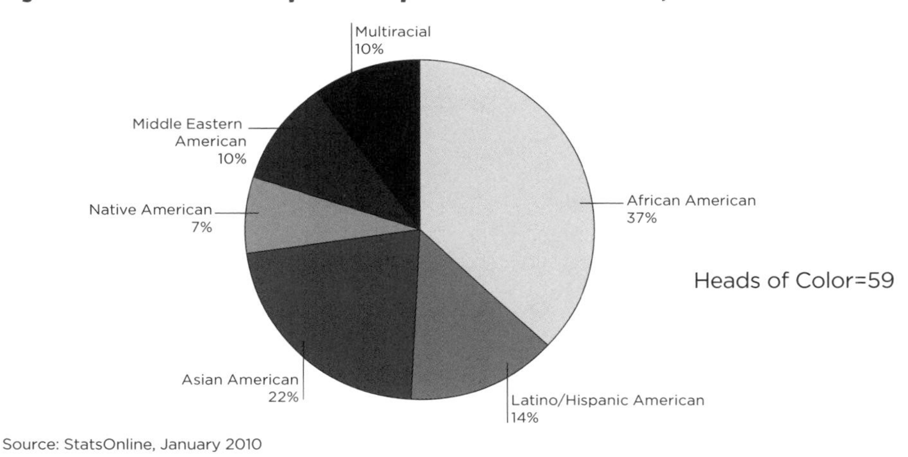

Source: StatsOnline, January 2010

have represented between 35 percent of the total (in 2001) and 56 percent in (2004). The 2009 numbers show that 37 percent of all heads of color/ ethnic minorities were African Americans, followed by Asian Americans at 22 percent.

From the perspective of many of the independent school heads and school administrators, the biggest contributing factor to the lack of people of color and those of ethnic minority groups as heads of school is that they have not come through the pipeline of independent schools, and especially that

PERSPECTIVE

SOME THINGS I LEARNED ALONG THE WAY

Bradford Gioia, Headmaster
Montgomery Bell Academy
NASHVILLE, TENNESSEE

Reflecting on some of the topics that I wish my predecessor had discussed with me before I took on the role of headmaster, I thought of the following suggestions:

Work closely with your board and alumni, always remembering that you work for the board and for the betterment of the school.

Keep a focus on both short- and long-distance goals.

Visit other schools to gain new perspectives, both daily and in the long-term.

Enjoy the students. They will remind you why you spend your time leading a school.

Develop genuine friendships with colleagues at other schools so that you can talk openly and honestly about your challenges.

Work at achieving empathy for the different people who work at the school and the different challenges they have. This means listening carefully to others, always remembering that you can usually gain more by listening than by talking.

Rejoice in the success of those you hire, who will carry on the important work of the school.

Refine your communication skills so they are void of platitudes and banality and fresh with new phrasing and ideas. Keep a file of your writing so you can look back and learn from your mistakes.

Continue to search for mentors, both younger and older, who can help you understand your challenges.

Find ways to enjoy the different aspects of the job and to handle its diversity with grace and a healthy perspective.

Stay conscious of your own health, both physically and mentally, so that you are clear in your thinking and stronger in your activity.

Find a balance within yourself and the school that will refresh you and your work. Give yourself permission not to do *everything* and not to stay to the end of every event.

Understand your family relationships so that you give of yourself to your family in the right ways and never confuse priorities. ■

they have not followed the traditional career ladder of senior leadership — not to mention consideration of people of color and ethnic minorities from outside independent schools. In fact, 54 percent of heads[5] and 48 percent of school administrators[6] participating in the 2009 leadership surveys considered that having few people of color and ethnic minorities in assistant/associate/division head positions in independent schools was one of the top factors in explaining why there were few heads of color or those of ethnic minority representation.

However, another remaining obstacle, in the view of the heads and administrators, is that boards and heads of school search committees are often reluctant to hire new heads who depart from the traditional model. Twelve percent of respondent heads cited this as the major factor when considering possible reasons why there were few heads of color, heads from ethnic minority groups, and female heads. Another 31 percent considered this reason as one of the top factors.[7]

The 2009 study of aspiring heads[8] also revealed that people of color and those from ethnic minority groups were a younger set of candidates with relatively fewer years of experience. In fact, two-thirds had fewer than 15 years of experience in independent schools compared with one-third of those who have become heads; few had been assistant heads when they joined the program. People of color and ethnic minorities in the Fellowship program applied for more positions than their Caucasian counterparts and were interviewed and considered finalists in roughly the same proportions; however, in the end, they were less likely to receive headship appointments.

Age

Not surprisingly, less than one percent of heads of independent schools participating in the 2009 leadership survey were in their 20s, and just 4 percent were in their 30s. Most heads (38 percent) indicated that they were in their 50s, followed by 35 percent in their 60s. When comparing these results with the numbers recorded in an NAIS study conducted in 2002, we notice that, at that time, the majority of heads were in their 50s (52 percent), while only 19 percent of them were in their 60s. The 2009 numbers indicate that there is an aging population of heads at NAIS schools.

In fact, this aging population issue could be exacerbated by the fact that around 37 percent of heads stated that they were planning to change jobs or retire in the next five years, and another 32 percent expressed similar plans for the next six to 10 years. This could represent a problem for our schools if there are not enough candidates in the pipeline for headship, especially, since 78 percent of school administrators participating in the 2009 leadership study said that they were not interested in pursuing a head of school position.

CAREER PATH

Education

The 2009 leadership survey revealed that the vast majority of heads have a graduate school education — and about half of the degrees received are from schools of education: 41 percent have a master's in Education and 11 percent have a doctorate in Education. Also, a majority of heads (51 percent) reported having an M.A. or an M.S., and 12 percent reported having a Ph.D.

Earlier in their careers, many heads said they were teachers (76 percent), department chairs (42 percent), or admission officers (31 percent). Immediately before moving to their current positions, a large number were assistant/associate heads (38 percent) or division heads (34 percent), suggesting a traditional ascent up the independent school career ladder. In fact, classroom teaching continues to be viewed by both heads and administrators as an

Figure 5: Degrees Held by Heads at NAIS Schools

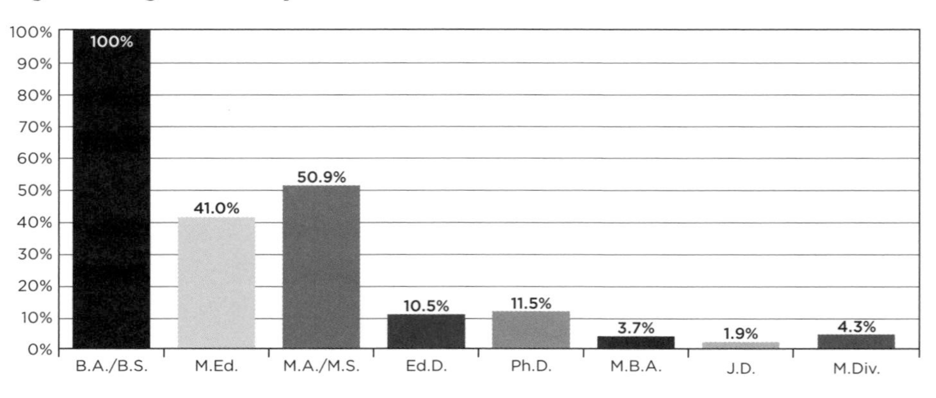

Source: 2009 Survey of Independent School Heads Regarding Leadership

Figure 6: Years Spent Working in Independent School Education by Heads at NAIS Schools

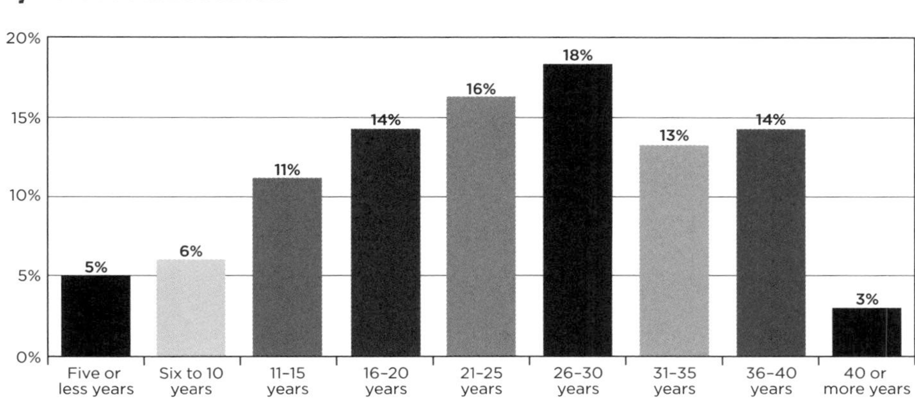

Source: 2009 Survey of Independent School Heads Regarding Leadership

absolutely essential type of background for head of school positions. Having a strong mentor, holding other administrative positions in independent schools, and having financial management experience are also viewed as absolutely essential for success as a head of school.

Another characteristic of heads is that they have spent most of their careers in independent schools. In fact, 64 percent of the heads participating in the 2009 leadership survey reported more than 20 years in independent

Figure 7: Average Number of Years Spent in Different Educational and Other Sectors by Heads at NAIS Schools

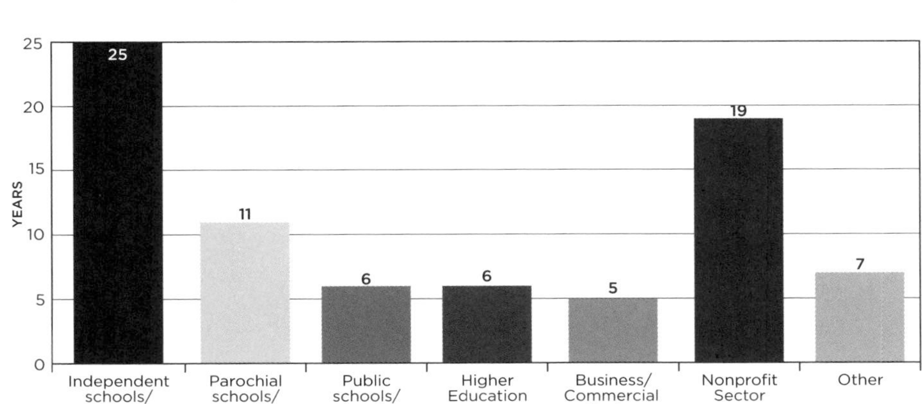

Source: 2009 Survey of Independent School Heads Regarding Leadership

school education, and 30 percent cited more than 30 years (Figure 6).

The same leadership survey revealed that heads have worked in independent schools for 25 years on average (Figure 7). Other sectors where heads have worked for a number of years include the nonprofit sector (19 years on average) and parochial schools (11 years on average).

Tenure

In spite of all their years of experience working at independent schools, the data demonstrate that heads do not stay that long in the same school. They tend to move around from school to school. The leadership survey revealed that 78 percent of heads were hired from outside their current school, but once in the headship, they stayed in that position for several years. Heads participating in this survey had more than 12 years in their current position, while the average tenure for heads of school immediately preceding them, as reported by the heads in the survey, was more than 13 years (Figure 8). These numbers are similar to those recorded by the more comprehensive NAIS StatsOnline annual survey. According to this survey, the median years of experience for heads was 15 years, while the median tenure as heads in their current school was only seven years.[9]

Figure 8: Average Head Tenure at NAIS Schools

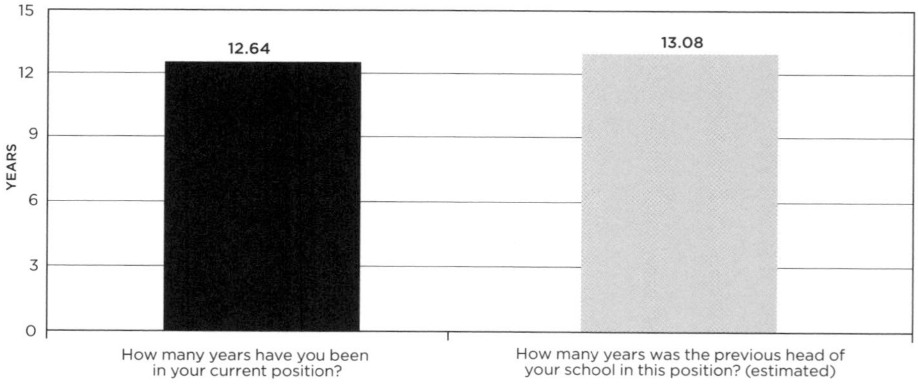

15
12
9
6
3
0
YEARS
12.64
13.08
How many years have you been in your current position?
How many years was the previous head of your school in this position? (estimated)

Source: 2009 Survey of Independent School Heads Regarding Leadership

Retirement Plans

A large number of today's heads of school plan to change jobs or retire within the next five years (37 percent) or the next six to 10 years (32 percent).[10] The 2009 leadership survey reveals that for responding female heads, the numbers are even larger, with 43 percent planning to change jobs or retire in five years or less and 33 percent planning to change jobs or retire in six to 10 years. Also, the number of responding heads of school who plan to change jobs or retire in more than 10 years is higher now. While in a 2002 study[11]

PERSPECTIVE

ONE THING I HAD TO LEARN THAT IN A MILLION YEARS I NEVER THOUGHT I'D NEED TO KNOW

Kay Betts, Head of School (2005–2010)
Episcopal High School
BATON ROUGE, LOUISIANA

I moved to southern Louisiana in summer 2005, five weeks before Hurricane Katrina devastated the Gulf Coast and flooded New Orleans. My school, Episcopal High School of Baton Rouge, became the school of choice for over 600 evacuees, attracted to our community by the reputation of the school and the city's proximity to New Orleans. Those students, and their desperate families, were waiting at our doors even as Baton Rouge itself was without power and suffering the residual effects of Katrina.

Like most new heads, I expected to chart a course through the pressures and conflicts inherent in school leadership. I never thought that I'd be called upon to lead our school community through a time of chaos, a period in which not only our school but also our region suffered devastating losses. These losses ranged from the shortage of gasoline, water, and food to major disruptions in communication. In a city that doubled in size overnight, over which Black Hawk helicopters flew ceaselessly, everyone was off balance and stretched to the breaking point. And I was on my own — literally — without home, friends, or family. I was, however, supported by a committed board, an extraordinary administrative team, and an incomparable parent and student community. Nevertheless, the responsibility for implementing (and defending) our shared decisions rested with me.

In the days that followed Katrina, the board established admissions protocols, and we accepted 100 students into our regular program. In less than two weeks, we had formed a new division, The Knight School (our school mascot is a knight), staffed by its own principal and teachers who had been displaced by Katrina. Meeting in the afternoon and at night, The Knight School served an additional 100 upper school students. It was designed to gradually contract as students and teachers returned to New Orleans.

So, to all you aspiring heads, here are my words of wisdom: You will never be able to figure out this job ahead of time. Give up on that idea. Recognize that your core values are what will keep you strong and give your work integrity. Find them. Hold tight to them. And remember, there are lots of us out here ready to help — as long as the cell phones are working! ■

Figure 9: Heads' Plans for Changing Jobs or Retiring at NAIS Schools

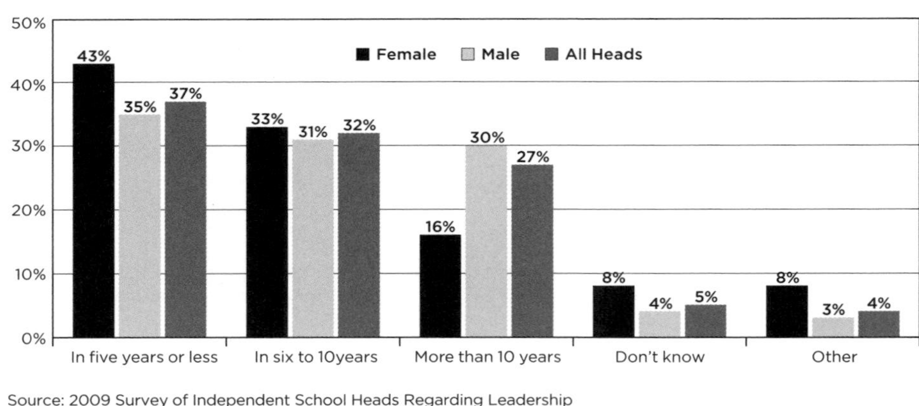

Source: 2009 Survey of Independent School Heads Regarding Leadership

this number was 20 percent, in our 2009 survey, it has increased to 27 percent. However, because of the recession that started in December 2007, some heads have decided to delay retirement by one to five years (21 percent) or indefinitely (6 percent).

PREPARING FOR HEADSHIP

Role of the Head

Heads identify the big-picture aspects of their job as their most demanding duties, including providing vision and leadership, managing the school's climate and values, and working with their boards of trustees. However, school administrators, in particular assistant/associate heads, have an exaggerated view of the demands put on heads in comparison to the heads' own perceptions.

Also, the demands of the job for heads seem to have changed during the past years. Nowadays, heads are more involved in managing the school's overall financial health, strategic planning, and fund-raising, as opposed to personnel management. In previous studies, heads and trustees had identified recruiting and hiring quality staff and faculty as one of the most important functions of the head[12] and managing teacher relations as one of the most demanding aspects of the job.[13]

Developing a Pipeline for Headship

Overall, independent school heads report very high levels of satisfaction with their work in independent education generally and other aspects of their jobs, including the level of discipline and behavior of students, sense of community at their schools, and the city or town where they live. The majority of heads of school would have sought a job as head elsewhere if they had not been appointed to the position they currently hold and would never think about leaving education and going into another field.

However, when they were asked about the number of candidates relative to the number of top positions available, such as head and assistant head, they responded that there are too few candidates relative to the jobs available. Only 22 percent of administrators participating in NAIS's 2009 leadership survey mentioned being interested in obtaining a headship at some point in the future.[14] This number is somewhat higher among responding administrators who identified themselves as people of color and from racial/ethnic minority groups. Respondents who show an interest in pursuing a headship are heavily male (66 percent), European American (86 percent), and in their 40s (45 percent).

NAIS and independent school leaders need to work together to prepare senior and middle level staff for leadership positions. This work can be done via an array of institutes and workshops (NAIS's Fellowship for Aspiring School Heads, for example) and one-on-one assistance, such as mentoring opportunities and leadership coaching. The new cadre of leaders for independent schools needs to develop management and leadership skills, as well as abilities to deal with the big-picture aspects of the headship, including how to facilitate the development of a vision for the school, manage the financial health of the institution, do strategic planning and fund-raising, and successfully partner with boards of trustees as stewards of the school.

NAIS's role will be to continue providing research on school leadership and encouragement through our programming, through leadership development initiatives and programs, and through our bully pulpit for the next generation of school leaders to aspire to the headship and to be trained to meet the challenges they'll face there.

NOTES

[1] 2009 Survey of Independent School Professionals Regarding Leadership, NAIS, October 2009.

[2] 2009 Survey of Independent School Heads Regarding Leadership, NAIS, October 2009.

[3] Belden Russonello & Stewart Research and Communications, "Still Aspiring: An Examination of Why Women and People of Color Are Less Likely to Attain Head of School Positions Following Completion of the Aspiring Heads Fellowship — Results of Five Individual Interviews and an Online Survey of Past Aspiring Heads Participants." Study commissioned by NAIS, April 2009.

[4] NAIS started collecting data on the ethnicity and race of heads in 2000. Since that year, NAIS has included the following options for heads to identify themselves racially/ethnically: African American, Latino/Hispanic American, Asian American, Native American, Pacific Islander American, Middle Eastern American, and Multiracial.

[5] 2009 Survey of Independent School Heads.

[6] 2009 Survey of Independent School Professionals.

[7] 2009 Survey of Independent School Heads.

[8] Belden Russonello & Stewart Research, "Still Aspiring."

[9] StatsOnline, National Tables, Administrator Salaries 2009-2010, November 2009.

[10] 2009 Survey of Independent School Heads.

[11] Belden Russonello & Stewart Research and Communications, "Perspectives on Leadership in Independent Education: Report of Survey Research Among School Heads and Administrators." Study commissioned by NAIS, 2002.

[12] "NAIS 2006 The State of Independent School Governance," NAIS, 2006; online at *www.nais.org/trustees/article.cfm?ItemNumber=149156.*

[13] Belden Russonello & Stewart Research, "Perspectives on Leadership."

[14] 2009 Survey of Independent School Professionals.

PART II

PERSPECTIVES ON THE HEADSHIP

BECOMING A HEAD

Ilana Kaufman

"DO YOU CONSIDER yourself open to feedback?" asked the search consultant facilitating the process for which I was a finalist candidate. "I'd like to think I am open to feedback," I said, trying to sound confident despite the criticism I assumed was en route across the phone line. "We'll see," he said, and then proceeded to say six words that promptly deflated my wanna-be head of school ego and returned me to my proper place. "Ilana, I have reviewed your portfolio. Nice layout …" he said, as if I were applying to be a graphic designer. And then he said, "… but *you sound like an assistant head.*" And then priceless feedback escaped his lips. "If you want to be a head of school, you have to sound like one, act like one, you must *be* a head of school." He went on to give me feedback about my curriculum vitae; the way I talk; the cadence, pitch, and tone of my voice; how I dress; the way I carry myself; and the impression I leave with people after we first meet.

After that conversation, several things changed about how I prepared myself to become a head of school. First, I revised and reformatted my CV. The activities I led in my role as an assistant head now boldly stated that I was the leader. At least on paper, I took credit for those accomplishments that were indeed mine and not those of my team. I also paid very close attention to the many dimensions of my personal presentation. I stopped ending words and phrases on an up tone. "Women tend to talk like that," the search consultant had said, "and it makes you sound unsure of yourself, as if you were really asking a question rather than making a statement." After additional reflection and soul searching, I made the decision to wear the clothes that made me feel exactly and confidently like the person I knew myself to be and not like an imposter. I decided that nothing I wore could give the illusion that I was older than I was or Ivy League educated. And it was clear that no matter how well groomed I was, I was still going to be an urban-flavored woman of color.

I began a new "practice" to get grounded in the reality that I was indeed well prepared to be a head of school. I made the decision to envision actually being a head. On my daily walks to BART, I repeated out loud to myself, "I am a head of school, I am a head of school, I am a head of school." While at first I felt self-conscious and like a bit of a fake, my personal mantra, an expression of years of training and preparation, affirmed for me that I was indeed prepared to be a head of school.

The head of school search process is for the most part predictable and, therefore, one that can benefit from strategy and planning. During the process, remembering these three concepts is key:

1. **Know the purpose** of every step you take, every meeting you attend, every process-related conversation you have.
2. **Know the process** of each experience or activity in which you will be involved.
3. **Know the people** with whom you will be engaging during these experiences and activities.

If you know why you are doing what you are doing, what is going on during those interactions, and the people with whom you are interacting, you can think proactively, strategically, and thoughtfully about how to be most effective.

Also, get in the loop. Sign up for the Blue Sheet. This is the list of head searches available from Educational Directions (*http://edu-directions.com*). Get to know the search consultants, the schools, and the "seasons" during which vacancies are announced. If an announcement debuts 12 to 16 months in advance of the start date, you can expect that the reason for the transition is healthy, such as a retirement or anticipated departure of the current head. If the announcement comes out eight months before the job begins or a shorter period of time, be circumspect about the conditions, but don't let that stop you. No matter the timing, the transition will be hard — it just may be harder if the current head is leaving under difficult circumstances.

Then get to work. Make sure your pre-head-of-school role is providing you with the technical experience that will help you thrive when you become a head of school. Higher education is important. Advanced degrees in education, educational leadership, and even business administration will serve you well on many fronts. That advanced degree will help your CV make the cut. And, no doubt, the actual educational experience itself was both enriching and relevant to the role of head of school. Finally, the rigors of advanced academic work will give you some of the skills and discipline required for the work of head of school. The mandate to "publish or perish" has a place in the work of the head of school. There is an extraordinary amount of writing, data analysis, and reading in that role. Graduate school will give you a tiny taste of the blistering pace and demands of the work.

Next, it is essential that you are exposed to and familiarize yourself with the operations and systems of a functioning (or dysfunctional) independent school. Work hard to understand schools through multiple lenses. Independent schools are nonprofit organizations, most with multimillion dollar budgets that require long-range financial planning and modeling; they are educational institutions working on curricular and pedagogical programs with facilities that must ensure the physical, psychic, and sometimes spiritual safety of hundreds or even thousands of students and staff; and they are organizations governed internally by a board of trustees and externally by legal and regulatory policies. While no head of school is expert in all areas of school operations, she or he must be familiar with all of the variables and able to contribute in meaningful ways that always advance the school's mission.

continued on page 33

PERSPECTIVE

LESSONS FROM THE FIRST FOUR YEARS OF HEADSHIP

Matthew J. Walsh, Headmaster
LaGrange Academy
LAGRANGE, GEORGIA

This piece is intended for aspiring heads of school or those just beginning their job. While the mechanics of finance, curriculum, development, and trustee work are obviously critical to the job, sometimes the intangibles can be the most important and the hardest to learn. Here are some lessons I learned, not always the easy way, in my first four years of headship.

Enjoy the present but hang onto your past. There is nothing quite so fine as the collegial friendships and associations of independent school life. The people are the best part of the job. They are smart, diverse, and interesting to be around. Enjoy the people who work in your school, and if you change schools, try to take those friendships and contacts with you. I haven't always succeeded in keeping up with everyone, but I now know how important it is to try your best to do it.

Dirty Harry was really smart. As Clint Eastwood's Dirty Harry raspily said to Hal Holbrook's corrupt police commissioner in *Magnum Force*, "A man's got to know his limitations." Work on your weak areas and seek help from other people. Your shortcomings may not be so obvious to you or others before you become head, but the array of different areas of responsibility in a head job makes it impossible to master everything, and you really shouldn't try. Hire the best people you can, let them do their jobs, and ask them for help with yours.

How do they fit? Try putting yourself in other people's shoes and see how they fit. If this doesn't come naturally, learn to do it. As head of school, you will need this ability. When you're dealing with different constituencies, imagine the plan or problem as viewed from their perspectives. What would a parent, faculty member, graduate, student, or trustee think about it? In dealing with people, ask yourself how you would want this person to be treated if he or she were your child, parent, or spouse.

Hold the line with the hard heads. This is a corollary to "How do they fit?" There are some people you simply cannot satisfy, try as you will to hear their concerns and work on solutions. Every now and then, you will run into someone who seems determined to be unhappy or to find fault with the school. And once in a blue moon, you will have to tell such a person that perhaps he or she might be happier somewhere else.

Go "old school." Consider doing things the old-fashioned way sometimes. A face-to-face conversation is very valuable. If this isn't possible, at least hearing someone's voice on the other end of a telephone line is important. There is nothing better than email to disseminate information quickly to a large audience, but email should never be used for the things that need to be said face-to-face.

Here comes the bride/groom. If you're going to be a married head, you'd better marry well. I am truly blessed to have married a wonderful woman. My wife Janet understands what it means to be married to a head of an independent school. We would all agree that family should come first, but a smart independent school couple knows that there are some events that are "attend or offend" for the head of school. Working until 10 or 11 o'clock on a Friday night or spending a beautiful Saturday afternoon 100 miles away from your family is inconvenient, but when it's prom night or a state final four appearance, people expect you to be there. This is not to say that an important event at home will *never* take precedence, but just know that you need to accumulate a healthy bank account of goodwill and appearances from which you can draw if you need to make that choice. And there will certainly be many times when you need to put the school first. A smart independent school couple knows this and makes peace with it.

Home improvement. Like a great carpenter doing a home improvement project, remember to measure twice and cut once. Take your time making important decisions. Just because someone else thinks an immediate decision is needed doesn't necessarily make this an institutional priority. You will find that most of the decisions you make do not need to be rushed.

More than "just the facts, ma'am." Remember to ask a lot of questions, especially if you feel that someone is pressuring you to make a quick call. It's amazing how much you will find out. It is important to gather information, benchmark against other schools, and make "data-driven" decisions. Just don't overdo it. This is a people enterprise and always will be. A lot of intangibles go into making good decisions. Getting the right people involved and choosing the right time to do something are usually the most important factors.

Don't be a freak — a control freak that is. Most heads, by temperament, are strong-willed people who like to exert their influence. But there are some things (economic circumstances, for example!) you just can't control. Work on the things you actually can change, and you will be amazed at how many of them go your way.

Gone "fishin." I don't fish, but you know what I mean. Most management books tell you to take vacations, and there's a good reason for that. Be sure to carve out personal and family time to recharge your batteries. Independent school communities will eagerly absorb whatever time and energy you can give, and most heads are people who are eager to please others and do things as well as they possibly can. This can lead to burnout in a hurry. But remember to **vacation with a small "v."** No matter how much you may feel you need some time off, you are the "boss." If something urgent comes up while you're out of the office, you will have to deal with it. There is not a lot more to say here. It is just part of the job.

Say what? Don't fight other people's battles for them and don't tolerate an atmosphere where some people act as the mouthpiece for those who are not willing to speak up for themselves. Encourage people to go to the source first before they complain to you or someone else. This is important in all independent school relationships: student-teacher, parent-teacher, teacher-teacher, trustee-trustee, etc. Beware of someone who tells you "everyone is saying" or "the faculty think that ..." Often, when you ask these people *who* is doing the saying or thinking, they are reluctant

continued on next page

LESSONS FROM THE FIRST FOUR YEARS OF HEADSHIP

to tell you. Sometimes that's because there is no "everyone." But even when there is, I am not a big fan of allowing people to carry someone else's water because it can prevent others from learning to speak for themselves. It can also give the "talkers" more influence than they may need to have.

Embrace the "dirty desk." Get used to the feeling that your work is never done. Most people like to have that "clean desk feeling," but as head of school, you will seldom have that feeling. Chuck Harmon, head of school at York School in Monterey and my close friend and mentor, told me this one before I started, and I have found it to be true. My beloved father, John Walsh, talks about the difference between being regular tired and "tired-tired." Tired-tired is feeling so exhausted at the end of the day that you don't want to fall asleep right away. You just want to enjoy lying there for awhile! If you're doing it right, you'll have lots of days like this in your first few years.

Let's go to the amusement park! Being head of school is like going to the amusement park every day and riding the roller coaster, especially in these economic times. Sometimes it's a real thrill, sometimes it makes you sick, and sometimes you get both on the same ride. Condition yourself to expect surprises. Since another twist is always just around the corner, you will learn to develop an internal equilibrium where you do not allow yourself to get too down when things go badly or too high when things go great.

Mission possible! In any major planning or policy pursuit, always start with the school's mission and philosophy. Process and plans should always come after mission and philosophy. In communicating about a project, remember to announce what's coming, report when it arrives, and comment on its implementation. As I advise our administrators, tell people you're going to do something, tell them when it's in progress, and then report how it went and what the school community learned from it.

Exit stage left now if ... You need to get off the stage now if you don't have a sense of humor. Happiness will be elusive if you can't laugh at yourself and all the crazy, unpredictable things that happen every day at your school. If you take yourself and the inevitable problems too seriously, you won't be much fun to have around either.

And last but certainly not least, remember how lucky you are. You get to work with teachers and young people every day. Teaching is a vocation more than it is a profession. People do it because they love children and they love learning. As a head of school, remember how privileged you are to be around people every day who genuinely love what they do and truly want to be there. This is certainly the case at LaGrange Academy, and I count myself lucky every day. ■

In addition to all this, you need to front-load the personal, social, and emotional work necessary to be effective in the role of school head. Work on your emotional intelligence. Know how to communicate effectively and compassionately. Know what pushes your buttons, and learn how to manage those emotions. Develop empathy and an ethos of care. As head of school, you must be highly skilled in working with many kinds of people. Without exceptional interpersonal, social, and communication skills, even the best-prepared head of school is bound to fail.

THE HEAD OF SCHOOL SEARCH PROCESS: PLAY-BY-PLAY

This outline will help you plan your search process.

Preparation

1. Start your research a couple of years in advance.
    - Get to know search consultants, timing, patterns of openings.
    - Get your current head on your side. Be transparent about your aspirations and intentions and ask for his or her help.
    - Join a board or your school's board committees (if the school's bylaws permit) to develop experience with finance, buildings and grounds, admissions, and/or marketing and development.
2. Thoughtfully and strategically prepare your portfolio to include items that will be requested by all search committees. This will include your curriculum vitae, letters of recommendation, writing samples, and an educational philosophy.

Phase 1

1. Identify a headship you are interested in and make a move. This might include reaching out to the search consultant to understand whether you are a good fit for the position. If encouraged by the consultant, send your portfolio. You will be expected to submit it by email, so finalize it in PDF format. Avoid being too cute or technically slick. The materials you produce must be easily portable, reproducible, and easy to use by the search committee members.
    - At this point, the search consultant will probably want to have a

phone conversation with you in order to get a better sense of who you are and whether you are a good fit for the school. He or she will have reviewed your materials, and the combination of your materials and this conversation will determine whether you are presented to the search committee for consideration.

- Wait to hear from the consultant about whether you are invited to the first round of consideration. If there is no invitation, ask for any relevant feedback, and then move on. The school probably was not a good fit anyway. Back to Step 1. But if the answer is "yes" …
- You will be invited for a first-round interview with the search committee, most likely at a location off-campus. This interview will be a formal Q&A about two to three hours in length.
- Remember to send thank-you notes!
- After this interview, ask yourself whether this feels like a match. If, in your heart of hearts, the answer is "no," contact the consultant to discuss your conclusion. He or she will help you withdraw from the process.

2. Wait to hear from the search consultant about whether you are invited to the second round of the process. Again, if you are not invited back, ask the consultant for any relevant feedback. Remember to send thank-you notes! But if you are invited back …
   - As part of preparing for the second-round interview, begin a dialogue with the consultant and, if applicable, your spouse about general salary expectations, geography, and "fit." At this point, it is your responsibility to make sure you know all you need to know about the structure of the role and the school.
   - If you are invited to the second-round interview and you accept the invitation to participate, be certain that if you are offered the job, you can say "yes." As one of three or four finalists, it is bad form to enter this round if you are not absolutely certain that this could be a fit for you. The stakes are simply too high in the interviewing community for you to say "no" or withdraw late in the game; it could send their search process into chaos. Of course, if at any time before you actually sign the contract, you find that the job is not the

right one for you, it's better to withdraw, no matter how late in the process it is.

Phase 2

1. The second-round interview will take place on campus (and in the community) over two full days, from about 7 am to 9 pm both days. You will be asked to meet with students, parents, staff and faculty, trustees, and alumni — in formal and informal settings. When you are meeting with various committees, the format will likely be Q&A sessions with most of their questions prepared in advance. Plan to give a number of prepared and extemporaneous speeches for formal and informal board interviews and for receptions that require your attendance.
   - A note about formal receptions: In advance, make sure you know how to conduct yourself when engaged in fine dining environments. The second-round interview will probably conclude with a dinner at a very nice restaurant or a catered experience in a trustee's home. While you might feel comfortable with the board by this time, never confuse comfort with casual. In advance of such events, have a personal policy about the kind of food and the amount of alcohol you will consume in this high-stress, high-stakes professional situation. Similarly, boards have their own cultural alcohol-consumption norms. Read those cultural cues and then decide how to proceed. And a warning: Never drink alcohol if it puts you at risk of behaving in a way that could be attributed to the booze. That is a sure way out of consideration for the headship!
   - Your spouse and family may be expected on campus and at dinners.
   - Again, always send thank-you notes.
   - Finally, when the interview is over, ask yourself if this continues to feel like a match. If, in your heart of hearts, the answer is "no," immediately after the interview contact the consultant to discuss your thoughts.

2. And then you wait, and wait, to learn the outcome of the search. Waiting could take a couple of weeks. Stay strong.
   - If you are offered the job, *mazel tov*! The hard work has just begun. Be prepared for a number of weeks of contract negotiations.

- Also, be prepared to carve out some time from the role you currently hold to phase in the work of your new role and school. As part of this process, make sure you stay in communication with the school you are leaving so that the overlapping times and responsibilities do not adversely affect the role, work, and efforts you leave behind.

3. If you are not offered the job, the truth is simply that the fit was not there. Debrief with the consultant. And be very gracious. The time and interest the school gave you was huge and an exceptional experience. Send those thank-you notes. Shake off any funk you might feel and go back to Phase 1, Step 1.

WHAT TO LOOK FOR IN A SCHOOL

You have to be part scholar, part scientist, part psychic.

The language of independent school leadership is neither cryptic nor difficult to decipher, but it does require familiarity — sort of like navigating Middle English. When looking at a school of interest, you can take several approaches to position yourself most successfully for the head and interview process. Begin by reading everything you can find about the school. While it is essential to read every word of the school's website (the search committee will "test" you on some of this), go far beyond the school's web presence and find media articles and even postings in local parent networks that discuss life on the ground in the school. And, of course, ask friends, colleagues, and heads whom you know and respect (and who respect you) about the school.

In tandem to the school research process, you must also do the introspection necessary to know what kind of school will be a good fit for you. Go deep and get clear on the kind of educator you are. What kind of mission and vision are you looking for? Do you want to be in a traditional or progressive school? Whom do you want to serve, and which schools fit that profile? Do you want to lead a school of 200 or 1,200? What kind of school are you prepared to lead? Even the most esteemed and solid schools have their own personalities, histories, quirks, and issues. Faculties have their qualities and foibles. Campuses and facilities have their challenges and opportunities. And even the most professional trustees who steward and sustain the school for the long haul — the school's super-volunteers — can be a tough bunch to have as bosses.

Because the stakes are so high for both a school and its head, there is no point in pursuing searches for schools that will not be a good fit for you. The work of a school head is demanding, and someday when you feel that you have given everything you have, all that might keep you going is the core passion that you have for the school, its values, its philosophy, and, of course, its students. So, in the first phase of your search, when you are submitting your portfolio for consideration, look for schools that align with what you think will be a good fit in the areas of mission, vision, and educational philosophy. If geography is a deal-breaker, limit your search to schools in regions in which you can thrive. If a gender or religious focus is essential, look only at schools that align with those basic parameters. In this phase, you are focusing on the public articulation, presentation, and reputation of the school.

Understanding the nuances of the first-round interview experience will give you invaluable insights into the board of trustees for whom you might soon work, the culture of the school community and its leadership, and whether or not the "vibe" is one that attracts, repels, or even exhausts you. If after the portfolio review, you are asked to a first-round interview and have the privilege of meeting the search committee, the list of what you are looking for will become more refined and focused. Through the first-round interview process and your interactions with the search committee, which undoubtedly will comprise trustees and community members with real or perceived power, you will be able to get a feel for the school's governance and leadership teams, their style, and their expectations regarding formality and approach. Through the questions committee members ask, you will get a sense of the school's current priorities and gain insights into what they are looking for as well as their tone and cadence as a community.

Observe the dynamic of the interview. Are the questions that are asked assigned to each committee member or delivered at random? Does the dynamic of the committee welcome dialogue or is the interview staid and structured? Is there an assigned or even assumed hierarchy present in the room, and how does that affect the dynamic of the interview?

On entering Phase 2 of the search process, you are looking for more concrete evidence of how the school community actually lives its mission and vision. Because this interview takes place over several days and involves interactions with perhaps more than 100 people, the experience will present opportunities for you to have process-related insights and "ah-ha's." During Phase 2, every interview and event contains clues and insights into what the community currently is, what it has been, and what it could be with you as head of school. Look at each person or group you have been asked to meet, and ask yourself why you are spending time with that particular representative of the community. Do you get to meet with students? Alumni? Just the faculty or also the office, maintenance, and after-school staff? Are all of your meals catered? Does some collective cook for others and for you? Or are you provided with a sandwich from the favorite sandwich shop? Are you being quizzed about your credentials, or is there delving into how you have put into professional practice what you have learned on the ground?

Through the Phase 2 experiences, you will better understand whether the school is one you can grow into and that is willing to grow with you. The perfect match is not the school that appears to be perfect (fiscally stable, perfect philosophical alignment, ideal location, etc.) because a school that appears perfect is an illusion. Look for a school that gives you an emotional and spiritual sense of trust, partnership, connection, and hope. With trust, connection, and hope in tow, even the biggest surprises or the worst days are situated on a healthy foundation.

WHAT TO LOOK FOR IN A BOARD

The sole employee of the board is the head of school.

The board of trustees of an independent school has just one employee, the head of school. Like other executive positions, the head of school has between 15 and 25 bosses. This kind of supervisory dynamic and relationship is at best complicated and at worst disastrous. A board deciding which head of school to appoint and support but also, in truth, *supervise* is sometimes like a 19th-century courtship facilitated by a professional matchmaker. Understanding the search firm and consultant the board has chosen is just as important as understanding the board itself because the firm and consultant represent the board to the candidate and the candidate to the board.

When looking for a job, look for a board whose members deeply understand their essential roles. Through your search process, work hard to understand the board's approach to the school. Can the board help realize the mission and vision of the school? In what ways does the board support and evaluate the head? How does the board realize its essential fiduciary duties? How has the board fulfilled its charge of taking on a leadership role during the school's development efforts? How does the board think about the ten-

PERSPECTIVE

ONE THING I HAD TO LEARN THAT IN A MILLION YEARS I NEVER THOUGHT I'D NEED TO KNOW

John Gulla, Head of School
The Blake School
MINNEAPOLIS, MINNESOTA

In my very first month as the new head of school at The Blake School in Minneapolis, the director of the physical plant told me that we had a problem in our ice arena. It seemed that during the previous spring break, the arena had lost power. To compound matters, the auxiliary power system had also failed. Only a skeletal crew was on campus at the time, and there was no automatic alarm that warned the school. As a result, no one immediately discovered this power failure, and the system that supplied heat to the subsoil beneath our ice sheet failed. The subsoil had subsequently frozen.

Unless we repaired this problem, I was told that we could suffer the equivalent of a frost heave that would crack our sheet of ice and shut down our rink. I was asked to authorize the expenditure of over $300,000 from the school's PPRRSM (provision for plant repair, replacement, and special maintenance) fund to "take down" the ice and excavate and replace several feet of subsoil that was ruined because it had frozen. Then we would have to re-create the ice sheet. Oh, and while we were at it, what did I think about moving to a more effective but more expensive "glycol cooling system"?

Huh?

This proposed expenditure was a big chunk of unbudgeted change, and the board members on the Finance Committee expected me to assess the need and urgency of this request. Although new to the scene, I was well aware that I was in charge of a school in a state where hockey had an almost religious devotion among its citizens.

I quickly had to learn about adiabatic systems, calcium-chloride brine water solutions, and the challenges that come with one of the state's first indoor ice arenas (where we had frozen subsoil under the ice sheet instead of a concrete pad, now commonplace). Was I willing to take responsibility if the ice sheet cracked mid-season? Heck no, but I made sure that we competitively bid all components of this work, and I regularly visited during the excavation of the subsoil.

And I made sure that our backup systems would not fail a second time. It was a long way from math and English curriculum, student discipline, and parent relations but — as I learned — part of my new job! ■

ure and eventual succession of the head of school? How does the board plan for and facilitate the transition of its chair? If you know the answers to these questions, you will enter the board/head relationship in a way that will serve your school well and make you successful in your work with the board.

How to Prepare for an Interview with a Board

How do you prepare for your interview with the board of an independent school? Begin by picking the low-hanging fruit and know who your trustees are! This information is available on the website of most schools. Not doing this research will make you look lazy and possibly uninterested. Don't be afraid of the trustees. Google them, look at their work locations, and then make some sense of their attraction to the school's board. Somewhere in the information you find will be the values shared by the trustees, the school, and, presumably, yourself. Find those connections and shared values, and hold onto them as part of your process. It will make your effort to connect with the trustees more meaningful and authentic.

Be proactive. Find out whether you — or anyone in your circle of friends, acquaintances, and colleagues — know any of the trustees. Depending on the school and the search process, it might even be appropriate for you to have a preliminary conversation with a trustee from the school you are interested in. But take your cues from the trustees. If you are invited to lunch or coffee, go. The contact and communication, if handled well, can be in your favor. Never pass up opportunities to research, network, and do the groundwork for relationship building.

In addition to the homework and relationship building that are essential when you are interviewing with a board comes the rigorous technical and professional pre-interview work required to impress and reassure a board. Ideally, you have had some experience on nonprofit boards and board-level committees. In the big picture, you must be able to make sense of various board dynamics so that you can understand the age and stage — the level of maturity — of the board you are interviewing. Board maturity level is neither good nor bad. It is simply one aspect of the developmental trajectory of the school and the board for whom you will work. Without the ability to make meaning out of the board dynamics you observe during an interview, you will be at a real disadvantage. In addition, the trustees will want to know that you understand how they operate so that the board and you as head of school can work together as an effective team on behalf of the school you hope to lead.

GATHERING THE KNOWLEDGE AND SKILLS FOR A SUCCESSFUL HEADSHIP

What do you need to know to be a successful head, and how do you gather that information? There are five areas of training and expertise that are essential to entering a first headship in a way that positions the school and you for success: business and finance, buildings and grounds, admissions, advancement, and governance. Last but certainly not least, you will need to be the school's educational leader.

Business and Finance

You will need practical, hands-on knowledge and experience with business and financial matters to be able to interpret and make financial leadership decisions for the school. Having financial literacy will enable you to participate meaningfully in the work of your board's Finance Committee. While this knowledge base is not necessarily native to educational leaders, we are surrounded by financial professionals who are generally eager to support the learning of those who demonstrate sincere interest in their areas of expertise. Begin by acknowledging what you don't know, what confuses you, and what boggles your mind. And then when you approach a financial professional, he or she can see your intentions and effort. When seeking mentorship and support, ask without being pushy to participate in projects and activities that can give you context-based, hands-on experience. Work with everything from operational budgets to investment approaches to cash versus accrual accounting models to bond management strategies will be energy well spent. Mastery of this skill set is key to running the business of the school.

Buildings and Grounds

Often connected to business and finance are the school's operations and buildings and grounds. This work includes everything from how the administrative offices execute the systematic work of the school to how the school plant is engineered and maintained. To familiarize yourself with the work, walk your current campus and all offices, and ask yourself how things work — what makes everything function and operate smoothly (or not). Figure out who does what and how the sequencing works, and, if you are able, talk to the people in charge of these operations. Their perspectives can be as good as gold.

Admissions, Advancement, and Governance

Literacy, technical expertise, and affection for the work of admissions, advancement, and governance are also needed for all heads of school. The best, most contextually appropriate way for an emerging head of school to develop expertise in these areas is to interface with them at the school committee and board level. Join your school's Admissions Committee. As part of the committee work, sign up to interview prospective students and families and to read admissions files. Work to understand the connection between admissions, enrollment management, tuition assistance programs, development, and the school's long-term financial strategy. This experience will help you jump into the intersections of this work with the ability to contribute, rather than sitting on the sidelines.

If you have nurtured your partnership with the head of the school for which you work *and* have been transparent about your aspirations, she or he might invite you to attend board and committee meetings and to participate in advancement activities. If you are without such an invitation, offer your favorite nonprofit organization help with fund-raising activities. I suspect that the organization would welcome the support.

Finally, as with all aspects of working as the head of school, the key to successfully navigating the job is the intersection between the work of the school and the people who do it. Learn how to be in meaningful connection with all types of people. Finance officers can be introverts, development officers extroverts. The school counselor will often want to "check in" and ask how you "feel" about various topics. Program directors can be visionaries, and assistant heads and division heads (the senior and middle managers) are always balancing the needs of multiple and often competing constituencies. It takes all kinds of people to support a school, but it is the head who is at the nexus of the relationships. If you aren't comfortable with a range of personalities, the essential positive relationships on which a successful school runs can't be in place. And without those relationships in place and regularly nurtured, the work of the school won't be at the high quality that kids, families, staff, and faculty deserve.

Teaching, Learning, and Best Practices

While the demands presented by running the business of an independent school are compelling and can appear to be all-consuming, as chief thinker and educational leader, the head of school must be a model of continuous and active learning. Students benefit from exposure to an adult who assumes a learning posture. They deserve to see the head of school engaged in challenging educational experiences that are similar to their own. And faculty, staff, and families need the head to be authentically impassioned by historic, current, and cutting-edge research and ideas related to education, child development, organizational management, systems thinking, and leadership development, as well as current events, social and economic trends, and popular culture. Resources are numerous, but the challenge is to identify and effectively use those that will be most helpful. Subscribe to educational periodicals. Frequently visit NAIS publications, Harvard University Press, and New Press websites. Most important, ask those whom you hold in high regard for their top five education and leadership books. The more diverse this group of people is, the richer and more dimensional the titles. And trust their advice. These titles will become treasured texts in your head of school library.

CONCLUSION

It's part humility, part chutzpah, part training, part destiny.

At the close of a speech I gave on Generations and Special Friends Day, a pre-Thanksgiving event to which the grandparents, aunts, uncles, and special friends of my students (and sometimes staff) are invited, a grandmother approached me and asked if I minded a probing question. She said that this was the seventh Generations Day she had attended, and she had been able to observe both the past head of school and me in context. And then, in a way that made me feel that the answer she wanted was not purely factual, she asked, "If you don't mind, *how* did you become a head of school?" As a handful of other grandparents leaned in to hear my answer, I took a deep breath and spoke from my heart.

I replied, "I believe becoming a head of school is my destiny. Upon reflection, I have always been a leader. And through the careful supervision and support of many extraordinary mentors, through extremely hard work and a bit of luck, I have become a head of school. I have been a classroom teacher, dean, and diversity practitioner and was for many years an assistant head of school. I was pushed and nudged to go far beyond what I thought my abilities and limits were. I was groomed and nurtured by mentors. And I was intentionally trained to be a head of school. I think my training was perhaps more similar to that of an 18th-century apprentice than a modern-day intern, but the approach and model really worked for me. And yet, even with all my training, I still had to take a leap of faith."

The grandmother took my hand and said, "How did you pick *this* school?" I said, "I waited for a sign." I mentioned that after years of training and preparation, I knew I was technically ready. I also shared that there was no way I could know everything I would need to know to confidently make such a change. I knew moving from a school and job I loved to something completely new required the harnessing of my courage and, again, a leap of faith.

I told the grandmother, "In order for me to jump into the unknown, I needed a sign. And while I was privileged to be a finalist for more than one head of school position at really great schools, only here did I experience something unexplainable. There was a sign." I told her that on what was an otherwise unremarkable, cloudy October day, as I was preparing to leave the campus after my final interviews, I stood at the top of the main staircase and looked west at a fogged-in San Francisco Bay. Caught up in the memory, I recounted that in that moment at the top of the staircase, "The skies parted, the late fall sun poked through the clouds, and just for a second, I could see clear across the Bay, beyond the Golden Gate Bridge, to the Pacific Ocean." A bit self-consciously, I looked around to see whether the other grandparents thought I had lost my mind. But they were right there with me.

And then the grandmother, still holding my hand, said, "Ilana, of course becoming a head requires rigorous training and exceptional skills. But actually *being* a head requires technical expertise coupled with owning the work as your destiny." This grandmother mentioned that fulfilling my destiny is what I do for the grandchildren, and she kindly suggested that unless I am in touch with my own destiny, I could never give the children all that they need. Still holding my hand and now squeezing it tight, she went on to say, "You became a head of school because you were trained and you were ready. But you *are* a head because of who you are and who you know yourself to be."

Being a head of school is the most rewarding, challenging, joyful, and sometimes heartbreaking work I have ever done. It has exercised muscles in my mind and in my heart that I didn't know I had, and it has stretched me in ways that I could not have imagined. While being a head of school has left me neither rich nor famous, the rewards of leading a school and being in deep and meaningful connection with a school community offer bounty of unimaginable scale.

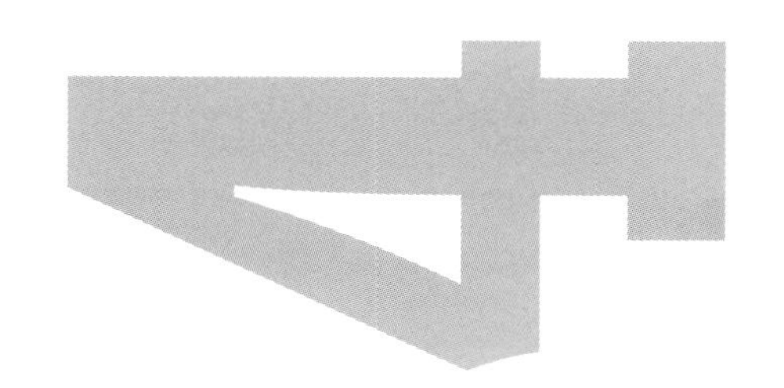

WHO ARE THE HEADS? HOW ARE THEY CHANGING?

PATHWAYS TO HEADSHIP

Mike Murphy

I AM THE SON of a roofing contractor who expected my siblings and me to appreciate hard work and to value the benefits that come from those efforts; that may be the most valuable influence that has led me to become a headmaster. Even though roofing was not my career of choice, my father taught us lessons about leadership, management of all kinds of people, finance and marketing, and adapting to change. He encouraged a passion for independence and a distrust of unions, government, or anyone who infringed on independence. He taught us the importance of personal relationships with the customers and suppliers who make the business work.

He modeled the importance of service and philanthropy to the community. Most important, he instilled in all of us a deep respect for people, regardless of their backgrounds and the work they do — as long as they worked hard and did it well. My father showed us the benefits of being "the boss." He, Edward J. Murphy, also passed on to me a respect and appreciation for Murphy's Law: "If anything can go wrong, it will." Understanding this rule has kept me out of trouble, both personally and professionally.

Another significant influence in my pathway to becoming a headmaster was the experience of attending summer camps from age seven to 22. I went from camper to kitchen helper, from junior counselor to counselor, from assistant director to director of various camps. I met teachers, administrators, athletes, and others who were passionate about young people and the potential of those children to become happy, successful people. To my father's disappointment, those people steered me away from his line of business and into the world of education.

At first, it seemed that I was not cut out for school. I was the classic late bloomer when it came to academic success. During my junior year in high school, my advisor counseled my parents to let me finish high school, forgo college, and go directly to work for my father. Thankfully, my parents valued education and were patient with their late-blooming son. After high school, they sent me to a PG year at the Bullis School. At Bullis, an inspirational math teacher who taught us as much about social issues as math had me dreaming math equations in color, and he opened up some new ideas for me. My life as a student changed that year. My career path solidified the next summer when John Mummy, an all-American quarterback from Ohio State, planted the idea in my head that I might be more successful teaching young children than high school athletes. Mr. Mummy was a guest coach at a sports camp where I was working as the head counselor. His two young sons were in my cabin. During a break from a practice session, John Mummy sat with me and shared his observation that I seemed to be at my best when I was supporting the younger campers. He confirmed something I was already sensing.

Upon returning to Dayton, I plunged into elementary education as a major at the University of Dayton. The university provided great opportunities to work with all kinds of children in a variety of school settings. My advisor was an inspirational professor of education and mathematics. He convinced me to student-teach in the second semester of my junior year. When he assigned me to teach math in a new open-space middle school and outdoor education center, I was sure he was trying to sabotage my career. But I was paired with a talented teacher/leader who loved her students and the challenges of working as a team of professionals. We wrote our own materials, never used textbooks, and worked in small groups with students. This opened my eyes to the excitement of teaching middle school kids. My experience at the Outdoor Education Center at Antioch College was life-changing. Not only was I exposed to the skills of teaching outdoors, I was also fortunate to work with men and women who were passionate about environmental conservation, birds, wildlife, camping, and all things outdoors.

A lifetime friendship was ignited the first day at the Center with Mike Zaccardi. I was fortunate to be supervised and befriended by outdoor education leaders like Stephen Kress and Dick Paterson. They opened my eyes and mind to birds, cameras, and outdoor exploration. All three areas continue to be avocations today. My student teaching experiences demonstrated just how influential talented teachers can be for children and their colleagues.

My first "real" teaching position was in Oxford, Ohio, the same place where I had been a camp counselor, and also the home of Miami University and the Institute for Environmental Sciences where I studied for a master's degree. The interdisciplinary program in environmental science taught me the importance of including many voices in decision-making. This was one of the most important formal lessons I have used as I have progressed from teacher to division head to headmaster. The inclusion of diverse voices with a range of expertise is an important way to approach problems and decision-making.

While in Oxford, I taught sixth grade at the Kramer School, a K-6 school with over 400 children. My principal, Karl Garnett, was a cross between Mr. Rogers and Captain Kangaroo. He was a gentleman farmer who loved children and adventure, and he was bilingual, having taught in South America. He trusted me enough to put his youngest daughter in my first class. In fact, he placed all the sixth graders who played string instruments in that first class — 36 of them. I actually thought I was pretty good until the next year when he assigned me 36 band students. (Note: String instrument players have exquisite listening skills and are not as apt to keep the beat on their desks or on their classmates' heads as band students.) Yes, you read that correctly: There were 36 children in those classes. Some transitioned from the LD classroom. They were special kids. But I never thought that there were more than I could manage. I was young, idealistic, and maybe a little stupid, but I was living my dream, and Mr. Garnett was there to support me. Mr. Garnett set me up for success by letting me try different methods with my class.

I moved from the Kramer School to the Miami Valley School, my first

PERSPECTIVE

MENTORING — WHO NEEDS IT?

Dennis Bisgaard, Head of School
Kingswood Oxford School
WEST HARTFORD, CONNECTICUT

It is ironic that more than 20 years after my initial strong skepticism about mentoring as an artificial type of relationship, I find myself reflecting about the mentoring I have received over the years. In 1988, when I arrived in the United States from Germany and Denmark, I knew nothing about independent schools, and the concept of mentoring seemed completely alien.

Through the years, mentoring has become the metaphorical training wheels I needed to find my professional balance to move ahead without crashing into walls or wiping out entirely. Most of my key mentors have been seasoned heads of school, both former and current, but one, most surprisingly, was a formerly incarcerated, 20-year-old, inner-city youth for whom I was a mentor. I was insecure, out of my comfort zone, and not at all certain I would be able to help him. He and I met over lunch weekly for a year, and as we spoke about struggles, missteps, life lessons, goals, and inspirations, I learned much from him in our give-and-take meeting of the minds. I hope I in turn provided some insights for him. When I moved away, I missed these lunches with my friend and confidant from a world so remote from my own.

I never set out to become an administrator, let alone a head of school. Yet, along the way, my mentors nurtured skills, talents, and potential I did not realize I had. I was given responsibilities and encouraged to lead. People nudged me along and always seemed willing to help — not necessarily to provide me with answers but to serve as sounding boards and to ask questions such as "Have you looked at it from this angle?" while shoring me up when self-doubt got in the way.

As an aspiring head and an individual of color, I was fortunate in having role models of color in Reveta Bowers, head of school at The Center for Early Education; Rudy Jordon, former dean of Bank Street School for Children; and Lucinda Lee Katz, head of Marin County Day School, whom I have always admired for their ease of leadership, their intellect, and their ability to deal with any situation. I was in three serious searches, and three times I was the "other" finalist. Several heads of school told me that once I found the right school, I would just know. I wondered how they knew that, and my skepticism crept back into my mind, sitting right next to "maybe I independent school, and then to the Columbus School for Girls — two very different schools, MVS being a fairly young school while CSG was steeped in tradition. I then took a position at the Kennedy School in Berlin, getting my first taste of administration.

Initially, the move to Berlin was more about seeing Europe than about engaging in an international school community. However, during my second year of teaching science to German and American students, I was asked to apply for the American assistant principal position at the school. The German assistant principal was already in place. The four years in Berlin and at

am just not cut out for this." David Thomas, a professor at Harvard Business School, gave me two simple yet profound pieces of advice: "Don't let others define you; define yourself so everyone knows your vision and key competencies." He also said, "Don't act like an aspiring head of school. Act like you are in charge and in the role already. If you don't, how will people get a sense that you can do the job?" I listened, read his book, *Breaking Through: the Making of Minority Executives in Corporate America*, and the next time, I landed the job.

I don't know whether I am the only person to have attended the NAIS Institute for New Heads (INH) twice. It wasn't that I failed the first time around! I attended the INH while serving as acting head of school at Shady Hill School during the head's sabbatical. I then stepped back into my associate head role for a couple of years before being appointed head of school at Kingswood Oxford School. Then I attended my second INH. Although many lessons and presentations were similar to those I heard the first time around, I approached each with a more profound understanding of the demands of school leadership. I know I learned more the second time as a "PG head."

Five years into my first official headship, I am still trying to find my balance, but I have been able to let go of the training wheels. I feel more confident, and I know my guardian angels, my mentors, are only a phone call or an email away. Even when I am not in touch, they "sit on my shoulder," whisper in my ear, and have my back. This is not an Academy Award "thank you all" speech, and my wife does not want me to write this, but I have to say that Monica has been my biggest source of encouragement along this journey. Without a spouse, a partner, or a close friend as the ultimate mentor, I don't believe you stand a chance!

I love being a head of school, for every Friday thus far, no matter what has happened during the week, I have been able to say, "Overall, it's been a pretty good week!" Yet apart from parenting, it is the hardest job I have ever had. Without my mentors, I would not be where I am today. And, without my current friend and fellow head, John Bracker from Watkinson School, a few miles down the road, I might still need help balancing my job and professional life.

Who needs mentoring? I do! ■

JFK School provided great lessons about working in a diverse community and allowed me to develop a greater appreciation for Berlin, Germany, and the people of Europe.

On my return to the United States, I landed on the doorstep of the Ensworth School in Nashville, Tennessee. The headmaster, Ron Fay, was then at the peak of his career. He had assembled a fantastic faculty. My division head/teaching position provided me with well-paced experiences in supervision, curriculum, admissions, and planning. I had time to nurture my career and my family. Ron encouraged us to attend NAIS and ISM professional development workshops. I was 32 when I started at Ensworth, and I was already chomping at the bit to become a head of school. In retrospect, those were the most formative years of my career. They would launch me into my role as head of Lower School at Pace Academy in Atlanta, Georgia. At Ensworth, I saw how important it is to hire people who will shape the school. Ron Fay was committed to seeking talented men and women to add diversity and strength to the school. His commitment made Ensworth a unique and special elementary school.

Pace Academy could have paid Ensworth for training me. Ron Fay provided me with experiences that helped me understand the complexity of running a division and a school. At Pace, I was fortunate to work for George Kirkpatrick ("GGK"), a devoted headmaster who gave me enough rope to hang myself but also plenty of guidance and support to avoid the hangman's tree. GGK knew his community. He loved the admissions process and took time to know each applicant and his or her family. He was a serious worker but found time to socialize and have fun with faculty, trustees, and other heads of school in the area. He had a ritual of eating lunch off campus at a local Houston's. If he did not have a guest, he had his yellow legal pad filled with numbers, tasks, and, more than likely, his fantasy baseball team. GGK had a profound respect for the history of the school and the men and women who had built it. He had the school's budget in his head at all times. He taught powerful lessons about the importance of the individual, and he showed how a headmaster could influence the culture of a community. Sincere in his appreciation for all volunteers, he was also deeply devoted to the faculty. He was a fine educator and modeled commitment to the school community. I carry

During my time at Pace, I was reminded of the importance of being humble in both giving and receiving acts of generosity. This is best illustrated by two stories involving my youngest son, Patrick, who had been diagnosed with neuroblastoma cancer when he was in kindergarten. Patrick entered the sixth grade the year I was named interim head at Pace. One morning, after having spent the night in the hospital with him, I arrived at my office and was greeted by a parent who was in deep distress because his very talented son was not meeting the standards the father had set for the child. My son was dying. A piece of my brain wanted me to tell the parent to get over himself. However, the educator inside my head reminded me that his issue was vitally important to him. He needed comfort and counsel, and I needed to give it to him. Being able to support that father was one of the few things that energized me that day. I think of that experience often and realize that we cannot ignore our own families and issues, but when we are in the office, we need to be able to serve others.

The second story took place right after I was named headmaster at Pace in February 1997. Since the headmaster's residence was vacant, I arranged to move into the house in late March. Patrick passed away a few days before the move. What might have been one of the most joyous times of my professional career was blunted by Patrick's death. Anyone who has been fortunate to live or work in a great school community knows what happened next. The school community, which had already been supportive of our family throughout Patrick's battle with cancer, united to comfort and support us in unimaginable ways. Among other far more important things, I was moved into the headmaster's residence and never touched a box. Headmasters, like other school people, can be the beneficiaries of enormous generosity. ■

—Mike Murphy

those lessons with me every day.

By the summer of 1996, GGK had retired and a new headmaster had come on board. I had been appointed assistant headmaster in addition to head of the Lower School and was attending a weeklong leadership program at the Center for Creative Leadership. Before I went to the program, a variety of people completed 360-degree feedback forms regarding my performance as a leader. The CFCL program then engaged participants in examining our leadership styles and understanding the feedback from people back in our work environments, as well as the professionals who observed us throughout the seminar. This was the single most beneficial professional development experience I have had prior to becoming a headmaster.

Ironically, during a workshop on crisis management, the director of the Center called me out of the session for a crisis/emergency phone call. The chair of the board of trustees from Pace was on the other end of the line. He informed me that the current headmaster would not be returning and asked if I would be willing to serve as interim head for the coming year, which was scheduled to begin in five days.

I accepted the interim position with no intention of applying for the headship because I wanted to head a K-8 school. After three months serving as interim head, however, I changed my mind and entered the search. To this day, I believe that there is no way someone with my background could have become the headmaster of the K-12 Pace Academy had it not been that people knew me from my role as head of the Lower School, combined with the unexpected change of leadership that summer. But it worked. I learned that by surrounding myself with great division heads and department leaders, I could play the role of conductor and support them as they addressed details that made their departments thrive. Unlike being a division head where I had some expertise, as the headmaster my focus changed to supporting others and implementing programs and plans. My support for students was not as direct although I continued to attend student activities and events. Strategic planning, fund-raising, and working with trustees became new preoccupations. And I was fortunate to be surrounded by trustees who were dedicated to the school and to my success.

In the spring of 2004, after 15 years at Pace, my wife and I agreed that we would take the leap and leave Atlanta for Shorecrest Preparatory School in Petersburg, Florida. The change from Pace to Shorecrest was far more dramatic than I could have predicted. A tragic death of my wife's ex-husband, our inability to sell our home in Georgia, my stepson's unhappiness with the move, and my wife's discomfort with the humidity in Florida all contributed to the stress of the move. Fortunately, Shorecrest's trustees and community members reached out to welcome and embrace us. Time is an important element and a salve to any change. Over time, the personal issues settled, and relationships of trust and acceptance took hold with faculty, parents, and students. Even though I still miss the friends and the school in Atlanta, the change has helped me continue to grow.

During all of these years I have met people who have seen my potential and have supported me. Being a head has helped me strengthen a strong internal value system instilled in me by my parents. I have found that loving people and seeing the potential in even the most difficult child has been important. Being able to drive myself, inspire others, forgive others and myself for mistakes, and laugh at the absurdities that life throws at us are equally important.

Attending parochial and independent schools, being an education major, being a classroom teacher, and serving as a division head all helped me on my path to headship. Nevertheless, the good fortune of having wonderful role models and mentors and the values, habits, passions, and internal drive to serve others have been far more important elements as I continue down my path. As traditional as my path may be, the skills and lessons from outside of school have been every bit as important as the skills learned in school. This combination of traditional and nontraditional experiences has given me rich resources to draw on as I continue to develop as a headmaster.

NONTRADITIONAL PATHS TO HEADSHIP

D. Scott Wiggins

I REMEMBER IT as if it happened yesterday: an angry phone call from an irate father to me, a seven-year teacher and administrator serving my first year as athletic director at a Boston area junior boarding school. The subject was a hockey-stick fight between two sixth graders that had occurred in an unsupervised locker room because of the late arrival of the teacher/coach. To make matters worse, the caller was a lawyer, and his son had sustained hand bruises in the skirmish. He wanted me to know that he had every intention of suing the school and having me fired as athletic director for failure to provide appropriate supervision. At the time, those angry words fell on impressed and slightly terrified ears, and it struck me then that a familiarity with the law might be a very good thing for an independent school administrator to possess.

Nine years later, I fielded another angry call from an attorney father. At the time, I was the dean of students and director of residential life at another junior boarding school in Connecticut. The caller's son had told his father that a disciplinary investigation was focusing on him for something he had not done. The highly agitated father called me to assert his status as an attorney, to warn that the investigation seemed heavy-handed, and to threaten legal action against the school. When I replied that I, too, was an attorney and that serving for five years as a criminal prosecutor in the Commonwealth of Pennsylvania had fully equipped me to conduct disciplinary investigations in an even-handed way, the whole tone and tenor of the conversation changed. We ended up having a productive conversation.

Fortunately or not, my J.D. degree and training as a lawyer have come in handy every day I have served in independent schools since I left the Chester County, Pennsylvania, District Attorney's Office in June 1993. Eighteen years later, I am in my eighth year as head of school at Lawrence Academy in Groton, Massachusetts. While the nontraditional portion of my background has given me both advantages and disadvantages with respect to my performance as head of school, I have also had several pivotal early-life experiences that gave me many of the skills and attributes needed to be successful as an educator, even as my sights were initially trained on a career in medicine.

Among those early life experiences were 10 summers spent in the mountains of a Colorado summer camp. My progression through the ranks over those summers — from camper at age eight to being in charge of the counselors in training at 24 — gave me the opportunity to develop personal responsibility and independence early on, to learn about leadership and life skills by watching superb role models, to practice and gradually take on the mantle of leadership, and then to discover success as a leader. Those years were truly transformative. Another added bonus of summer camp was the opportunity to form close friendships with kids and colleagues who had independent school roots and experiences, something that I — as the product of public school — did not have. Those relationships would eventually provide me with my entree into the independent school world.

Another early-life experience was active participation in youth sports through grade school, middle school, and high school. Familiarity with and the ability to coach a number of different sports are a huge plus in boarding schools: I knew football, ice hockey, and baseball, and I had also come to have a supreme regard for sportsmanship, teamwork, and commitment to something larger than myself. These qualities and skills are highly valued in the independent schools in which I have worked.

My third major early-life experience was the revelation during my first year in medical school that I wasn't fully committed to becoming a doctor. While this was quite an epiphany to have so late in the game, it enabled me to take stock of those qualities I had wanted to possess as a doctor, qualities valued and admired in my physician father and the colleagues he allowed to care for his family. What I internalized as the greatest thing about practicing medicine was the opportunity a doctor has to touch someone's life, to give them undivided attention, to listen to them, to care about them, to encourage them, to be kind to them, and to treat their physical ailments while being equally mindful of their emotional needs. I now find that I am able to do more of these important things as an educator than I would have been able to do as a doctor! I get 10 minutes with my primary care physician once a year. She is an excellent doctor but busy beyond belief, and she doesn't have the time to get to know me. As a teacher and administrator in independent schools, I have the luxury of being able to spend the time that needs to be spent with my students and my colleagues. I value those opportunities and the relationships I am able to forge.

After I left medical school in spring 1978, I began to think about what I might want to do with my life other than practice medicine. Because of the satisfaction I had experienced as a camp counselor and the expertise I felt I had in connecting with kids, it occurred to me that teaching might be something I'd be really good at and would enjoy.

That fall, I visited the head of school at the Fessenden School in West Newton, Massachusetts. (His son had been a fellow staff member at summer camp.) I asked him whether there were any coaching or tutoring positions open at the school. He hired me on the spot, and within a very short period of time, I was tutoring every academic period of the day and coaching in the afternoons. From the moment I started, I knew I had found my calling. The following year, I was hired as a full-time math teacher, coach, and dorm head. I loved every aspect of the job.

During the December break in my second year at Fessenden, I visited a boarding school in the West. My East Coast junior boarding school credentials must have impressed the head and admissions director who showed me around that day, as I got a call that evening asking whether I would be interested in becoming an admissions assistant at the school the following year. I accepted, and in August 1980, I moved west to begin my new role. After my first year as assistant director of admissions, I was promoted to director of admissions and given the head varsity hockey coaching position. Perhaps it is the linkage between admissions and securing impact athletes, but in the two years I coached hockey, the team distinguished itself as one of the best in the state and was collectively inducted in spring 2009 into the school's athletic hall of fame.

While things were going great on the hockey front, I faced significant challenges in admissions from several powerful trustees who were too involved in the day-to-day operation of the admissions office. As I worked my way through my three years at the school, one of the critical lessons I learned was that I needed more cachet (education, experience, clout) in my role as an administrator if I was going to play successfully with the "big kids," the trustees.

One of the defining moments in my career occurred during a trustee weekend. I was reporting to a trustee committee on admissions and college counseling and explaining that, rather than trying to increase the numbers of visits and applications in order to show increased numbers in our admissions statistics, we were employing a strategy devised to achieve a board-directed mandate to improve the caliber of the applicant pool. This strategy encouraged visits and applications from students we were reasonably certain had the wherewithal to gain admission and do the work at the school. By way of example, I told the committee about a family from Chicago that was planning to fly out for a school interview. I had received the boy's grades, test scores, and recommendations and realized that there wasn't a chance we were going to admit him. Rather than encourage the family to fly out for the interview, I had suggested in the kindest way possible that their trip would be a hollow exercise. While *they* appreciated my candor, one of the school's trustees did not. Hearing the story, he brought his fist down hard on the conference table and shouted: "Who do you think you are, God?" At 27 years of age, I was completely undone. Ultimately, I resigned my post at that western school because of changed admissions expectations and directives that I believed compromised the work I had been asked to do as director.

As luck would have it, Fessenden was looking for a full-time math and science teacher, and so I returned there that fall. During my first year back at Fessenden, I formed a vision of what I wanted to do. First, I decided that I wanted to become a head of school. Second, I knew I would need an advanced degree; my bachelor's in chemistry just wasn't going to be enough. Finally, I wanted to pursue a degree that would empower me to do the job of head of school but that would also enable me to land on my feet if I were ever fired or needed to walk away from a head position for any reason.

It was for all of these reasons that I decided to attend law school. In fall 1985, I entered Arizona State University College of Law. During law school, two things happened that proved critical to my career path. First, I met my future spouse in summer 1987 when I was visiting friends at Fessenden. At the time, she was the associate director of admissions at Fessenden, and without her wholehearted support, encouragement, and willingness to play a critical role in what I hoped we would do, we would not have gotten where we are today.

Second, even though I had intended to return to independent education immediately after graduation from law school, my plan was modified by a special internship course that allowed me to practice law and try criminal cases as a city prosecutor in the Tempe, Arizona, City Court. The experience was exhilarating and humbling, and because of that prosecutor internship, I decided to practice law for a few years before heading back to education. After I got my J.D. in May 1988, my future wife moved to Westtown School outside Philadelphia to become the assistant director of admissions. I joined her there, spending my summer studying for the bar exam and looking for a job. During the five years we spent at Westtown, I had the opportunity to be a faculty spouse — a real eye-opener and an important perspective for any head of school. After I passed the Pennsylvania Bar, I worked for a short time with a high-profile patent law firm in downtown Philadelphia. Although it didn't satisfy my desire to be of service to others, it was extremely lucrative!

In spring 1989, I was hired as an assistant district attorney in Chester County, Pennsylvania. As a prosecutor, I handled preliminary hearings in the county circuit courts for a year, served as the county juvenile prosecutor for another year (a great experience for a future head of school!), and then spent two years as a trial prosecutor in the adult division. In this position, I was assigned a good number of child sexual abuse prosecutions because I knew how to talk and work with kids and support them through painful trial experiences. But when I was asked in late 1992 to head up a new unit dedicated exclusively to child abuse prosecutions, I turned down the offer. I knew that I couldn't take on that new role and still leave myself time to fulfill my vision of returning to education.

In 1993, I began my search for a mid-level administrative position in an independent school and was hired as dean of students and director of residential life at Indian Mountain School in Lakeville, Connecticut. It was the only job offer I received! Many of the schools I interviewed with were leery of my eight-year absence from independent school education, and they were not sure what to think of my pursuit of a law degree and my experience as a prosecutor. I got the job at Indian Mountain because the head was the person I had worked most closely with when I started at Fessenden 14 years earlier.

After three years at Indian Mountain, I was encouraged by a head of school search consultant to take the next step toward becoming a head: taking on a division headship. In winter 1997, I applied for several division headships and ultimately was hired as upper school head at Metairie Park Country Day School in New Orleans, Louisiana. One of the things I value most about my experience at MPCDS was the relationship I had with the head of school, David Drinkwater. He gave me an open invitation to prepare myself to become a head of school during my five-year tenure there. (Every aspiring head should have a sitting head mentor to school him or her for the rise.) In my fifth year at MPCDS, I pursued a handful of head of school searches and advanced to several semifinalist rounds, although I did not make it to the finalist round in any of the searches.

The following year, the experience I had gained during the previous year's searches paid big dividends, as we (my wife and I) made it to the finalist round in three searches. (I say "we" because we do this work together as a family, understanding that it is a joint effort that comes with but a single salary.) I ultimately accepted the offer from Lawrence Academy.

As an independent school head, I have found that the training, experience, and familiarity I have with the law are of inestimable value in performing my job day in and day out. Legal issues that present themselves or that lurk undetected on the horizon can be intimidating, confusing, and difficult to understand, parse, and recognize; and they can be paralyzing to non-lawyers. Thanks to my nontraditional background, I never feel out of my element in this regard. Heads who are not familiar with the law may find themselves calling the school attorney when they don't really need to or not calling him or her when they absolutely should. I have a good sense for when I need to pick up the phone to my school counsel, and my conversations with him tend to be collaborative rather than instructive.

Interacting with lawyers (especially parents who are lawyers), law enforcement personnel, and regulatory authorities can be extremely uncomfortable without training, expertise, and confidence in how to handle these interactions. Moreover, in many cases, they can be turned to a school's advantage. For example, here at Lawrence Academy, we open up our dining facilities at all meals to the town police officers who are on duty. It sets a good tone; we find that the officers take a caring interest in our kids, our faculty, and our campus. In those rare cases where we get paid an official call, the police know us and are keen to work with us to resolve a matter.

Sadly, we live in a litigious society, and nowhere have I seen this more in evidence than when a student runs into serious disciplinary trouble and has been asked to leave the school. I can recount only a few occasions in my tenure as a dean of students, division head, or head of school where parents didn't hire or threaten to hire legal counsel with an eye to fighting a dismissal. In serious disciplinary matters, attention to thorough investigation, adherence to published disciplinary procedures, and an understanding of when it is in the best legal interests of the school to pass a matter off to the school attorney can rule the day and the ultimate outcome for the school.

As a result of my tenure in the law, there is relatively little I do, say, write, or think that is not first processed through a legal lens. At times, this works to my disadvantage. As head of school, my constituencies expect me to behave like a head of school and not like an attorney, and I struggle at times to fulfill that expectation. I tend to write like a lawyer, and I am often criticized for this. When I use life experiences in the talks or speeches I give to different school groups, I have found it is best to focus on my "traditional" school self rather than my "nontraditional" legal self because people generally don't have a high regard for attorneys. When I have to rely on legal reasons for taking a particular course of action or for not being able to speak publicly about the details of a matter (e.g., terminating an employee midyear), I spend political capital as penance for being the "legal" me rather than the "headly" me.

In addition to having a law degree where some folks expect an education degree, I know that some of my faculty would want to see heftier academic credentials in my background, and that, too, has worked to my disadvantage at times. At the end of the day, however, I could not do my job as head of school with the confidence I have without my law degree and training, and I appreciate the extra punch this nontraditional aspect of my background gives me.

Each of the following educators also draws substantial strength and empowerment from a nontraditional pathway to independent school headship.

Paul M. Krieger spent the first 12 years of his working life in sales, marketing, and management with an international architectural firm. He had only one job offer when he graduated from college: selling aluminum in Saudi Arabia for a U.S.–Saudi joint venture. He spent four years in Saudi Arabia and two in Athens as a Middle East marketing manager. He then moved to the company's corporate headquarters in New Jersey as international marketing manager. But by 1989, after 12 years with the company, Paul yearned for something more. He had powerful memories of his own independent school experience at Newark Academy in Livingston, New Jersey. He realized that he wanted to work with young people because he wanted to have the impact on adolescents that many of his teachers had had on him. He figured he could do this best by teaching history, coaching, and mentoring young people in an independent school setting. But his business background and lack of teaching experience made breaking into teaching in independent schools a daunting task. Ever the visionary, Paul secured a position in the advancement office at The Hill School in Pottstown, Pennsylvania, eventually becoming a full-time history teacher, houseparent, and coach.

After eight years at The Hill, he became the assistant headmaster at Montgomery School in Chester Springs, Pennsylvania, and began work on his master's degree in educational leadership at nearby Immaculata University. He was recruited to fill the role of principal at Christ School in Asheville, North Carolina, in 2000 and ultimately ascended to the position of head in 2003.

Paul counts the time he spent working in the business world and traversing the globe as a pivotal experience that he calls on daily in his role as head of an independent school. The ability to interact with people from all sorts of backgrounds and sensibilities gives Paul unusual access and effectiveness in connecting with each of the constituencies within his school community. Moreover, he has a strong understanding of the financial workings and underpinnings of his school, an exceptionally valuable skill in these challenging economic times.

Marcy E. Cathey grew up in Silver Spring, Maryland, attended public school there, and went to Duke University, earning her bachelor's degree in public policy. During two of her summers at Duke, Marcy worked for IBM, developing a knowledge base in technology and the soon-to-be-booming computer industry. After graduation, Marcy returned to Washington, DC, to work for NBI, a company that was marketing its own word-processing system and other software packages. Marcy became a marketing representative with a natural talent for teaching her customers how to use NBI's products.

Marcy left NBI in 1985 after her first child was born and, shortly thereafter, got a call from the International Monetary Fund (a former NBI customer), seeking her assistance as a trainer in technology for employees and as a computer systems troubleshooter. Marcy could work part-time and have plenty of time to be a mother.

After Marcy's second child was born in 1990, she saw a classified advertisement for a computer teacher at a nearby independent school in Alexandria, Virginia. Despite having no experience in teaching children in a formal school setting, Marcy's experience teaching adults and her understanding of technology earned her her first position in an independent school. Shortly after she was hired, her school merged with a neighboring school to become St. Stephen's and St. Agnes School. After the merger, Marcy was asked to head up the newly created Computer Science Department.

In her fifth year at the school, Marcy became an internal candidate for the position of director of technology. Although she was not successful, when the Madeira School in McLean, Virginia, began a search for a technology director, she threw her hat into the ring, and this time she won the appointment. Under the tutelage of Headmistress Elisabeth Griffith at Madeira, who had a high regard for Marcy's excellent multitasking skills and easy way with people, Marcy was elevated to the role of assistant head of school for technology and was encouraged to start thinking about becoming a head of school herself.

In 1997, she began coursework through Nova Southeastern University in Florida to earn her master's degree in instructional technology and distance education. She wrote her master's thesis on teaching mature classroom teachers how to integrate technology into their classrooms. In her last years at Madeira, she began to pursue headship opportunities and found the match she was looking for at Holy Trinity Episcopal Day School in Glenn Dale, Maryland in 2005.

During Marcy's tenure as head of Holy Trinity, her experiences in marketing allowed her to communicate the right messages about her school to all sorts of constituencies in a way that was interesting and exciting. She helped her faculty and staff understand the importance of conveying messages in the proper way as well. Marcy's facility and expertise with technology have served her well as a head of school, unlike many of us who must rely on our technology professionals to tell us what is going on.

Marcy has recently been named the head-elect of Good Shepherd Episcopal School in Dallas, Texas. She will assume her duties there in July 2011.

Hugh McIntosh grew up attending local public schools in Collins, Mississippi, and, like many of his small-town classmates, playing football and other team sports. After logging some hours on the gridiron at Mississippi State, Hugh graduated with a general business degree in 1967 and immediately entered Officer Candidate School, serving three years as an officer in the U.S. Navy (aboard a destroyer for two years and as a naval advisor in Vietnam for one). He then attended law school at the University of Virginia and practiced law in Houston, Texas, and Washington, DC, for the next 25 years with the nationally recognized law firm of Vinson & Elkins.

But when he was 50, Hugh began to contemplate career opportunities in the not-for-profit sector to expand his horizons and satisfy his desire to be of service to others. In this soul-searching process, Hugh received one particularly valuable piece of advice: Act like an adolescent for two years. When Hugh asked what that meant, he was told to try the things he wanted to do and drop them just as quickly if he didn't want to stick with them (I love this definition of adolescence, by the way!).

Hugh decided that he really wanted to attend divinity school and become a chaplain at a college or independent school. In 2001, he earned his master of divinity degree from Harvard Divinity School. In July 2001, Hugh accepted a one-year chaplaincy at Punahou School in Honolulu, Hawaii, beginning his new life as an independent school educator. In addition to his chaplaincy, Hugh served as advisor to the school's president for character development. He quickly realized the impact that a great teacher and leader can have on the lives of young people. Together with Head of School Jim Scott, Hugh worked with a group of colleagues to refresh the chapel program and explore the territory ahead for Punahou's character education curriculum. He also began to imagine himself as leader of his own school.

When Hugh's one-year posting at Punahou ended, he returned to Houston and did some consulting on leadership development and character development at The Kinkaid School. When Don North, the head at Kinkaid, told Hugh about a head vacancy at Keystone School in San Antonio, Hugh entered the search and was named head of school. He began his tenure in January 2004. After serving as Keystone's head of school for six and a half years, Hugh moved to his new post as head of the Episcopal High School of

Baton Rouge, Louisiana, in the summer of 2010.

Hugh believes that his experience on the legal end of corporate finance taught him to quickly discern strengths and weaknesses in organizations and to understand the complexities of their operating systems. His time as de facto COO in the DC offices of a high-powered law firm gave him experience in assembling teams of folks to work together toward common goals. His time at Harvard Divinity School gave him insights into what it takes to build a cohesive, meaningful, and stable community and how important it is to be

PERSPECTIVE

ONE THING I HAD TO LEARN THAT IN A MILLION YEARS I NEVER THOUGHT I'D NEED TO KNOW

Deborah E. Reed, Head of School
Polytechnic School
PASADENA, CALIFORNIA

I never thought that I would need to know about the construction of parking lots or parking garages.

Most schools that are in urban or suburban neighborhoods have increased enrollment since their founding or in the last 30 years. We impinge on our neighborhoods and complicate the lives of our neighbors. One reason we have increased traffic in our neighborhoods is that, these days, for many of our students, both parents work. This means that when parents come to events on campus, they often must arrive from different destinations in different cars. In addition, more and more of our students drive to school as we draw our student bodies from greater distances. And because the laws now mandate that new drivers may not have passengers other than family members, carpooling is often not an option.

As a result, we need to attend to our neighbors in ways we may not have in the past. That includes providing both ample parking for students and visitors and managing the traffic in our neighborhoods. I would never have thought that I would need to know about the city's parking and traffic ordinances and city master plan requirements.

In a sense, all of this falls under the topic of neighborhood and civic relations. Schools are to a greater extent expected to be good citizens— and rightly so — and this includes submitting plans for approval, holding neighborhood meetings, and participating actively in the community. Our contributions to the community have included tutoring in public schools, summer programs in collaboration with Pasadena Unified and other independent schools, food drives, and working at homeless shelters. We expanded our definition of service to include being a better neighbor. When our master plan met with neighborhood resistance, our city councilman and a friend of the school suggested that we take the time to meet with the people who lived near the campus and to listen to them. Regular communication with the neighbors about school events, invitations to plays and the school fair, the delivery of poinsettias at the holidays —these all spoke to our recognition of the people who lived next door to the school and improved our relationship with them. ■

inclusive. From practicing law, Hugh learned important lessons about being collaborative, which have helped him work with teachers. (Although I find it amusing when Hugh mentions that his time in the U.S. Navy pre-Vietnam training gave him the ability to spot insurgencies and prepare to fend them off, I have no doubt that this skill comes in handy as a head of school from time to time!) Hugh also feels that being the father of three children who went through independent schools gave him an appreciation for the important contributions parents make to our schools, even as the rest of us sometimes wonder why they can be so demanding or prickly.

Margarita O'Byrne Curtis has alternated between postings in independent schools and university settings for most of her career. A native of Colombia who moved to New Orleans with her family at age 12, Margarita was greatly influenced by the high regard her parents placed on education. After she graduated from Tulane University with a bachelor's in French literature in 1973, she undertook a year of study at Minnesota State University, Mankato, to pursue teacher certification in French and Spanish. In the fall of her first semester at Mankato, however, the professor of one of her courses died unexpectedly. In a scramble to find a replacement, Margarita the "student" was hired to be Margarita, the "teacher." Once she began teaching, she knew that she had found her calling.

She returned to New Orleans and secured her first position in an independent school as a French and Spanish teacher at Metairie Park Country Day School. Three years later, she moved with her physician husband to the Boston area and began work on her master of liberal arts in Spanish and Latin American Literature at Harvard University while serving as an instructor in the Department of Romance Languages and Literatures. After she earned her degree and spent another year teaching at Harvard, she was encouraged to apply for a position as chair of the Spanish Department at Phillips Academy in nearby Andover, Massachusetts. Margarita took famously to life in a boarding school and happily wore all of the hats that boarding school teachers wear. When she decided to return to Harvard to pursue her Ph.D. in Romance Languages, she took a three-year leave of absence from Andover and once again taught full-time at Harvard while she was pursuing her degree.

Margarita returned to Andover in 1991 on a full-time basis while she was finishing her dissertation. In 1993, she reclaimed the Spanish Department chair, became the head of World Languages in 1997, and was appointed dean of studies of the Academy in 2004. As Margarita took on administrative roles of a larger magnitude during the late 1990s, she began to think more and more about becoming a head of school and was finally appointed as the 55th head of Deerfield Academy in 2006.

Jack E. Creeden grew up in Boston, attended Catholic Memorial School, and earned his bachelor's degree in English in 1974 from the College of the Holy Cross. He then moved on to the University of Wisconsin to pursue a master's degree in English literature while working his way up the administrative ranks to become assistant dean of the College of Letters and Sciences at the university. Along the way, he earned his doctorate in educational administration. In 1986, Jack returned to the East Coast to become assistant provost of student affairs at Rutgers University and was later promoted to associate provost. In 1991, he moved with his family to Great Britain for a year to become the director of Rutgers' Study Abroad Program.

Jack describes his year abroad overseeing the 100 students enrolled in this program as one of his most transformative career experiences. Working closely with this small group of students, Jack found that he could really make a difference in their lives and have an impact on creating a community ethos that supported and nurtured its members. Jack began to focus on finding a professional environment that replicated this experience. A colleague suggested that he become the head of a boarding school. Jack met with a search consultant who encouraged him. In 1995, he became the sixth head of Fountain Valley School of Colorado in Colorado Springs. He served in this position until 2007 and then he served as head of Providence Day School in Charlotte, North Carolina, from 2007 to 2010.

At this writing, Jack is enjoying taking on some projects and work that he didn't have time for when he was a sitting head, including assisting the KIPP School in Charlotte, writing articles for educational publications, conducting workshops on governance at independent schools, and providing fundraising expertise to local foundations.

Stephanie J. Hull has been the head of school at the Brearley School in New York City since 2003. During her formative years, Stephanie's heart was set on becoming a fashion designer. Indeed, becoming a professor, a college dean, an assistant to the president of a college, or the head of school of a highly regarded independent day school in New York City couldn't have been further from her thoughts when she set off at the age of 10 to position herself for a career in fashion design! Realizing even at that tender age that Paris was where the action was, she decided to prepare herself to mix in the world of fashion by studying French with great purpose and zeal.

Throughout her education, Stephanie continued to embrace the goal of a career in fashion design at the same time she was excelling in all her academic disciplines, especially French. Upon her graduation from high school, her parents urged her to apply to a high-caliber liberal arts college, thinking that she would be well-positioned for success if she were to decide that her fashion design career plan was more of a romantic notion than a purposeful goal.

After enrolling at Wellesley College and putting herself on track to graduate in three years, Stephanie went on a few job interviews with major corporations that came to campus to recruit aspiring corporate titans. She found out in short order that those career opportunities did not resonate with her.

At the urging of her French professor, she applied to graduate school at Harvard University and, over the next five years, she earned her M.A. and Ph.D. in romance languages and literature. As an added plus, during her time at Harvard, she spent two years as a teaching fellow at Wellesley College. It was through her Wellesley classroom teaching experiences and transformational interactions with then-president Nannerl Keohane that Stephanie fell in love with teaching and was inspired to adopt the career goal of becoming a college president.

After graduating from Harvard, she joined the Dartmouth College faculty as a tenure-track professor in the Department of French and Italian. After she had been at Dartmouth for four years, she jumped at the opportunity to become an assistant dean of the college. She served in that role for three years, citing as one of her most significant accomplishments the expansion of an integrated academic support program for at-risk freshmen. To her surprise, Stephanie took some real heat for moving into the administrative ranks from colleagues who had earned or who were seeking to earn tenure at Dartmouth. She believes that this was because the college had put so much effort into recruiting her to the faculty, particularly because she was a person of color who was an academic and a scholar.

Still moving toward her goal of a college presidency, in 1998 Stephanie took on the job of assistant to the president of Mount Holyoke College and also served as secretary to the college. In that role, she served as chief of staff to the president and to the board of trustees of the college.

By her fifth year at Mount Holyoke, fashion design had fallen off her "must-do" list, and becoming a college president had moved to the forefront. Then something strange happened. A search firm contacted her to see if she knew anyone who might be interested in being a candidate for head of school for a K-12 girls' day school in New York City. When Stephanie read the job description, she was intrigued. She pursued a search interview, visited the Brearley School, and fell in love. She saw that the girls at Brearley were engaged in the life of the mind and embraced the discussion of ideas as regular social discourse.

Eight years later, Stephanie Hull continues to revel in her good fortune at having had the presence of mind to look at something else when her sights on a college presidency were all but etched in stone. One of the most memorable things I have heard her say was in response to this question: "Why be a head of school when you could be a college president?" Her response: "Because as head of school, I get to play with kindergartners at snack time when they come to visit me." If you are an aspiring head, this quote should resonate with you, too.

CONCLUSION

What interests me most about all of these heads of school is that none of them ever envisioned working in independent school education when she or he first set off on a career path. Yet after making the transition to independent school education, each was a natural as an educational leader.

As the role of the head of school in independent schools continues to expand into myriad areas of responsibility, more and more people from nontraditional backgrounds will be looked upon as the preferred candidates to run the independent schools of the future. If you are reading this chapter because you bring a nontraditional background into the world of independent education, you have a strong wind in your sails as you move toward becoming a head of school!

DIFFERENT EXPERIENCES OF HEADSHIP

Andrew T. Watson

THE PAST SIX MONTHS *have gone by in a blur, but it all seems to have fallen into place — the search, the move, helpful new friends from NAIS's Institute for New Heads, successful opening speeches and letters — and now, three months into your first headship, you truly are bonding with the school. From "acting" like a head of school, a leader, you have progressed to actually leading: Today's difficult but open, productive, and successful faculty meeting set the path for the coming months and years of work. This is what you were hoping for. Were you just lucky, or did you and your school actually create this hopeful moment for each other?*

IT STARTS WITH THE SEARCH

"I want to be a head of school some day."

We have all heard this phrase spoken by colleagues along the way, sometimes uttered in a soft-spoken, humble fashion but at other times (more frequently, actually) immodestly, particularly when spoken in certain tones or at certain times. We also know many school heads who, quite possibly, never once uttered the phrase aloud until the day they threw their name into a search or accepted the entreaties of a search consultant to learn more about a particular school.

"I want to be a head of school some day."

The phrase is too generic. Independent school headships differ as much across schools as administrative jobs differ within a single school. And while most independent school administrators realize that they aren't well suited, by temperament or skill set, to take on all of the jobs within their current schools, some don't transfer this knowledge as they envision a headship in generic terms rather than as a match with a particular school.

The head's job can vary from driving the bus to town every Saturday in one school to not knowing the names of any of the (presumably outsourced) drivers within a fleet of school buses in another. There are equally wide differences (though no need to discuss them here) in school cultures when it comes to student and faculty expectations, willingness to attempt change, and (sigh) the politicized attitudes of groups and individuals pushed to dogmatic polarity in today's lightly informed, but highly opinionated, culture.

In addition, schools have widely disparate cultures of governance, though this isn't easy to assess as well-behaved search committees go about their work. After a bit of training, most boards are eager to convey the notion that they "get it" when it comes to best governance practices. But while many eager board members can quote Dick Chait verbatim, some still have the tendency to work at cross-purposes with the board as a whole, to forget their duty to confidentiality when speaking outside the boardroom, and to bring up topics that belong at the staff level if there is a break in the action during a board meeting. This is human nature and, before judging, we should recognize that at times we may do the same on the boards we serve, despite knowing better.

Practically speaking, the aspiring head has to envision having 20 or so bosses, rather than the more predictable one boss from the past. If the details of the past head's departure make it possible, confer with him or her about the school's culture of governance, knowing that, in some cases, this culture might be repairing itself even as you go through the interview process.

Potential school heads live with these challenges already and should examine themselves and prospective schools thoroughly to determine whether

PERSPECTIVE

TEN THINGS I LEARNED ALONG THE WAY

Margaret W. (Sissy) Wade, Head of School
Franklin Road Academy
NASHVILLE, TENNESSEE

1. **Surround yourself with good people** — people you trust to be honest, both with you and with themselves. Create a leadership team and form a bond that allows for the free flow of ideas.

2. **If something doesn't seem right, it probably isn't!** If you know that someone is not in sync with you and your core values, don't hesitate. Trust your instincts. A good head has good instincts. The trouble is, we like people and want to see the best in them, sometimes to our detriment.

3. **Establish for yourself and the board a yearly set of initiatives** — you are there to lead as well as manage. You need to have two or three initiatives to accomplish each year, goals that are agreed upon by the trustees. It's good to see progress, and those initiatives will show it, to yourself and to others.

4. **Get with the students.** I do it by "making rounds" once a week, in and out of classrooms. One day a month is set aside for "going to school." I just sit in on classes and leave a note of thanks behind for the teacher. It renews my heart and also my resolve.

5. **Be sure to have a great financial officer.** Independent schools are accountable to our constituents. A financial officer who looks both down at the books and out at the school will lessen your load and be an invaluable partner on your leadership team.

6. **Tell the story.** Don't be shy. You have a compelling story to tell — one that is important for your constituents to hear and your donors to consider. At the heart of good fund-raising is authentic and heartfelt storytelling.

7. **You need a good school attorney — on speed dial.** In today's world of suit and countersuit, you need an ally as you confront legal issues.

8. **Phone a friend.** A fellow head, probably not in your city, is essential when you need advice. Be it a difficult disciplinary situation or an initiative you are considering, a fellow head knows where the land mines are lying as well as how to get to the mountaintop.

9. **Mission, mission, mission** — it should be posted everywhere and known by everyone. It is the heart of every message you send, and it needs to resonate with every person on your campus, student, and adult.

10. **You are *always* the head of school.** Whether grocery shopping or watching an athletic contest off-campus, you are the head of school. Accepting that role as your lifestyle is part of the job. ■

a new school is potentially the right fit. The job of head begins with the search, not on July 1 *after* a successful search. I very nearly learned this lesson the hard way. After doing what needed to be done to receive a headship offer, I realized, hours after getting off the plane from a final visit and hours before receiving the offer, that I would be a miserable fit with the school — both in the eyes of the community and in my own estimation. I would fail in this school, my tenure would be short, and harm would befall us both. My error and perhaps hubris? I went into the search and then into the finalist interview simply wanting to be a head of school. Thank goodness I woke up before making a very big mistake.

Arriving with a discerning eye about school-head fit, head candidates should also be doubly, indubitably, themselves during the search process. Doing so increases the probability that the school knows, and wants, what it is getting when it offers the job. The school community has seen the real person, not one altered by the interview process into an inauthentic but successful candidate. Aspiring heads shouldn't want a job unless it is attained because of personal qualities that will endure every day of their lives.

It is very important, before accepting a headship, to fully understand the task at hand, particularly on the financial front. While not an overwhelming trend, this has been the number one "I was surprised" category expressed by heads at NAIS's Institute for New Heads over the past few years. It is natural that search committees want you to experience the uniqueness and the mission of the school when you visit, leaving the less-scintillating financial details in the background; find your way to this area before your visit ends, or soon thereafter, for your own sake and for the sake of the school.

As the search ends, and despite a wise candidate's efforts to be authentic, prospective heads who truly know themselves probably end up with a truer sense of personal fit with a school than the search committee and search consultant have about school fit with the candidate. It is a moment of decision when being true to oneself is vital for the future of both the candidate and the school.

Bottom line: By the end of the process, if all goes well, the head candidate will have shifted from "I want to be a head of school" to "I want to lead *this* school and serve its mission."

THE WORK, AND THE JOY, BEGINS

One hears wonderful, varied stories from sitting heads about the enjoyment of leading an independent school. These stories connect to mission, making a difference in an entire community, watching children grow and prosper, and creating a better country — and world — through the lives of graduates. Some heads gravitate toward an "I-am-the-symbol/figurehead-of-my-school-community" attitude, born of a feeling of responsibility more than a statement of ego, while others talk of service and passing through the history of a school as an advocate for a mission. Good heads are well-meaning, and few seem at all self-serving.

New to independent schools altogether? As you look at your possible headship, make sure that you actually like the independent school model — faculty members will sense ambivalence about this in a heartbeat. Your training has been different and, particularly if you've been in public schools, some portion of this training needs to be discarded (while other aspects, of course, will be invaluable). Find an experienced independent school mentor, and be open to his or her advice. You will probably love working in an independent school, but beware of treating it like a superintendency, particularly in areas such as administrative structure and relationships with individual faculty and staff members. And be aware that many on campus will expect intellectual leadership among the many traits they seek in their new leader.

I asked several head colleagues what aspects of their schools or jobs they most enjoyed. Here are some of their answers:

> What I had not expected as a new head, yet soon came to recognize, was the pastoral aspect of leading a school. It is humbling, sometimes deeply moving, and always an opportunity for learning, to be in a position where members of the community may seek one out to ask an urgent question, express both joy and sorrow, or struggle with personal pain or private fears. Being fully present to celebrate or console often has been the most important thing, more than any counsel or expertise I might offer. It has meant saying that in fact the door to my office is not always open, that privacy can be as important as access, that simple witness can matter as much as sound advice.
> — Mark W. Segar, Waynflete School (ME)

> The way I think of it is that we have the privilege of all of the tools — knowledge of the system, knowledge of the wishes and aspirations of others, human and financial resources, etc. — and can use them to advance our schools,

their missions, and the lives of the people (student and adult) who are a part of them. That's the part of the work I love.

— Lisa Darling, Armand Hammer United World College of the American West (NM)

Being the head of school feels like my ideal job. There are challenges, certainly, but to shape the educational experience and help to influence the culture of my school feels like a rare privilege. I don't take my supportive board of trustees for granted for an instant, and I feel fortunate to have an outstanding faculty willing to innovate, create, and think with me about what is in the best interest of our girls. The children and families in our school are remarkable. Personally, I haven't been bored a single day in five years, which I think is an indicator that I love what I do.

— Ann V. Klotz, Laurel School (OH)

And as for joy and goodness and headship ... for me, it boils down to being able to set the tone (just as teachers do in a classroom!) ... you get to lead the shaping of a language, the naming of the values and the modeling for young people ... it doesn't get much better than that! It is the joy of collaboration, of witnessing and of being part of something that just can't be about one person. And every day is the same in that call, but different in the specifics.

— Bodie Brizendine, The Spence School (NY)

I could not imagine doing anything else and always go "arrgh" when I hear a speaker say we have it so rough, etc. ... . I love going to work each day.

— Mark Desjardins, St. John's School (TX)

The good is easy: This is by far the most fulfilling job that I have ever been a part of — it is not about one aspect of it but about all of it. Every interaction and experience has a sense of import, meaning, and purpose that I had never felt in a prior position, and I absolutely love all of it.

— Jeff Leahy, Colorado Rocky Mountain School (CO)

For me the joy of the job comes in knowing that what I'm doing, many times behind the scenes and out of the conscious thoughts of parents, students, and faculty/staff, is creating opportunities for a life-changing education. Equal joy comes from getting to personally know and share the experiences of life with dedicated faculty, close colleagues, great parents (most of them are, you know), and talented/unique students.

— Bob Windham, St. Mary's Hall (TX)

As for my greatest joy in the job: it is having so much stimulus, from so many directions, that challenges me to do my best in so many ways. As Frost writes in "Birches," "Earth's the right place for love/I don't know where it's likely to go better." I feel that way, particularly about running this school: I'm in it head and heart, feet and wallet!

— Jim Leonard, Santa Fe Prep (NM)

A simple joy for me is the first week of school. I spend it listening to great summer stories, high-fiving students, and walking around our great school witnessing the magic of a typical day.
— T.J. Locke, Isidore Newman School (LA)

Favorite part of the job? It has to be that I am always doing something different — that each day brings a new and different challenge; I cannot imagine a job that is more stimulating, both personally and professionally. I also find that I still am a teacher (which is how most of us got here), although not necessarily in the classroom; there is always something to be taught.
— Stephanie G. "Penny" Townsend, The Pennington School (NJ)

It is enjoying the little things; they are happening all around us every day. The daily accomplishments of our wonderful students and teachers are uplifting and rewarding. They are the things that feed my soul in this job. Raising money, building new buildings, and other big and important milestones provide only fleeting moments of satisfaction. They can feel big, but they are not what is important. At the heart of it all, we are all teachers trying our best to help our kids.
— William Moseley, Ensworth School (TN)

If you finally get into the right school for you, one that closely matches your philosophy and ideals, AND you have a high-quality, high-functioning board (both hard to find), then one cannot have a better job … it is almost like not working … sort of … .
— Ray Griffin, The Chinquapin School (TX)

The enjoyment is as varied as our independent schools, our independent selves. It expresses itself in poetry and in prose, in philosophy and in practicality. And while no one respondent can capture it all or predict where it will live the most for the next new head, the combined voices of all (well, almost all) the heads I know create a chorus of satisfaction.

Speaking personally, the head of school job never ceases to surprise me, while also satisfying so many temperamental and existential needs. You want to know why?

- Ask me about language labs; solar arrays; the HSSSE, CTP 4, and WrAP; performance engineering; the documentation of adherence to standards; branding; D&O insurance; mezzanine debt; LYBUNTS; websites, database integration, and T3 lines; the federal free and reduced price lunch program; ERISA, UPMIPA, and intermediate sanctions. Ask me about that mysterious good governance thing. Go ahead, ask!

I won't always have the best answers in these areas or in many others that were completely new to me as head, but I've enjoyed exploring them amid the constant growth and exhilaration of the job — all without leaving educational areas behind, for a head's educational knowledge also expands due to constant practice, communication, professional development, and intellectual stimulation. I once had a colleague who started his teaching career in the British army. His routine consisted of getting a packet of materials on almost any topic under the sun on Friday and then stepping in front of a room full of enlisted men on Monday to teach the topic. It isn't always quite this frantic for a head of school, but it is a constant joy to be learning new aspects of management and leadership, education and psychology, buildings and grounds, the global and the local, throughout one's headship. And after learning in so many areas along the way, like that British teacher, we quickly turn around and teach some of what we've learned to our community as we make (and explain) decisions, enlist support for initiatives, and generate enthusiasm for our school as it moves forward. The stimulation never ends, and it constantly creates new connections among bodies of knowledge, quite to the satisfaction of the lifelong learners who become school heads.

- Most aspiring school heads are already highly creative in their current jobs, but a new feeling arrives with the headship; it is a loosening of restraints and a lessening of "having to check/get permission" when a great idea comes along. This comes, of course, with great responsibility but also with great liberation.

  How annoying when, in your middle-management administrative position, a decision made after great care and communication is rejected by a parent or faculty member who then takes the matter to the head of school's office for further consideration. You feel as though you've let your head down by not settling the matter yourself, and the anger of the parent/faculty member weighs heavily upon you. You might even have doubts about your decision and worry that the head will overturn it and think less of your decision-making. Even worse — you might absolutely know that you've done the right thing but worry that political pressure will cause the head to change the decision anyway, perhaps weakening the community and lowering your estimation of him or her. It is surprising how these concerns fall away in the head's office. The irate parents leaving the division head's office (you have been more than amply warned by the worried division head) are much more reasonable, most of the time, when they get to your office. You aren't looking over your shoulder because you have taught your board (or they already knew!) that it is the head, not the board, who serves as the final stop along the way for almost all school matters. Beleaguered heads of school (there are some out there) bemoan the fact that the buck stops at their desk, but, in reality, the head of school's desk itself changes the tone of the conversation and makes tough conversations seem easier. In sum, you will be dealing with the toughest issues in the school, but many of them won't feel as difficult as they were in the past.

- "I'll miss working closely with the students and teaching if I become a head … ." There is a little truth here, but boy, does the "you-must-miss-working-with-the-students" statement get old. It's bad enough that this question is so often asked of heads, but worse still when the sentiment is brought up by heads themselves (are they somehow being forced against their will to do this job instead of working in the classroom?). While student contact changes and can diminish when you are a head, the types of contact available are very rich. They come in moments of beauty and endeavor as you watch student performances, speeches, and athletic competitions. They arrive in life-defining moments as you take advantage of disciplinary situations, even dismissals from your school, to counsel students and show your belief in them for the future. As you walk the campus, you have the power of surprise when praising students about their efforts ("Wow — how did he/she know about the Science Olympiad contest over the weekend?"). The notes of gratitude, congratulations, and sympathy that you write to students are pinned up on bulletin boards and stuck into the frames of mirrors that you will never see, making a difference well after your memory of writing them fades — even

> your most aloof students have these private places where they note triumphs that they don't share with their friends. You'll miss teaching? Forget about it — you will never be more of a teacher than when you are a head of school. The audience shifts to older "students," but the meetings you run, speeches you deliver, plans you make, and counsel you give all invoke your strengths as a teacher. You will need to design these moments just as carefully as you designed your curriculum and classes in the past, and the result of a good "class" in this setting is just as satisfying as it was in the classroom.

And when things go wrong (as they will), you learn about yourself, and you reach a point where your worries diminish as long as you know that you have done your best. When at fault, you learn how to apologize to individuals and groups more broadly than in the past and, in doing so, you model authenticity, goodness, and humanity. And as you think about your doubts and mistakes, you grow stronger in knowing what works and what doesn't. This, in turn, improves your chances of making even more of a difference in the life of your community in the future.

AND THEN IT ALL SINKS IN

Finally, long after the thrill of hearing that you've been chosen to lead a school that fits and long after the thrill of that first head-of-school paycheck ("You've got to be kidding me — I'll be able to settle debts that I've carried for years since beginning this noble, but non-lucrative, profession!") — long after these startling first moments, you will reach a point when the meaning of your work sinks in, when you catch a glimpse, from the middle of your career, of how satisfied you will be at the end of both your career and your life with the difference you have made in the lives and histories of families other than your own.

We first read the existentialists in college at an idealistic time of life, but, at least for me, true understanding of the importance of creating one's meaning in life dawned in the classroom and reached its peak as a school head. We all have the ability to create this meaning through our personal lives and actions. I have to marvel, though, that I also have a job that allows an expression of this essential human need.

So, by all means, aspire to be a head of the right school, know yourself well in the process of finding that school, and then prepare for the most stimulating blend of challenge, learning, and joy imaginable. I just wish that everyone I know could have equally satisfying opportunities to serve others in such full lives of meaning.

Sitting at graduation, two years into your headship: Most of the work has gone well, and you are very pleased to have so many local experiences under your belt to add to the general knowledge you brought to the job (including the local intricacies of all of today's graduation traditions). The student speaker begins, and she starts talking about the school and its newly described purpose. She quotes, from memory, powerful phrases (including the ones you use the most) from the mission statement. You are stunned and emotional. It feels as though she is giving one of your *speeches, though so much better as she brings her wide-eyed idealism to the task and utters words that are fresher coming from her lips than from yours. You want to poke someone nearby and say, "Can you believe it? Our top student has internalized what we are trying to do, and she has chosen, on a day and moment like this in her life, to tell everyone about it." Looking around, you can't tell whether others share an understanding of the beauty of this moment. You hope, though, that they do, and you can't wait to hear reactions after the ceremony. For now, you smile inwardly and think, "I'm in a mission-driven school with students and adults working together; I've made a difference in the culture here. The beauty of the school and its mission are personified at the podium today." And though there is so much more you hope to accomplish, you feel at home, you feel alive in the fullest sense possible.*

LIFE AFTER THE HEADSHIP

NEW ROADS TAKEN

Richard Barbieri

F. SCOTT FITZGERALD ONCE commented that there are no second acts in American lives. If that were ever true, it certainly no longer holds. Today, in fact, we often hear of a Third Age, Third Chapter, or even "Third Half" — that period after a long career when new roads are suddenly open and ready to be taken. For those wondering what life after headship might hold, former independent school leaders can provide expert guidance about the coming years. As one of these heads said, "It's amazing how folks have distributed their talents far and wide, using the great training we got in schools."

PART ONE: STILL IN SCHOOL

Many former school leaders continue a lifelong commitment to independent schools. Among the largest group are those who enjoy headship but without long-term commitment. In any given year, two or three dozen people, almost all former heads, take on interim headships. Helping a school that has lost its leader (through illness, late resignation, or a parting of the ways between head and board) offers special challenges but also draws on the skills honed over years or decades as a school head.

More and more, this cadre of experienced heads takes on a series of interim headships, sometimes taking successive jobs for a decade or more. Joan Beauregard is on her fourth interim, all on the West Coast and the first two in her home base, Seattle. She describes interim work as being "something of an in-house consultant. You need to ask lots of questions, advise the board of what you see, and help them find boundaries. The main satisfaction of interim headship is the intellectual stimulation of solving a puzzle." The differences between interim and long-term headship are significant. "New heads and interim heads operate at different speeds," she observes, and "Your connections are much more to parents and trustees than to students." While it is difficult to move on and lose new friends and colleagues, she noted that technology makes it much easier than in the past to keep in touch.

Some former heads enjoy the chance to vary their experience significantly, whether that means leading schools in different parts of the country or the world or simply leading schools that are different from those of their previous experience. Susan Kluver, for example, who had run two progressive elementary schools in Massachusetts (Touchstone Community School and Fayerweather Street School), has been an interim head at both an adult education program for nurses and New York City's School for Children at Bank Street College. She notes that "your ability to recognize the patterns at an institution gets better with each experience" and you learn to "operate at the [faster] pace needed for an interim."

For those seeking an interim headship, traditional search firms are often helpful, but just as many placements come through long-standing relationships, particularly in the local area, or through referrals from association executives and word of mouth among trustees and other school people.

Other former heads are happy to stay on in independent schools but no longer want to be in charge. Descending (if that is the right word) the hierarchy, they take a position that uses the skills acquired in their headship or one that hearkens back to the years before they stepped onto the leadership track.

Some of these former heads draw on a major headship skill, such as fundraising, while others return to their earliest love, the classroom. Chris Mabley, former head of St. Mark's School (MA) and St. Stephen's Episcopal School (TX), has done both. After 10 years at Noble and Greenough School (MA), the site of his first teaching job, where he directed graduate affairs, managed the development office, and taught math, he moved back to Austin and to part-time teaching. He said of this choice, "I entered this profession because I enjoyed working with adolescents. Because I am also professionally the product of the classroom, I always felt that I wanted to finish my career teaching." When asked if he felt any sense of moving back down the ladder, Chris replied, "No, the goals I had set for myself in my thirties — opportunity, challenge, responsibility, authority — were different from those of my fifties — to mentor and to give back. I felt that relationships were more important to me than opportunities for professional advancement."

Are there any difficulties in being a part of the team instead of its chief? Chris commented, "I miss the opportunity to affect the strategic direction the school takes. I can see what could be done, but I have no responsibility or authority. On the other hand, I don't miss the stress that went with 'ownership' of the whole institution." Another former head noted, "The jolt of not being the head, of not walking in the door and having wide interconnections, is stunning at first."

For those who choose not to return to headship, work as a search consultant is an extremely popular alternative. More than 40 former heads are active in search work, some with large, multi-service organizations, others in small or even one-person shops.

Experienced school leaders bring a great deal to the task of head searching. They know intimately the skill set needed by a head, as well as how to work effectively with a board of trustees to ensure a successful outcome. They have a wide network of professional contacts and are focused solely on the needs of independent schools, not on generic not-for-profit or CEO positions.

There is a great difference between being a school head and helping a school find one. Clay Stites, now with RG175 (a consulting group) after heading Friends Academy (MA) and the Curtis School (CA), suggests that "the respect that heads are used to goes away immediately," to be replaced by the feeling of being "a 'hired gun' of sorts." With the field of search consulting having increased markedly in recent years, "you have to be prepared for the competitiveness of a for-profit business in which you don't get nearly all the jobs you pitch, and you often take a job that may not be ideal because you're not sure a better one will come along." Nevertheless, he says, "The work itself is wonderful, and much more nuanced than it seems to be at first, drawing on all your skills as you respond to the complex dynamics of search committees." Though search consulting is time-consuming, he says, it is "infinitely less stressful than the work of a head."

Dick Jung, former principal at the John Burroughs School (MO) and head of the Bullis School (MD) and SEED Public Charter School (DC), is now the principal of his own firm, Education Access Strategies. He focuses on finding division leadership for large schools and heads for small and medium-sized schools. He says, "The predicate of a healthy school is the board chair–head

PERSPECTIVE

TEN UNCONVENTIONAL PROFESSIONAL DEVELOPMENT ACTIVITIES FOR THE HEAD OF SCHOOL

Keith Evans, Head of School
Collegiate School
RICHMOND, VIRGINIA

1. **Serve on the board** of a not-for-profit organization outside the independent school world.
2. **Serve on the accreditation team** of a school outside the United States.
3. **Complete an online course** in any area of interest.
4. **Subscribe to and read the *Harvard Business Review.***
5. **Visit and tour your board members' businesses or organizations.**
6. **Enroll in the Center for Creative Leadership's Leadership Development Program.**
7. **Watch at least one TED (*TED.com*) lecture** each week.
8. **Create a series of one- or two-day exchanges** with a non-competing, out-of-town school most like your own. Focus the exchanges on areas of strength as well as challenges. Work toward a trustee-to-trustee visit.
9. **Read** *What Would Google Do?*, *The Innovator's Dilemma*, and *Presentations Zen*.
10. **Spend a day divided between the campuses of two great schools** that are *not* similar to your own. ■

relationship, and I can assist at that nexus while still wearing jeans three out of five days and taking time for bike trips around the country and the world, one of my great satisfactions in life at 60+."

On the other hand, Agnes (Aggie) Underwood, former head of National Cathedral (DC) and Garrison Forest (MD) Schools and now leader of the Search and Consulting Group at Carney, Sandoe & Associates, says, "The work is the hardest I've ever done. It's 24/7." She emphasizes that "search is much more than making a match. There are hundreds of other decisions along the way that will lead to the right kind of outcomes, up to and including helping the old head leave gracefully and the new head arrive with the best chance of success." For Aggie, "Head search is in some ways a continuation of the mentoring you used to do internally. There's a great deal of satisfaction in preparing 'rising stars' in some modest way and especially in seeking people from diverse backgrounds as future heads."

PART TWO: A BROADER EDUCATION

Since independent schools make up only a small sector of American education, it's not surprising that some former heads remain in schooling but enter new terrain. From charter schools to educational think tanks and urban initiatives, former heads have continued to work with young people on a professional or an extensive volunteer basis.

Edwin Fredie, for example, former head of Milton Academy (MA), has spent the past decade working for school improvement with for-profit educational companies. Today, as vice president for school solutions at K12, he directs improvement programs at three post-Katrina New Orleans schools. "This is where the battle is," he says. "If we fail here, we're going to fail as a nation." He credits his independent school days with setting a standard: "Milton taught me a level of quality in teaching that I try to extend into public schools." And although he worries that "public schools are driven by metrics that work against the private school model," he finds that "even under the testing system, kids can achieve when engaged in learning and not practiced and tested to death." Perhaps the ultimate lesson he draws from independent and public school headship is that "there's no one formula for success except the culture and the leadership."

Ed Fredie's former Boston colleague, Carolyn McClintock Peter, was freshly retired from The Winsor School headship when she read about Beacon Academy, a school being formed in Boston to provide a "gap year" (actually lasting 14 months) for urban eighth-grade graduates who were capable and ambitious, but unprepared for entry into competitive independent secondary schools. The concept immediately resonated with her: "I'd sat for years on admissions committees and seen wonderful urban youngsters whom we wanted to have at Winsor but found many of them academically unprepared. Even those public middle school graduates who had the potential to succeed often needed extra support and struggled with the curriculum." Beacon was a chance to change the pattern. "I wanted to be involved with this new school committed to helping students succeed at strong schools from the beginning," she says. "The stereotype of students of color at the bottom of the class limits everyone." Her interest led her to volunteer to help found the school, join its board, and finally become board chair, a position she has held for three of the school's five years. Carolyn talks with delight of Beacon's achievements: "Watching the transformation is astonishing. On the first couple of days of summer school you think, 'This is not going to be possible,' but in two months a transformation is underway. First the students' attitude toward school and work changes; then they become willing to ask for and accept help; then they develop confidence based on academic competence. It's breathtaking to observe!"

Like many others, Carolyn relishes the diminution of responsibility. She says, "I work hard for Beacon Academy, but there's still time for concerts, yoga, grandchildren, study, and reading." Another former head put the change even more pointedly: "Stress is the biggest difference between the school world and the volunteer world. I am taking only half the blood pressure medicine now that I took then."

PART THREE: FRESH FIELDS AND PASTURES NEW

A growing number of former heads have turned their skills to not-for-profit organizations outside of classroom education. Along with association work, museums, foundations, and community agencies are among the possibilities. In recent years, for example, the Baltimore Community Foundation, the Geraldine R. Dodge Foundation in New Jersey, California's James Irvine Foundation, the Shelburne Museum in Vermont, and the Mystic Seaport Museum in Connecticut have all been led by former independent school heads.

These leaders credit their school experience as vital to their new work. Tom Wilcox, former head of Concord Academy (MA) and for 10 years president of the Baltimore Community Foundation, says, "My 19 years as a school head were a perfect preparation for handling the leadership of a community foundation. I needed every day in that seat to learn how to fill this one." Similarly, Steve White, former head of Fay School (MA), describes a conversation with an octogenarian member at Mystic Seaport Museum: "He asked me, 'What does someone like you bring to museums?' After I had told him some of the ways boarding schools and museums were alike, he concluded, 'I guess you are prepared for this.'"

Each former head has a different way of describing the transferable qualities. The answers include these comments:

- "It's all about building the strengths of the individual into a powerful institution."

PERSPECTIVE

ONE THING I HAD TO LEARN THAT IN A MILLION YEARS I NEVER THOUGHT I'D NEED TO KNOW

Kathleen G. Johnson, Vice President and Senior Associate
Carney, Sandoe & Associates
BOSTON, MASSACHUSETTS

One thing I learned that I never thought I'd need to know was all the issues associated with building. My first headship was in a school with lots of land, and as a capital campaign was being planned, the feasibility study showed that many people said, "Sell some land!" It was prime land along the Potomac River, just outside the Washington, DC, beltway. But in the course of assessing selling perhaps 100 acres or so, we learned that the land would not perk and hence was undevelopable. I learned about gray water and black water and much more about the building and sewage process than I ever thought I would need to know — all a far cry from my experience as an academic dean.

I learned from the wise chair of the committee exploring the possible sale of land that it was a good idea to put some people on the task force who were known to be in total opposition to the idea of selling *any* land. In case the decision was made to sell the land, there would be respected voices to help explain the decision. It was a very open, transparent process.

I valued that learning experience, too, and afterwards brought opposing perspectives to the table on a number of occasions. And, as it happened, when we could not develop the land, the money that we had initially sought came in from constituents! ■

- "Just like a school, to reach excellence you need to have a big vision and raise the funds to accomplish it."
- "Trying to help a group of people collaborate, respect each other, communicate decently, build solutions together — what's new about that?"

But novelty is also an attraction. David Sheldon, for more than two decades the head of Middlesex School (MA), is supposed to have commented about his position at the Shelburne Museum that, after a lifetime spent with adolescents, it was a pleasure to work with things that were over 100 years old and didn't move. On the other hand, his fellow museum director Steve White says, "Everything here is paper or wood, and they decay, so trying to care for this stuff is an unbelievable challenge."

Yet even those who move furthest afield find parallels. Tom Evans, head of Cape Cod Academy (MA) for 26 years, was committed to staying in his local community after retirement: "I couldn't imagine picking up and starting life all over again in a new place after many years in one that I've known and loved." The area knew him as well, and a number of agencies began calling on him for help. Tom currently serves on the boards of a nearby special needs school, a conservation organization, a regional community foundation, and — most unusually — the Cape Cod Five Cents Savings Bank, where he is a paid board member.

He explains how this last came about: "Our application for a mortgage loan impressed the local mutual bank, and the president later asked me to join first the corporation and then the board. I said that I knew nothing about banking and he replied, "At the school, you don't put all educators on your board, do you?'" Tom notes, "Because ours is a mutual bank, its responsibility is to the community and not to shareholders, making it mission-driven in much the same way an independent school is." Perhaps surprisingly, he says "I have yet to see an issue arise at the bank board that has not been an issue at independent schools."

Former head Peter Buttenheim has moved away from school leadership in two stages. Leaving the headship of Berkshire Country Day School (MA), he first worked in the alumni office of his alma mater, Williams College, and then became a teacher and administrator at several mid-Atlantic and midwestern schools before formal retirement. He now spends his time volunteering at the Food Bank of Delaware and St. Stephens Food Pantry in Wilmington, Delaware, because "I just don't believe anyone should be hungry." Peter comments on the difference between headship and these other positions: "When I was head of a small elementary school, everything I saw from the moment I came onto the campus in the morning was in some way my responsibility. Moving to a job in advancement, or even to division headship, I could walk by many things and know they weren't my responsibility and then reach my desk and tunnel into what I had to do. Now, at the end of each volunteer day, I feel very satisfied from the work I just did — and because I am not leaving behind a long to-do list, as I always did as a school head."

Finally, a few former heads moved away from the organizational world altogether. Two who found new lives as published writers are Peter Tacy and David D. Hume. After leaving the headship of The Marvelwood School (CT), Peter spent 15 years as executive director of the Connecticut Association of Independent Schools (CAIS), a period he describes as "sort of an airlock preparing me for the next transition." While at CAIS, he also served on the board of the Round Square Conference, an international affiliation of service-oriented schools. Almost immediately upon his retirement, Peter was asked to write that organization's history and to explain its approach to a wider audience. (He was also asked to raise the money for the publication, drawing on another headship skill.) After completing *Ideals at Work*, a project that took him around the world twice, he was invited to write the history of Round Square member Appleby College, a Canadian institution that is over 100 years old and which Peter describes as having been founded "to develop leadership for a nation that didn't quite yet exist."

Peter commented, "Like most of us, I went to grad school and thought this was all going to lead to research and writing. In a way, that was a dormant part of me that I'd longed to get back to, and I didn't discover that about myself until I was doing it." Learning about the history of Appleby, he says, was "like going into your grandmother's attic and trying on clothes that nobody's worn in a long time."

For David D. Hume, writing was also a return to earlier enthusiasms, as well as a new exploration. "I had built one small sailboat while still a head [at St.

David's School in New York City for 37 years]. After retirement I built *Blueberry* and wrote a book about building and sailing her, which has sold pretty well." David also explains that his doctor advised him to take up a new activity to keep mentally active. Rejecting crossword puzzles and Scrabble, David began to study Italian, and he and his wife traveled regularly to Italy. The result was four volumes (to date) on their travels through various regions of that country.

David's latest book and first novel, *Beyond the Long-Eared Mountains*, is dedicated to his six children. The book began many years ago with stories he told them on vacations. The whole thing started, he says, with "a map drawn on a shirt cardboard." This book, like his others, is illustrated with his own watercolors and pen-and-ink drawings, another enthusiasm that goes back to his college days. It is filled with nautical lore and literary allusions, blending almost all of his passions into one volume.

David contrasts the life of schools with that of a writer: "As a head, I was partly responsible for the welfare and behavior of 400 or more children, over whom I had limited control, and of 800 parents, over whom I had no control, as well as the faculty. It began to be wearing. Although I'm 81 now, I'm in good repair, and if I can't run up the stairs so well, I can sit down at a desk and bang away at a book."

The roads to these post-headship positions were many and varied. Some heads developed long-held relationships or personal passions, while others simply answered an advertisement. A few roles, like the foundation and museum directorships, called for extended commitments and drew most heavily on heads' fund-raising and institutional skills, while others tapped different talents and lasted for a shorter term.

Former heads all offer encouragement to their colleagues. Tom Wilcox says, "The notion of reinventing yourself is really exciting. From the promontory of school headship, there are so many directions in which you can go."

Peter Buttenheim's advice is "go do something else, because it's good for your spirit." Finally, in the words of Peter Tacy, this phase "gives you a chance to do some of the things in your life that you had the potential to do but that just didn't fit in. It changes the slope of the challenge in your life and makes the road steeper again, and I've always enjoyed most the times when the slope was steep."

ENDINGS AND NEW BEGINNINGS

Fran Norris Scoble

ONE DOESN'T DISCOVER new lands without consenting to lose sight of the shore for a very long time. — André Gide

PART ONE: ENDINGS

At the press conference when Bart Giamatti announced his retirement as president of Yale University in 1986, he was asked why he had decided to retire at the young age of 48 and at a time when he was widely admired and respected. He answered that, no matter how well you are doing, there comes a time when "you hear footsteps." He went on to say, "I've always thought it was important to be the first to hear them."

That was Giamatti's way of describing his own process of deciding when to leave. He was lucky. He left a great job as president of Yale to take what many thought was an even better one: Commissioner of Baseball.

To put it even more succinctly: He quit while he was ahead. In this chapter, I am talking about what *New York Times* columnist Gail Collins calls "a timely and well-planned leave-taking — like George Washington, refusing a third term. Or the end of 'The Mary Tyler Moore Show.'"[1] Those of us who get to do deeply rewarding institutional work for a big chunk of our lives and then get to choose the timing and the manner of our departure are lucky for sure. But such decisions also require self-awareness and self-discipline.

There is always what might be called the institutional version of Newton's First Law of Motion. There are the voices that will want you to stay "until my daughter graduates" or "until I leave the board." In any school community, there is always some unfinished business. The truth is, there are always reasons to yield to inertia and stay put. Another way of understanding Giamatti's "footsteps" is to think of the Law of Diminishing Returns. While I believed I could continue to do good work as head of school for several more years and still take great satisfaction in that work, I also knew in my gut that each year I was finding it a bit harder to find the energy to begin anew. I recognized that I was still effective in my job but with less zest.

Other friends and colleagues who have made the same decision have shared similar feelings. Sometimes the pivotal year is related to a life change — a health crisis or a personal issue. These jolts of circumstance can trigger a shift of perspective. Suddenly things look different. My own jolt occurred when I broke my ankle, which, though not by any stretch a permanent or life-threatening injury, was a startling message about physical fragility. It also gave me an unexpected period of reflection. As I sat at home recovering, I began to think about what it would mean to just … stay at home.

Over the following summer, my early ambivalence and doubt shifted to desire — the desire to live a different life. Even though I was still not sure about the precise shape of that life or its particulars, I knew in my bones that I wanted my life to be different. I see the shift from the negative ("I want out") to the positive ("There are other things I want to do and another way I want to be") as pivotal. That summer I did an exercise of organizing my life as though I were separated from the school in order to think about the particulars of that change. It was illuminating — and encouraging.

Feeling anxious about leaving the familiar environment of school is a common thread in my conversations with friends who have left their headships — or are thinking of doing so. After all, we have spent our whole lives in school. Two of my colleagues spent virtually their entire adult lives in the school from which they eventually retired. The power of the familiar is formidable. Imagining a new life is difficult. One colleague says this about his own transition, "Leaving the headship and coming up out of that deep sea and walking onto the dry land of the … self-directed life is an environmental change of seriously massive proportions."

To leave the headship means leaving a community. We walk away from a network of relationships that has dominated our lives for so long we can scarcely imagine ourselves outside that element. We are, as my friend's metaphor implies, like fish leaving water. The change is further complicated by the fact that our own exit changes the lives of those who remain engaged in the community. For that reason, it is important to plan the leadership transition in ways that reassure the community and provide for continuity.

So let us assume that the decision has been made for the right reasons. You feel increasingly confident that the time is right. You and your board work together to create a timeline for the transition. You climb on the conveyor belt of farewell events. The spring is a blur of mixed feelings and farewells. Graduation is over. The boxes have been packed in the office and delivered to your house. This is the moment called "Now what?" While there are many individual answers to that question, there is a road of transition that everyone must travel.

PART TWO: THE NEUTRAL ZONE

Every life change, however joyful and voluntary, carries with it what Sara Lawrence-Lightfoot calls "both loss and liberation." I read her insightful book, *The Third Chapter,* during the year I was leaving the school, and her phrase echoed in my head and heart on a daily basis. As my colleague says, "When you are making this change, proceed mindfully and carefully: You are going to be in recovery for a while." Good advice!

"Recovery" is another word for William Bridges' "Neutral Zone." An authority on managing change, Bridges makes an important distinction between "change" and "transition." Change, he says, is situational. "Change is taking a new job, moving to a new city, or getting married. Change is visible and definitive. Transition is a psychological, interior process of responding to change. Whether the change is by choice and voluntary or something thrust upon us, it sets in motion a psychological adjustment."

In his book, *Managing Transitions: Making the Most of Change,* Bridges breaks down the transition process into three phases: Endings, The Neutral Zone, and The New Beginning. The first phase is easy to understand. Something comes to a close. We may have chosen our own time and our own way to end it, but life goes on, insisting that we move with it. To echo my friend's advice, enter the Neutral Zone with care. His approach to the Neutral Zone was to be disciplined about refusing to commit to any new professional obligation or long-term plans. He is fortunate that he has the luxury of such a decision, and I recommend that, to whatever extent possible, those leaving long-term headships make some provision for what the Italians call *far niente.* Do nothing for a while — at least no externally structured work. Bridges calls

continued on page 100

PERSPECTIVE

YOU DON'T KNOW WHAT YOU DON'T KNOW

Amy Richards, Head of School
Crystal Springs Uplands School
HILLSBOROUGH, CALIFORNIA

The new field will have a surface grade of approximately point seven-eight percent. The synthetic turf material has been certified lead-free. The manufacturer has a recycling program in place for the field material at the end of its lifespan, approximately 10 years. The heat differential between the air temperature and the surface of the turf is approximately 10 to 15 degrees but can be reduced, if not eliminated, with 15 minutes of watering.

I couldn't believe these words were coming from my mouth. In my wildest dreams, did I ever anticipate knowing so much about synthetic turf? I was standing in front of a group of neighbors, talking about my school's latest project, the installation of a synthetic turf field.

I became a head of school five years ago, after 20 years in independent schools. My experience prior to becoming a head included serving as a mathematics teacher, summer program director, dean of students, and division head. When and where was I supposed to learn about synthetic turf?

As a candidate for the position of head, I recall thinking that there were only two tasks I would take on as a head that I had not done before: fund-raising and firing employees. Looking back, I realize how naïve this was. I clearly didn't know what I didn't know.

For example, nowhere in my earlier responsibilities did I have to deal with facilities management, the appropriate administration of the physical plant as well as the renovations and new work every school plant requires. In my first year as head, we renovated four science labs, one of which was the chemistry lab. My school is located in a leafy green suburb, a town that doesn't have another high school, public or private. As a result, the town authorities had no experience with the state and local requirements regarding the storage and disposal of chemicals. Fearful that the town was going to put in place some (costly) requirement we didn't actually need, I engaged in a crash course on local regulations regarding chemical storage. I also called other heads of schools who had undertaken such projects.

And then there were the legal issues! When I moved to California, I recall a New York lawyer telling me that California labor laws were unlike those of any other state in the union. The personnel issues I have had to deal with made this observation prescient. I had to fire an employee in October of my first year. It was one of those hand-me-your-gradebook-and-we'll-walk-to-your-car dismissals. Thank goodness my school had already secured good legal advice from a lawyer well-versed in California labor laws. Sarbanes-Oxley, protected class, and FMLA have all become part of my vocabulary.

Furthermore, I knew very little about marketing and admissions processes. As a young teacher, I used to think that the very word "marketing" sullied the noble nature of teaching. Admissions efforts were simply another manifestation of this despoiling of our chosen profession. Again, this was my naiveté at work. As head, I know that I have a responsibility to ensure the long-term viability of my school. This includes ensuring that my school captures its share of the school-age market. I now listen closely to my admissions director whenever he suggests some new marketing technique designed to bring my school's "story" to a new school or geographic area. When my director of development tells me about ideas regarding institutional advancement, I pay attention.

I also knew very little about investing and the school's endowment. This became apparent when, in the fall of my first year as head, the Investment Committee of the board decided to change the fund managers of our endowment. We reviewed and interviewed representatives of several companies. I remember coming home from those Investment Committee meetings and telling my husband that I felt like the school's Norwegian exchange student; I could understand only every eighth word. "REITs, small caps, large caps, and emerging markets" meant nothing to me. What percentage of the endowment should be allocated to these investments? Despite the language barrier, I was acutely aware of the fact that, in eight or 10 years, the Investment Committee's makeup could turn over completely, and I would be the only member who was present when the decision regarding the new fund manager was made. I might be the only one who could explain or justify the committee's decisions. In the five years that have passed since we switched fund managers, it is safe to say that while I may not be the most financially literate member of the Investment Committee, I certainly know far more about how the endowment is invested than I did when I started.

What about those things about which I *knew* I knew nothing: fund-raising and firing? It turns out that fund-raising isn't as difficult as I anticipated. It boils down to believing in my cause and pitching the need to prospective donors — donors who, because they have already agreed to meet with me, are open to the idea of supporting my school's projects. Dismissing employees? I have since realized that this will never become easy, nor should it. In fact, there may be nothing more difficult in this job than terminating an employee.

What's an aspiring head to do about all this? Talk to your head of school about his or her job, especially the low-profile responsibilities, the tasks not immediately apparent. Pay attention to the minutiae that punctuate your head's day. Ask questions. *What do I need to know about this? What do the parents/neighbors/local authorities want to know about this issue?* Make peace with what you don't know and, in all likelihood, can't learn until you are in the position. Once in that position, connect and stay connected with other heads of schools. Their experiences will help you as you confront your own. Use the online community of schools, including NAIS. Make sure the folks around you — your legal counsel, facilities director, and your architect of choice — know their stuff. How to ensure that? Get recommendations from other local heads.

I spent 20 years as an independent school teacher and middle administrator and five as a head of school. It is easy to say that, with the exception of my first year as a teacher when everything was new and when I didn't even know where the photocopying machines were, I never had to learn as much as I have in these past five years. Is it daunting? You bet. Is it also exhilarating? Beyond belief! While the responsibilities and required knowledge and skills increase dramatically when you are head of school, your perspective also broadens. Like the vista from the top of a mountain, the view from the head's position is much more expansive and, as a result, much more exciting. ■

the Neutral Zone "a nowhere between two somewheres."

Some plans are perfect for the Neutral Zone. Plan a trip — especially as school starts the following fall. Virtually every recently retired school head I know found a way to shake up the calendar when September rolled around. Smart move! First, you will be having fun at a time of year when you normally returned to the routine, and second, your opportunities to meddle or worry about the school will be significantly curtailed.

While in the Neutral Zone, do more of whatever has given you joy but for which there never seemed to be enough time: grandchildren, travel, reading a book from start to finish, golf, yoga, exercise, taking a nap because you can, cooking. Pursue activities that are so satisfying you can easily lose yourself in them for hours. You may hear familiar inner voices whispering that you should be "doing something useful." That is understandable. Our lives have been driven by schedules and calendars and the needs of others for so long, it is surprisingly difficult to compose our own lives. One colleague tells me that the hardest part of starting his "new" life was allowing himself to "just be." He sees the Neutral Zone as moving from a life of action (doing) to a life of reflection (being). In fact, he plunged immediately into a busy life as a consultant and now confesses that he thinks he may have made a mistake. He realizes that he did not take the time to savor the chance to be reflective and to focus on those parts of his life he had had to neglect for so long — to make those paramount.

The term "neutral" can be misleading. While it is a time of consolidation, it can also be a chaotic time when life feels disorganized. As heads, our lives are defined by a calendar that is almost liturgical in its predictability. Schools have very particular seasons: opening ceremonies, traditions and celebrations, commencement. These seasons are deeply imprinted in those of us whose lives have been bracketed by those occasions for so many years, and it is a part of our work many of us deeply miss. My friend says that he misses the opportunity to be "a maker of meaning and an interpreter of experience." One reason for taking advantage of this processing stage — the Neutral Zone — is that chaos fosters creativity and fresh thinking. It is a time to create new, more personal "seasons" and rituals. My colleague and I agree that the boundaries between the three stages of transition are permeable, and we move back and forth among them as we adapt to new realities.

In anticipation of my retirement from the headship, I enrolled in a year-long course to become certified as an executive coach. My idea was to develop skills and a knowledge base that could form the basis of my "new work." Indeed, that has happened, but there were also unexpected gifts that I received from that course. The course required that each student engage a coach for several sessions. Thinking that this was one more thing to check off, I quickly realized that it was an opportunity to be reflective about the step I was about to take. What a gift! Two moments of my coaching stand out.

In one session, I was bringing my coach up-to-date and relating a kind of ordinary event of the day when I suddenly realized I was crying. With my coach's help, I began to focus on the ways I was ignoring the emotional layer of all that was happening. She helped me make a decision to pay careful attention to those feelings and to experience them mindfully. Without that counsel, I might well have missed an element that made that last year so rich. The second powerful coaching occurred when she asked me to describe an "ideal day" after my retirement. I was amazed by how such a simple exercise could reveal so much about those parts of my own soul and being that had been locked up for all the years I headed a school. That was the moment I began to understand — to *feel* — the liberation. The truth is, institutional leadership requires one to be what psychologist Robert Kegan calls a "mediated self." That means that not only are we suppressing certain parts of our selves, we are also presenting other parts that those we serve need. Stepping out of the institutional frame can liberate parts of the self that have long been ignored. Work is an important component of a meaningful life, but it is not the whole of life or of identity. I appreciated a colleague's observation that the Neutral Zone is a chance to "reinvent the self."

After I left the school, I returned to teach a senior seminar in which the students had asked me to talk about my experience of leaving the school. I talked about "loss and liberation" and about my own interior journey. We then found ourselves comparing experiences. They were themselves poised on the brink of leaving the school (and home) for their college lives. One student exclaimed, "We are doing the same things!" Indeed we were. I talked about the spiral of life experiences in which we cycle through similar forms of loss and liberation, but we are different beings each time. I also told them that I sometimes felt as though I were 12 again — getting to decide each day how I want that particular day to be. Being in that room with the students resonated with a colleague's comment about the loss of the daily opportunity to be connected to "the spirit of optimism and hope of the students." That is one thing we both dearly miss.

I recommend that anyone taking this important step find a coach, someone whom you trust and to whom you can tell your truths. It might be a coach in the formal sense, or it could be a mentor, a minister, a counselor — but it should be someone outside the school and family who can listen deeply and uncritically to provide a safe space for reflection along the journey. Keeping a journal can be both instructive and cathartic.

PART THREE: NEW BEGINNINGS

One question I brought to the coaching conversations was this: How can I redirect my skills and experience in new settings? One answer is to volunteer for other nonprofit organizations. One colleague became increasingly concerned about the gap between the resources of the public school system and the independent school he headed for many years. Once he retired, he ran for the local school board and was elected. That experience was a revelation and galvanized a whole new commitment to education from a different perspective. As he says about his work on the school board, "We seven folks came from very different backgrounds: age, education, and, most importantly, life experiences. While this made it difficult a lot of the time, I would not trade what I learned for anything." In some ways, his "after-retirement" volunteer work with the public schools is the most satisfying of his life and is aligned with his own deepest commitments.

Sometimes what we intend to be a temporary system or placeholder in the Neutral Zone may in fact become a durable part of our New Beginnings. The boundaries between the stages of transition are permeable. Returning to an interest or enthusiasm from an earlier time can enable us to push the learning edges as much as taking up something entirely new.

One common thread I hear from my colleagues who have retired from heading schools is that they want to make a difference: to find work that matters and to feel useful. These are the ingredients of a meaningful life, and all of us feel lucky for all of the years we led such lives. It is something we fear losing as we leave our work as heads. But there are many other ways to achieve these values. There are important nonprofit organizations in every community that benefit from the experience we bring to their boards or as ad-hoc volunteers. My colleague's work with the public schools extends not only to service on the school board but also to volunteer work as a tutor in several local schools. I have carefully chosen some local nonprofits that offer rewarding opportunities to use my experience and knowledge. I have combined leadership coaching with governance consulting and find it a deeply satisfying blend that also allows me to remain, for the most part, in control of my calendar and my time.

And what of that elusive quality of life we spent years trying to achieve: balance! Each of the former heads I have mentioned — myself included — now intentionally builds in time for fun. That may mean saying no to some new set of commitments from time to time. I may have to miss a meeting because I want to travel with my family. My colleague may say no to an invitation to lead a retreat because it falls at the time of year he travels. Another colleague wryly observes: "The fact is, I love schools and the people in them ... and I have a possibly perverse interest in how boards of trustees work and really enjoy working with them ... and I have absolutely *no* interest in working *for* them." At a daily level, I offer the perspective of the principle that underlies the practice of Tai Chi. It is the principle of alternating work with rest. One movement works the muscles; the next rests those muscles. Work and restoration: This dynamic balance is possible in a self-directed life.

To use William Bridges' phrase, beginning anew means "redreaming the dream." We do not become new people, but we can become more fully ourselves. We can pick up the dropped stitches of our earlier lives and integrate those into the fabric of seasoned, reflective experience. The New Beginning is not only the "stuff" we do, it is also a dynamic. One colleague who is now several years into his "new life" observes, "I had been so enmeshed in the guts of the school for so long, it took years of separation to see myself there in the third person." That is an observation from the far side of the Neutral Zone.

I recognize that anyone who reaches what Sara Lawrence-Lightfoot calls

The Third Chapter with options, choices, and reasonable financial security enjoys some level of privilege. We are lucky! Indeed, being well-educated and having the opportunity to lead an educational institution are privileges in themselves. As is often observed, with privilege comes responsibility. In essence, that is what my colleagues and I share in our own third chapters: commitment to the importance of living responsible — and self-directed — lives. Lawrence-Lightfoot speaks of the 40 subjects of her book seeing their own third chapters as "both exciting and adventurous, and tender and treacherous." She goes on to say, "Their failures offered opportunities for recovery; their awkwardness helped them learn a new humility; their slowness demanded that they practice patience; their intensity and impatience required that they go deeper, rather than farther and faster."[2]

I find these thoughts both moving and inspiring. Paradox is the great gift of this new beginning: We are both subject and object of these new lives, surprising ourselves every day. No comeback tours for us!

I am indebted to colleagues who were willing to share their experiences — their journeys out and their journeys in — to enrich my own experience of writing this chapter. My thanks to Roger Weaver, former head of Crossroads School in Santa Monica, CA; Mike Babcock, former head of Polytechnic School, Pasadena, CA; Tom Clarke, former head of Campbell Hall, North Hollywood, CA, along with others who shared more casual conversations. Our journeys are both unique and universal. I am grateful that we continue to share stories and resist the urge to take ourselves (or one another) too seriously.

NOTES

[1] Gail Collins, "Putting the Fond in Farewell," *New York Times*, November 21, 2009.

[2] Sara Lawrence-Lightfoot, *The Third Chapter: Passion, Risk, and Adventure in the 25 Years After 50* (New York: Farrar, Straus and Giroux, 2009), p. 228

PART III

ROLES OF A HEAD

THE QUESTION OF HATS

Vince Durnan

ANY NEWLY APPOINTED HEAD of school can count on being asked, within a matter of weeks, by self-proclaimed insiders, "So, how much time will you spend fund-raising?" That's one of those questions that opens wide the issue of roles and responsibilities within the job, invariably leading to a consideration of the professional hats we heads wear. My response, now offered with an ease conferred by frequency of opportunity, is "100 percent of my time" — since it's never clear when the moment might yield an opportunity to provide a philanthropic boost for our school.

That answer correspondingly invokes the interconnectedness of the facets of the positions we embrace and the beauty of the blurred lines that accompany this profession, not the least of which is the boundary between work and play. Still, there are fundamental headings worth exploring. Let's limit our list to 10 and see how far those 10 reach, working from practical, pecuniary functions to philosophical futurecasting. Interestingly, each of these roles likely comports with some part of a school community's view of the appropriate and best use of a head's time — it's just that those views differ. The challenge (and the magic in a job balanced right) is to touch all these bases so that the roles reinforce one another without appearing to be zero-sum or overwhelming. Nobody likes that.

Now to those 10 hats:

CHIEF FINANCIAL OFFICER

Perhaps it's best to start with (1) the CFO, or more correctly the *executive* CFO, since most schools count on quite able specialists as directors of budget and finance. Still, budgetary authority ultimately rests with school heads, responsible to their boards, meeting the fiduciary responsibilities of a CEO, as stipulated in bylaws and accreditation processes. For those of us who came to the job through the teaching ranks and not by climbing some corporate ladder, reading balance sheets can be a daunting prospect. Do whatever it takes to develop a detailed understanding of your school's financial algorithm. Without that appreciation for the trade-offs inherent in every budget decision, we risk making fundamentally uninformed choices affecting people and programs. Informed answers to tough budget questions, answers born of at least monthly sessions with your board president, Finance Committee chair, and director of finance, build broad confidence and establish ground for consensus.

CHIEF OPERATING OFFICER

Similarly essential and perhaps unglamorous would be (2) the COO role, also at the executive level, underscoring the imperative to direct the daily operations of the school, albeit with the help of an administrative team. Seeing to the effective functioning of that group, allocating time to each member as calendar and circumstance dictate, puts the school on a footing to deliver on its promises to constituents: students, families, faculty, staff, alumni, and community. At the top of the list of opportunities in all operating areas is the hiring process. None of us will do anything more important than choosing great people to become colleagues and then seeing that they receive meaningful evaluation and support. The legacy of those choices, probably even more than whatever help we provide in attracting and admitting great students, will form the legacy of the school. Time spent on ensuring thoughtful hiring in the role of chief employer is time well spent.

SCHOOL EMBLEM

The message conveyed by being available for the annual processes of financial and personnel analysis additionally carries powerful symbolic value, bringing to mind the hat heads wear as (3) an institutional hood ornament — or school emblem. Where we go during the day, how long we stay at each destination, what we wear (on our backs and on our faces), and the level at which we engage set a tone for how the pieces and parts of our school communities should get along — how autonomously, how harmoniously, and how purposefully. It defines our brand, our culture of interaction. That culture will surely translate to admission efforts as well. Sorting out how many hours to spend in the office, or in the halls, or in conference room meetings, or at the playing fields/performance hall, or at home, for that matter, provides another equation to be balanced one school, one year at a time.

CHEERLEADER

A highly visible dimension of the symbolic role heads assume by voting with their footsteps is (4) the cheerleader role. There's no substitute for just being at school events, budgets and committee meetings and returned phone calls notwithstanding. The range, variety, and duration of our schools' jam-packed calendars can overwhelm even the most eager, but an earnest effort will generate goodwill. While working the crowd is always appreciated (and expected), it's important to remember that the crowd probably didn't assemble just to see the head of school. What's more, the resulting stories after the event concludes will be more interesting if you actually paid attention to what happened — and you were careful not to *be* the story. Seeing enough to make an honest claim that you were there is the key — past that, it may well make sense to visit three games rather than choose one to witness in full. Those choices and that allocative process offer another balancing act.

Turning from the literal to the metaphorical, heads serve as cheerleaders in a broader, symbolic sense. Virtually every item on the calendar offers a chance to communicate and amplify the school's accomplishments to a range of audiences. Carrying that megaphone in the form of official speeches, informal coffee sessions, sideline conversations, website columns, blogs, and available media appearances is an essential part of the job, crossing all roles. So my taxonomy sticks with a stricter definition of cheerleader: eager (and frequent) attendee.

PASTOR

Facing the tough news, the tragic situation, places heads in the role of (5) pastor, whether connected to a defined faith tradition or not. With so many independent schools now embracing families of varied (or no) religious affiliations, our schools constitute a form of modern congregation. The larger our enrollment, the greater is the chance on any given day that someone is hospitalized, or in family crisis, or about to lose a job or a home. The collective energy of our school communities can be channeled to reach out in a variety of ways, each of which can benefit from a head's direct interest in the helpers and in those being helped.

Sadly, it's just a matter of time before any new school head presides over a memorial service for a life ended too soon. While we may not have benefitted from divinity or counseling graduate work, lessons are readily at hand, and the same communities that ask of us so much can provide a great deal by way of support from experienced, capable people in our midst — parents, colleagues, and alumni. Response in time of need, not to mention attendance at weddings and funerals and coming-of-age rituals, will be remembered and appreciated for years to come. Of that I am sure, and for that reason probably an hour or so daily goes to tending the flock, as it were.

HISTORIAN/STORYTELLER

Reflecting on what finds a place in memory, heads should also serve the important function of (6) historian/storyteller for their schools. Each institution has an origin tale worth knowing, a pantheon of heroes and heroines worthy of recollecting, and a series of turning point moments that could help move the whole enterprise forward in the present day. Learning those stories will open doors with alumni, show respect to senior faculty, and place what may otherwise be head-scratching, venerable practices in context. If there is no written history available, it might be time to commission one — and strengthen the archives in the process before it's too late. Without a consensus view of a school's past, anchored in facts, a certain rootlessness can prevail, making it difficult, ironically, to effect change. And past all that, the case studies in decision-making available in our school histories offer a treasure trove of examples from which our students might learn.

TEACHER

And what of the school head wearing (7) the teacher hat? It may serve best for the head to embrace that role in a broader sense, as resident scholar sharing an occasional lesson in print or from a lectern, telling the school's story or a story generated by the school. But it may also be that the classroom beckons, as a statement of solidarity with colleagues, or an opportunity to connect directly with students, or a refuge from roles 1-5 above. At some point, the possibility is guaranteed to arise, as it has in schools for centuries. Whether head of school means head teacher, or even adjunct department member, is another issue entirely, a function of one's circumstance and one's constitution.

Two things, though, could be said on this topic with some certainty. First, even great teaching by a head of school cannot excuse poor performance in other areas essential to the job. Any choice to spend time in a classroom is a commitment to lengthen one's day since the rest of the work remains waiting in the wings. Those things that heads alone can do deserve focused and thoughtful attention, period. Second, while colleagues may appreciate the object lesson crafted by a head who teaches a course, a single class does not confer complete credibility — nor can a head expect to be in top teaching shape with so part-time an assignment. Perhaps the key question is whether the time invested in teaching a class generates better work for a head in other areas, whether it increases rather than limits effectiveness in other roles. If the answer is yes, then taking on that class can be a well-justified delight, a glimpse into the reason our schools exist. Not to belabor the point, but the same considerations hold double for coaching a team.

COMMUNITY PARTNER

If teaching provides a micro-lens, then stepping beyond campus as (8) a community partner offers a valuable macro-perspective on a school's place in the world. Opportunities to practice active citizenship, to open doors, abound for heads of school, given the range of contacts and resources running through their offices. It may be a nascent neighboring charter school or a summer academic enrichment program for children with few other options, a service

PERSPECTIVE

THE PASTORAL ROLE OF A SCHOOL HEAD

Don North, Headmaster
The Kinkaid School
HOUSTON, TEXAS

I first noticed Melody's loss of weight right after the Thanksgiving holiday. I asked her if she was feeling all right, and she said, "Not really." She told me that she had been feeling ill lately and thought she might have cancer. I asked if she had been to the doctor. She had not.

Three weeks later Melody received a diagnosis of stage-four breast cancer.

In her 30th year at this school, Melody was an absolutely superb teacher. Her students' feelings for her began in fear, traveled through respect, and came to rest in love as they understood her passionate commitment to their learning. A recipient of the school's Distinguished Teaching Award, Melody had led student trips to Hawaii, Central America, and Africa; she had persuaded Jane Goodall to visit the school in celebration of our Roots and Shoots program; and she had pushed the school to convert a backyard dumping ground into an outdoor classroom. In all ways, she was a remarkable teacher and human being, and she had planned on retiring at the end of the school year.

I wrote to our faculty and staff about Melody's diagnosis during the second week of the Christmas holidays and let them know that she would take some time off for radiation treatment. The first day back from the holidays, I wrote the parent community with the same news, and later that day, I visited Melody in her home. Two days later, Melody died.

In some form, this story will be familiar to veteran school heads, but it brought home to me, again, the considerable pastoral needs of the school community at such a time and the pivotal role of the school head in addressing these needs.

I see three distinct pieces to this pastoral role, each important.

The first is the school head as grief counselor and manager. The morning that Melody died, I was scheduled to go out of town. I cancelled the trip and spent most of the day in communication, both formal and informal, with faculty and staff, students, trustees, parents, and alumni. There were those with especially strong connections to Melody. It was not possible to speak individually with all, but I reached out to several personally — by phone, face to face, or via email. One was an alumnus and school parent who was also Melody's general physician. He was devastated and blamed himself for not questioning her hard enough in her last annual checkup. Another learning program in another hemisphere or a link with a community arts organization — the spectrum is wide. Identifying organizations and initiatives compatible with a school's mission broadens the reach and relevance of a school's message to a wider audience, with possibilities to draw interest from potential applicants, donors, or power brokers who might otherwise feel distant from the cloistered culture of many independent schools.

With the changing landscape of education in this country and with the

was the parent of a senior who told me that her daughter had just lost her best friend. A third was a faculty member who had been helped by Melody three years earlier in her own fight against breast cancer. At such a time, the school head must make a number of decisions about how to spend his or her time. Those decisions must be made strategically as well as personally.

The second piece is the school head as public speaker. Early in my tenure as a school head, I made a mistake that hurt the manager of our cafeteria, a wonderful woman. She had just lost her mother to illness, and I thought I was being a good school head by attending the funeral. During the service, a woman I did not know walked up the aisle and asked if I would like to say something about the deceased. Flustered, I declined. I learned later that our cafeteria manager wanted me to speak about her mother — or her. She had hoped for a public recognition of the respect the school had for her family, and I blew it. Now when I go to funerals of employees, retired employees, or even close family members of employees, I am always prepared to speak. If the opportunity arises, I take it, quickly. Invariably, I hear later from family members and others how important those words are, not because of any eloquence but because the head of the school communicated publicly how the school felt about a former member of the school community.

The final piece relates to the ongoing needs of the community. Because Melody was so attentive to detail as a teacher, her sudden death from breast cancer frightened several members of our faculty and staff. They feared that if Melody could develop stage-four breast cancer so quickly, then so could they. They also worried that perhaps there was something about our school — something in the air or the water — that put Melody, and them, at risk.

Soon after Melody's death, I asked her oncologist to talk with interested faculty about the disease, and she agreed. Thirty members of our faculty and staff attended this session, and this generous doctor answered questions for nearly two hours. She could not speak about Melody, but she made it clear that one could not get to stage-four breast cancer quickly, and she set at rest some of the fears present in our faculty.

All of us serve our schools well when we understand the pastoral needs of the school community at such a time and do our best to meet those needs. ■

increasingly visible resource disparity evident across school types, we can expect more attention focused on the public purpose of private schools. Beyond membership in civic organizations, beyond responding to regional and national member organization requests to attend conferences and conventions, the choices heads make aligning schools with nonprofits in their home communities can make a life-changing difference for students and faculty. To be too busy for that role is really to settle for less.

FUND-RAISER

It would be disingenuous to catalog these roles without a specific reference to (9) the chief fund-raiser hat, the one heads are assumed to don first and wear most. The balance to be struck *within* this role weighs the relative importance of help grinding away on annual fund efforts compared with time spent on long-term cultivation labors to meet endowment or facility needs. Connecting board members to the scores of volunteers necessary for a successful annual or capital campaign is work that a head is uniquely situated to lead. Connecting development office staff to the daily life of the school may also be a task uniquely positioned for the head of school. And connecting the thousands of potential donors to the message a school most wants to convey should be a constant back-of the-mind consideration that reaches the front of the mind at least once a day — in the form of thank-you notes, impromptu check-in phone calls, and careful review of everything communicated by the school online and on paper.

BOARD MEMBER

Processing all that information, eating that elephant a bite at a time, gives heads a chance to synthesize a perspective of inestimable value as (10) a board member. Whether part of the group in an ex-officio capacity or as a full member, a head of school walks an interesting line guiding and responding to guidance from trustees. What might regrettably be lost in the shuffle is the opportunity for a head to see the school from the strategic distance boards should adopt. Any decent board features wisdom in great measure and support for ideals that transcend the immediate urgencies piled on a head's desk. For that reason, it seems a fitting final element in this brief catalog of intersecting roles essential to the head's position.

From a board member perch, framing questions of direction over the long haul, personally and institutionally, may work best. The commitment necessary for a head to do right by the school requires a clear understanding of what is expected, and those expectations draw directly on the vision (dare we say it?) articulated by the head to the board. That circular flow takes effort, honesty, and understanding born of at least weekly conversations with the board president and executive committee members. Absent that communication, roles 1-9 above will ring a bit hollow. To state the obvious, this board stuff really matters — accepting a head of school job should begin with an assessment of what the board needs to make things work.

If you're still reading, this would be the point where you might ask why other roles were not mentioned (e.g., head of communications, lead admissions officer, curriculum czar, technology visionary). My answer, however idiosyncratic, would be that those responsibilities are subsumed in other headings identified already — readers may guess which ones. The other predictable reaction is that no one could actually make all this work, at least no one who didn't reside on Mt. Olympus. The answer there is yes — no *one* could make this work. It takes a whole orchestra of skilled players to bring harmony to all these roles, to create the impression that the conductor is on just the right measure of the score. Without a trusted and capable set of administrative colleagues, the weight, seasonal and cumulative, of these responsibilities would bow the back of any would-be leader. With that support, though, and with the freedom to embrace the combination of vocation and avocation schools provide for heads, it really can work — if you find the right school.

PART IV

A HEAD'S RESPONSIBILITIES

THE HEADMASTERS' WIVES' COOKBOOK: EXPECTATIONS OF THE HEAD'S FAMILY

Katherine Dinh

YEARS BEFORE I BECAME a head of school, I had heard about an infamous, well-loved, but ridiculously titled book: *The Headmasters' Wives' Cookbook*. In our early years of marriage, my husband (who is also a head of school) and I were amused by what the book implied about the traditional role of the head's spouse — to put out the appetizers at development parties, mix the cocktails for trustees, and bake the casseroles for faculty dinners. As it turns out, my spouse is an impressive cook and the food and wine connoisseur in our family. My kitchen credentials include boiling pasta, using a rice cooker, and throwing together peanut butter and jelly sandwiches.

To be honest, I have never seen a copy of the cookbook, nor do I know if it actually exists by that name. Nonetheless, both my husband and I have held the roles of head of school and head's spouse, managing the complex expectations our school communities have for the head's family. While I hope one day to learn how to make a delectable roast or casserole, it's likely I won't reach these aspirations while I'm a head's spouse. The traditional model of the head's family is evolving, and independent schools are well served by acknowledging and adapting to these changes.

EXPECTATIONS OF THE HEAD'S FAMILY AT SCHOOL EVENTS

We live in a school-owned house, and as such, I can expect to come home to school parties several nights a week during those opening months of school. Families are being welcomed to the community, hellos are being made, and the head's family is being checked out. While this sounds like a bit of work for our family, we have it rather well-orchestrated and swap our roles quite smoothly, depending on what is expected on any given evening. The one who is not hosting the event will commit to attending the cocktail hour, being introduced in a welcome speech, and then, when the time is right, making a surreptitious departure if possible or necessary. To be sure, we support one another. We also can only do so much.

Both my husband and I have heard this question: "Does your spouse exist?" We are very familiar, comfortable even, with living constantly at the intersection of our professional and personal lives. Nonetheless, in order to sustain the most important aspects of ourselves, which is a sense of home and family, we have negotiated a few structures that have helped.

- Work in partnership with your board to manage expectations. Your board will understandably want both you and your partner/family to be at most events. Be assertive about your needs, but also be flexible to the school's needs.
- If you have young children, negotiate childcare reimbursement for those events when both of you will need to be present.
- Share calendars with one another's assistants.
- Go over your calendars every week. For us, it's a Sunday ritual.

Finally, if you can't do any of the above, do this: Create a few family routines that are sacrosanct. We schedule several sit-down dinners a week, and on those nights, we are strict about our arrival time at home. The routine gives our family some much-needed time to share stories and be with our young child. Nothing is more important than your family.

Often the search for a head is described as the search for a spouse. When the right person is chosen, analogies are made about the marriage between the new head and his or her school. The analogy is apt, given the all-consuming nature of headships, and I believe the comparison is made mostly to remind boards that, like marriage, the relationship between the head and the school community requires constant attention and work. Unfortunately, I've also heard enough stories about real marriages that have suffered because of headships. A friend and long-term head, who has been married more than 30 years, once said to me, "We need to keep in mind that we're married to our spouse, not our school." In the end, be prepared to walk away from a job opportunity if the prospective school community has expectations of your family that you cannot meet.

BEING A DUCK

A cliché I have heard often is that successful heads of schools are those who can channel a duck. Above the surface, appear serene and in control. Below the surface, paddle like crazy. This metaphor is less about balancing the stressors in life and more about faking it if you need to. And, unfortunately, it describes my own modus operandi more than I like to admit. However, faking calm and competence does require a certain level of preparedness, confidence, and discipline. If done well enough, acting the part can become a habit, and soon, we realize we're making good, thoughtful decisions and being a successful leader. In other words, being a duck works. It doesn't, however, address the fatigue involved in paddling like crazy. New heads may choose the duck strategy for the first year or two, but it can't be sustained.

My journey to becoming a head of school was both a whirlwind and a long, bending road. The short story is that I became a head after having worked in independent schools for a dozen years as a teacher, department chair, and division head. The long version is that I had also founded two schools, and in the aftermath of Hurricane Katrina, as a division head in New Orleans, had my job doubled and ran two divisions at the same time. All the while, I fantasized about being a stay-at-home mom for my young son and

PERSPECTIVE

WHEN ILLNESS HITS

Evan D. Peterson, Head of School
Fort Worth Country Day
FORT WORTH, TEXAS

Cancer Survivor

School had started about a month before. It was still as hot as a frying pan, but there was hope that September would bring a reprieve from the 100-degree days. I had been working out in the school's weight room three days a week or as my schedule would allow. On a Friday afternoon, I noticed a lump on the right side of my neck. It didn't hurt, and I figured I had pulled something while weight lifting. The next week was busy so I missed my workout on Monday but got to it on Wednesday and on Friday. I noticed the lump again as I showered after my workout. That Saturday, my wife and I flew out to Bald Head Island, North Carolina, for the wedding of our older son. Our days were filled with events as we prepared for the wedding on Saturday. When we returned home, the lump was still there.

The next Saturday, I played golf with a doctor. He looked at the lump and told me I should have a CT scan of it. Later that day, my neighbor, another doctor, suggested the same thing. On Thursday of the next week, I had the CT scan. On Friday, I played golf with three alums. On the 16th tee box, I got a phone call from my doctor. The lump was cancer. I didn't finish the golf game.

On that Monday, the process started. I was scheduled to see three doctors in four days. More tests told us that the cancer was the worst kind (if there is such a ranking). With my head spinning, I needed to talk to my board chair. I was to deliver my goals to the board at the October meeting and had presented them to my board chair only days before I learned I had cancer. I wrote an email telling her that I needed to add a goal to the list I had given her. The additional goal was *to survive*! In that email, I explained all I knew at that time.

During the next couple of weeks, between doctors appointments and lab work, I met with the board chair and vice chair. We talked about how and when to announce my diagnosis to the faculty, students, and parents. In the end, we wrote two letters, one from the board chair and one from me. These would be sent to the parents after I spoke to the faculty and students. I met with the faculty the morning of October 8 and during the day with the students in each division. That afternoon, the letters were sent to the parents. The word was out, and the well wishes and prayers started flowing in.

Almost immediately, the executive committee of the board gathered to put a leadership plan together. We decided to adjust our administrative team by asking our senior director of operations to oversee the running of school when I was unable to be on-site. The three division heads would meet with the senior director weekly. As it turned out, I was able to be on conference call during those meetings. We also asked the board chair and vice chair to be available to the group continuing to play the part of the spouse of a head of school.

After my husband took a new head position at a wonderful school in Marin County, California, I hardly imagined I'd be starting my first headship

should a major issue arise. The two of them attended the first administrative team meeting. I don't think they attended any other meetings. During the seven weeks that I was housebound, I called in every week to participate in our weekly team meetings. These were run by the senior director. This process seemed to work well for the administrative team. The school year moved forward, and the daily operations seemed to go smoothly. I attended one general board meeting and joined another by conference call. Looking back, I think that my inability to attend committee meetings and my lack of contact with board members were the downside of my absence. My sense today is that the board moved more slowly on topics and spent more time discussing issues that should have been resolved easily and quickly.

Our concern going into the announcement of my illness was always how our school families would react. After their initial shock and well wishes, we worried that they might ask, "Who is leading the school and how will the absence of the head of school impact my child's education?" To prevent those concerns, we tried to keep our families informed and up-to-speed with push pages, letters home, and teacher-parent contacts. I think all of those worked to some degree but maybe not as well as we had hoped.

Some things did fall by the wayside. Our curriculum committee did not meet during my absence. This group is made up of teachers from all three divisions and representatives from the arts and athletics. They manage and evaluate our curriculum. I'm finding out that proposals and recommendations are slowly coming to the surface and will not be ready to impact our curriculum for next year. I also think that simply meeting as a group has benefits that we lost this year. Other than that one group, I think the teachers and staff did a fine job of keeping the ship afloat and moving forward.

When I returned to a normal schedule on January 5, I found that many small issues had been allowed to be blown out of proportion. Middle school parents complained about the sports program and the coaching expertise at that level. This is not a new issue, but this year, it took on a life of its own. I found myself spending hours defending our program and explaining the complicating factors of middle school sports. I got the feeling that some parents felt that "nothing is being done." I believe that they were frustrated when they did not get a definitive answer.

The board of trustees continued to move forward. They were always respectful of my situation, and they allowed me the time to get back on my feet, contacting me only a few times. More often than not, I contacted them. The board chair and I spoke maybe once every two weeks, usually in regard to a committee or some other general issue.

Make no mistake about it. Returning was hard. When I came to campus, everyone knew I was

continued on next page

at the same time. Making a smooth transition from New Orleans and putting our son in school were priorities. Finding a job was not. Then I got the call from the search consultant.

I love being a head of school — don't get me wrong. I just didn't plan to

WHEN ILLNESS HITS

ill. They were glad to see me, but the demands on my time were sometimes overwhelming. After three days of being back, I had to take two days off because I ran out of steam. I worked too long and tried to do too much. I learned my lesson and stopped pretending that I was operating at 100 percent. I shortened my days and avoided early morning meetings and late night athletic events.

For anyone facing a similar illness, I have these recommendations: When you return, be sure to pace yourself. Plan your days like you plan your week. Juggling work with doctor appointments and lab work takes some real planning because you never get out of a doctor's office when you think you will. Give yourself plenty of time! Make sure the board understands that you are not operating at 100 percent and won't be for weeks, if not months. We are now about six months out from the conclusion of my treatment. Each day, I gain a little more energy. Even though it's only been a couple of weeks, the pace is already back to normal or very close to it.

So what have my board, my administrative team, and I learned? No matter how well you plan any announcement, you will leave many questions unanswered. You need to have a strong relationship with your board and especially your board chair. You should use your webpage to keep your families and staff informed. We also consulted an outside agency about what and how we should announce the situation to our constituents. I think this helped the board feel that they were covering all the bases. Someone suggested that I use *Caringbridge.org* to keep everyone in the loop about what I was going through. Caringbridge also allows people to write comments in an online "journal." I questioned its value but did it anyway. The last time I looked at my page, over 16,000 contacts had been made. The notes and comments were humbling and heartwarming. I am still amazed at how many people learned of my battle and wanted to offer words of support and prayers.

I also learned that you should keep the students in the loop. Every time I came back on campus, I made an effort to walk around and visit with the students, and I spoke at assemblies after I was back. I learned that you should write to the parent body as often as you can.

I told the other local schools what was going on. In every case, everyone was supportive and showed concern. We learned that every school needs a plan addressing situations that might cause the head of school or any major player to be, as they say in the South, "out of pocket" for an extended period of time. You have to give yourself time to heal. Be honest with yourself and others about your illness and your ability to "carry on" the duties of your position. Allow others to help. When you return, things will be different. People will look at you differently. You will look at your life and your job differently. One parent who is also a cancer survivor told me that going through what you have to will, in the end, make you a better person and a better headmaster. I hope she was right! ■

be one. The search process was too much fun to be true and the next thing I knew, I had fallen in love with the school. And there you have it. Thus began my life as a dual-head (and dual-head-spouse) family with a preschool child. There are no fail-safe strategies in balancing work and life beyond work. What people don't seem to realize is that guarding your own time can maximize your abilities to be successful at work. While there will always be unplanned crises that get in the way of your personal life, consider selfishly developing some outside-of-work interests that may result in a boost in your professional productivity.

- Create things. Whether you knit, cook, paint, write, or do carpentry, cultivate hobbies that require you to create something. Not only can making something of your own be gratifying, it can also sharpen your creativity and problem-solving skills.
- Cultivate friendships outside of work. Take a class, register for an adult team sport, or get involved in your chosen religious organization. Note: Making friends with other heads in your area is rewarding and, in some cases, life-saving. That said, spending time with other heads will inevitably lead you back to work conversations. Try to get together with friends on a regular basis who don't have any connection to your work.
- While it seems counterintuitive, the busier you get, the more important it is for you to find time for physical exercise. No one will argue that exercise is good for your body, but research now points to the relationship between physical fitness and optimum brain function. The 30-minute walk or run you squeeze into your busy day will reward you with more stamina and a clearer head to do your demanding job.

All the juggling of work and family cannot be done at the expense of your own health. This is basic wisdom, but we often fail to heed it, sometimes with very costly consequences to our professional and personal lives. I'm terribly guilty of pushing my needs all the way to the bottom of the list, and perhaps this is the most problematic aspect of being a duck. No one can see you paddling like crazy below the surface, so no one will be able to tell you to take a break. You're the one who has to gauge your own emotional and physical health and take the steps necessary to care for yourself.

To that end, I did something seemingly insane after my second year of headship: I signed up for my first triathlon. I did it in order to make exercise a priority as well as to meet new people in a training group. Ironically, even with all my (metaphoric) duck-paddling experience, I didn't know how to swim. I had to learn how to do so in the weeks before the triathlon, an endeavor that was like going from zero to 60 in no time flat. The first time I jumped into the pool, the reality of kicking, fighting for air, and being stricken by fear and exhaustion hit me hard. Learning to swim in the pool, however, doesn't begin to describe the terror I had about swimming in open water. I put in many extra hours and extended my workout beyond what my coaches asked of me in order to overcome my significant emotional and physical obstacles. The challenge, however, was exhilarating. It also forced me to admit that I wasn't always in control, that I was scared, and that I had to rely on others for support.

In the end, as terrifying and difficult as the process was, learning to swim — with efficient, long, graceful strokes — showed me the benefits of committing myself to being taught how to swim the right way, to overcoming my fears, and to stop faking it. Being a duck can get you through the first year — maybe the first two years — of your headship, but don't make a habit of it. Instead, if you are honest about your shortcomings but work hard to overcome them, there will be people around you who will be there to support you, coach you, and teach you how to swim well and with grace.

BEING A ROOM PARENT: PRIORITIZING OUR CHILDREN OVER OUR STUDENTS

I adore my son's teacher. She is the epitome of everything one could hope for in a preschool teacher — patient, kind, loving, and thoughtful. Without any feeling of self-doubt or guilt, I completely trust her to fulfill my son's intellectual and emotional needs — in other words, to be his mother — when he's at school and I'm not around. This is a hidden part of the contract that I sign with his school — that I trust them to educate and nurture my son in the same way I do for all the parents who send their students to my school. But I can't help wishing for what all educators strive for: to give their own children as much time as they offer to other people's children. Is this even possible? I like to believe it is.

Just to give a little more context to my situation. I live on the campus of the school where my husband is the head. Our son attends an independent Montessori school near our home. I commute to my school, over the San Francisco Bay, about 20 miles. Needless to say, I don't have much wiggle room when it comes to commuting and school schedules.

We are involved parents: We care about nurturing our son's interests, reinforcing the lessons his teacher exposes him to in school, and attending back-to-school nights and parent conferences. When we can, we get a babysitter and volunteer for the admissions events or come to the parent education nights. I am desperate to be more involved, but it's a challenge.

So when my son's teacher called and asked me to be a room parent for his classroom, I had some initial reactions. First: Did she dial the wrong number?

As a working mother, I can't help being somewhat intimidated by the very put-together moms who seem to have an endless amount of time and energy to devote to their children's class activities. There are a handful of dads as well who are real-life superheroes. In the sea of stellar parent volunteers at my son's school, I simply wasn't among the most obvious choices for leadership. His teacher must have meant to call someone else. But she didn't. Perhaps she was serious.

Thus my second reaction: What if I couldn't find the time? This is when all doubt had to be erased. Above all else, parenting is the most important job my husband and I do. Regardless of the myriad appointments, board meetings, athletic matches, and performing arts nights on our schedules, we decided to team up. We wanted to do this thing. I told my son's teacher that yes, I would be honored to be a room parent.

Still, it's not easy. I missed the opening class picnic, even though my name was on the invitation as a co-host, because of a board meeting. Each of these conflicts is enough to throw me back into the darkness of working-mom-self-doubt. But what's the point? I can only do what I can, which is often late at night. With support from my husband, I helped organize another class picnic, hosted the parent potluck at our home, stenciled and cut countless paper pumpkins and hearts for holiday classroom decorations, and baked cookies for the teacher appreciation lunch. The bond I developed with my son's teacher made me adore and trust her even more. I also came to love the other parents in my son's class for their diversity of talents and collective enthusiasm. I saw that they were human, too, and that their volunteer hours were as hard to come by as my own.

Working as a parent volunteer taught me a great deal about how many parents in my own school struggle to find the balance between work and family — and how none of us can do it perfectly. Parents who are educators (not to mention heads) are especially at risk of having to prioritize their students' needs over those of their own children. I hope you embrace the opportunities to give your children the time and energy you surely give to the children at your school.

FINAL THOUGHTS: DON'T JUGGLE OR BALANCE — NAVIGATE!

Even though this chapter may seem to be about the need to "juggle" or "balance," I should clarify that neither word aptly describes the task of being a head of school and having a life. Turbulent waters, such as those in which I have swum as a professional (and in my first triathlon), are a much better metaphor.

Juggling and balancing require great skill and coordination, and we can all benefit from cultivating the kind of grace and focus that these actions require. The words, however, evoke the image of a circus act that requires acrobatics and showmanship that only temporarily stave off the inevitable pull of gravity. Juggling your life is impossible. You may keep a few items from crashing down, but you do not have the stamina to go on forever. Balancing assumes that you have the ideal situation — a tight enough rope on which to walk or a strong enough partner who will hold you — so that you won't eventually fall. If you find yourself juggling or balancing, you need to stop.

Navigation through the unpredictable seas is the only way to manage your professional and personal lives successfully. In order to cross any body of water, you must have a fortified vessel in which to travel, outfitted with the right tools and the right crew of people, without whom you cannot survive the roughest voyages.

After Hurricane Katrina, I found myself in Houston, having just weeks earlier moved to New Orleans with my husband and our then one-year-old son. My husband and I had both taken new leadership positions in two excellent independent schools in New Orleans, but with one giant crack of the levees, our plans were washed away, and we were hundreds of miles from where we had only begun to put down roots. We set to work, somehow navigating through enormously difficult waters and at times nearly crushing waves, to help our respective schools reopen their doors in a few short months. I also founded a temporary school for pre-K-8 students who were displaced in Houston, with a staff of displaced faculty. The school was called New Orleans Academy of Houston and lovingly referred to as NOAH. Pun intended.

When I face the hardest challenges, I think about navigating through Katrina, with my essential tools and my crew, and creating a safe harbor such as NOAH. When your journey becomes rocky, may you build a strong ship that will withstand the storm and lead you toward the horizon.

DEMANDS ON HEADS

Carolyn Chandler and Joseph Cox

CORE RESPONSIBILITIES: THE CHILDREN, THE MISSION

The foremost obligation any head of school has is to the overall well-being of the children attending his or her school. Second is the obligation to the mission of the school and the demand to make every decision with the long-term success of your institution and the accomplishment of its mission in mind. Heads of school bear direct responsibility for delivering the programs that nurture and develop children and for keeping the business affairs of the school in order. If those two priorities are kept, they will generate a system of values that will help in your management of a very complex operation. Adhering to a value system that keeps children first and the health of the school a close second should be and will be your moral compass and the source of your most demanding concerns. However, you will find that there are many ancillary demands that will consume your time and energy beyond what you anticipate to be those core responsibilities.

It is easy to feel overwhelmed by the many decisions you face as a head of school, but remembering the Latin origin of the word *demand* sheds light on how to approach your duty. *Demand* comes from the Latin *demandare*, "to entrust." You are *entrusted* with the responsibility for your school's care, protection, and performance. It is a weighty task and one that perhaps only other heads of school will fully appreciate. Thus, for your own peace of mind and for the sake of the profession you have embarked on, one of the most important demands that you have is to foster positive relationships with your wider community of school leaders. You will find those who share in your unique calling to be a source of wisdom and support. Despite the competition that may exist between or among schools, what you give to build a healthy network of school leaders will enrich you personally and professionally. If you find yourself entrusted with the leadership of a geographically isolated school, you will find the support of your peer group of school heads even more valuable. Seek out relationships with other school heads — trust and share. What you give to building those relationships will support you in the difficult times and delight you in the best times. At first, it might seem risky to share with those whom the larger marketplace perceives to be your competition, but there are no copyrights when it comes to educating children. More than any other profession, educators share their best practices because we put children first.

DEMANDS OF THE BOARD

You may find the demands of your board (often made up of business professionals) to incorporate hard-nosed business practices difficult to deflect, but your overall obligation to providing the best learning environment for children trumps purely commercial considerations. At the same time, although you are in charge of a nonprofit enterprise, you have to realize that you do have financial responsibilities. Heads of school are quintessential entrepreneurs with all the risks and responsibilities that go along with any independent business venture. Therein lie many demands on your leadership that you may not have anticipated.

For example, you may find yourself responsible for a new building, not only supervising its construction with the help of a professional project manager but also raising the money to fund it, stewarding the approval process through your local governmental agencies, sharing the news with your neighbors, and accommodating your many constituents during the construction. All will look to you for the overall success of a construction project, and you will learn more about zoning, union relations, HVAC systems, and building materials than you ever thought you would need to know. Yet these demands make your job fascinating. In the learning communities schools aspire to be, you will find that you are indeed the chief learner, but don't expect your experiences to be the status quo. Expect the unexpected.

LEADERSHIP IN A TIME OF CRISIS

Consider the following scenario:

> Hurricane Katrina hits New Orleans, and the flood walls are breached. Your campus is flooded, contaminated, and deserted; restoring it will cause the school to incur financial loss far beyond what federal flood insurance will cover. Your own house is flooded and will be uninhabitable for months to come. The future of your city is in doubt, and dire predictions abound. Students, faculty, and administrators are scattered to the four winds. Just over a quarter of your student body will not be returning. You are asked by the school's board of trustees to step up from your position as assistant head of school to shepherd the school. Though employees are still being paid, the board is contemplating staff reductions that you know will be emotionally devastating in this tight-knit community. Simple recovery will be hard enough, but you know that simple recovery won't be enough if the school is ultimately to succeed. It's your first headship, and it follows on the heels of the very successful tenure of a respected leader. You are deeply grateful to have an extremely strong faculty and a wonderfully talented administrative team, but now all are looking to you.

The demands of headship in a time of crisis are particularly great, yet embedded in the challenges of rebuilding a school in trouble are insights into the full range of leadership demands faced by school heads.

Fear management tops the list. All of us who love our schools have strong feelings about them. As leaders, we must also contend with correspondingly strong personal fears of failure, of loss and of defeat in tough times. The necessity of confronting and dealing with one's personal 3 am bundle of fears before the next day's faculty meeting is one amazing way to get to know yourself, a personal opportunity to be the "chief learner."

Heads of school never have to carry the ball alone; indeed you cannot and must not. Following Katrina, our school's board chair stood up immediately to insist that the school would reopen. No matter the cost, we would raise the money and present our students with a clean and fully restored oasis as soon as possible. A strong board chair, executive committee, and board of trustees are a head's essential partners in good times and bad. While an executive committee may need to take on much of the board's leadership in times of crisis, the committee must also have the wisdom to relinquish that aggregated power as soon as possible.

One of the great benefits of working through a crisis is the bonding that develops between administrators, faculty, staff, trustees, parents, and students when all are working together with great determination toward the same high purpose. During the recovery from Katrina, in order to build morale, all employees needed to pitch in with the physical labor, so when the environmental firm we hired gave the green light, faculty were called back in organized work teams to help gut and clean the school and sod the grounds.

The extraordinary goodness of the still-anonymous donor who gave our post-Katrina school an early gift of one million dollars brought hope and boundless energy to the in-town faculty who had banded together to open the school early, upstairs, and away from the construction. Their tender care of the students who came home to devastation also brought hope and energy to parents whose volunteer efforts can never be sufficiently credited. The manifest happiness of the children and young people to be back on campus and back together brought great joy to those of us who were privileged to work with them in those days of a small preliminary fall reopening before our full program reopened two months later. The nonstop all-hours work of some inspired others to contribute the same. The wives of our two on-campus work crew bosses (our director of facilities and our athletic director) assured us that they understood why their husbands worked seven days a week and came home only to sleep. With hugs and smiles, they affirmed that they stood firmly behind us all. We were humbled by all those who came forward with financial and moral support and kindness beyond measure.

The support of other heads across the country in opening their doors to our evacuated students was an extraordinary example of educators putting children first, and it must stand as a point of pride for years and years to come for solidarity within NAIS. We who were on the receiving end of this largesse will never be able to adequately express our enduring gratitude.

Communication with all constituents is never more important than in a crisis, offering a healthy mix of truthful reporting, reassurance, optimism, and forward planning. Sharing stories of the heroines and heroes who emerge in crisis generates more heroism. Shared news of fund-raising success generates more success. The parents who ask to see you or linger around your office door really do need to see you, and time must be found for all their concerns. Through all the angst, the head must stay closely attuned to the emotional tenor of the adult community. We created occasions to laugh together and party together, and when we had to move forward with layoffs, we also cried together. We told each other our personal evacuation stories over and over again, but we also celebrated everything we could think of to celebrate. We encouraged one another to face forward more and more.

Whatever your leadership style, you as the head must be genuine. Part of fear management is not being afraid to let your faculty know the real you, in sorrow as well as in celebration.

FINANCIAL MANAGEMENT

And then there are the numbers. Some you will confront as head may be grim indeed, others heartening, but the head's challenge is to face the objective reality of enrollment numbers, annual fund collections, increasing requests for financial aid, tuition receipts, cost of debt, and so on, and to make clear-eyed decisions and plans. When board-funded New York business consultants came to our school after Katrina, we immersed ourselves in the numbers, studied spreadsheets modeling multiple scenarios, discussed every detail of school operations, and explored options so exhaustively that when the analysis was complete, even the most die-hard, hard-headed advocate had to agree that faculty and staff layoffs were necessary to save the school.

Because children must come first, our layoffs were proportionately fewer for faculty than for staff and administration.

Managing finances is always a challenge for the head but less so with an excellent CFO at the helm.

Only the patiently intrepid could successfully wade through multiple insurance claims, application of shifting guidelines from the federal Hurricane Education Recovery Act, working with myriad and ever-changing FEMA personnel, and the necessity of fielding multiple requests from the state bureaucracy for the same data and the same documentation year after year. Persistence was the order of the day, but once again we all celebrated our CFO when the major FEMA project check came through some three and a half years after Katrina.

The head must be a constant source of encouragement to staff throughout long-haul efforts. We found shared sputtering verbal outrage to be therapeutic on occasion.

Surely an applicable lesson of crisis management for heads must be that planning is not an easy game. Beware of lengthy, detailed strategic planning processes that result in predictable but unfunded grandiose plans. Take advantage of work that must be done on a regular basis for reaccreditation, and create a thoughtful planning model with maximum flexibility for your school so that you can face forward and dream big or hunker down as circumstances change. Increasing demand for financial aid when your community is badly damaged or when the economy is rocky gives us all the opportunity to be creative in meeting the needs of applicants while keeping the school solvent.

Even in the most well-endowed schools that do not experience national disasters, a great deal of your energy will be spent managing finances. You will have to work openly and honestly with your board of trustees to determine yearly budgets that efficiently support the programs necessary to accomplish your school's mission. You will find yourself in the middle of many a tug of war over resources, and somehow you must navigate the many interests and be the final arbiter of how you spend your board-approved budget. Key to the amount of money you have to spend is the tuition you charge, and you will find yourself in the best position to recommend appropriate tuition levels because you have the best sense of the programs needed to serve your students and the best sense of the value of the program you offer. Don't be shy in stating the honest needs of your school. You know those needs best, and very often your trustees do not see the human impact their financial decisions have on your students, families, and employees. You do, and you have to live with the consequences.

SOCIAL JUSTICE

You will also be the final arbiter of financial aid — how much you "discount" your product and how you distribute financial aid to ensure socioeconomic diversity. In your role as a school leader, you must be sensitive to the demands of social justice. Independent schools take pride in their educational innovation and success and strive to create in their students an appreciation for the richness that is the cultural tapestry of our communities. We make every effort to prepare our graduates not only to serve our local community but also to make greater global contributions. It may be difficult to instill these important values in homogeneous, predominantly affluent communities. The costs of true diversity lie in making funds available to ensure a socioeconomic mix of families and in creating an accepting, inclusive, and equitable community where all families are welcome. Heads of school must balance the demand for the prudent financial planning that makes financial aid accessible and the obligation to articulate and lead their community's understanding of the educational value of socioeconomic diversity. They must lead by example. Heads of school must get involved in the financial aid process and advocate for greater diversity, but they must also listen to and balance the competing demands that come with a more diverse school community.

SELECTING AND SUSTAINING FACULTY AND STAFF

Most important, diversity begins with the faculty and staff hired by the head of school. Although selecting and sustaining your faculty and staff should be a team effort, it demands your full attention. Since every person working at your school will represent you and the school, you should have the final say in each person's employment. Your budgetary responsibilities will demand that you administer the salary budget fairly while still setting salaries at ap-

continued on page 140

PERSPECTIVE

ADVICE FROM A LAWYER

Nick A. Boodrookas, Partner
Steyer Lowenthal Boodrookas Alvarez & Smith LLP
SAN FRANCISCO, CALIFORNIA

When do I need a lawyer?
Independent schools are increasingly complex organizations and must deal with a wide variety of legal issues. Successful heads of school understand when to seek legal counsel for themselves and for their schools. Good lawyers can help you with planning, prevention, and protection. Savvy heads know that waiting until friction occurs or a crisis happens can be a mistake. Experienced counsel can help you with strategy and tactics that nip problems in the bud.

Finding the right lawyer — what kind, which one, and who is the client?
First, assess what kind of lawyer you need and who that lawyer should represent. Ask yourself a few questions: Do I need a lawyer to represent me personally, or am I looking for a lawyer to represent the school? Does the lawyer have experience dealing with independent schools? Does the lawyer have experience with the types of matters commonly faced by independent schools and heads of school?

Ideally, legal counsel for a head or a school should have experience representing independent schools or school heads or both. Time spent as a respected independent school parent or trustee can also be very valuable. Independent schools often deal with personnel matters, student or adult misconduct, public relations or crisis management situations, and related transactions and litigation. Try to find an attorney with that skill set. At times, schools deal with issues that may require additional expertise, such as bond financing or criminal law. It may not be possible to find one lawyer to fit all projects, but having a relationship with an attorney familiar with independent schools can help you find other experts when the need arises.

Independent schools wisely focus on "fit." They seek students and families and employees who will fit the ethos of the school. Fit is just as important when choosing a lawyer. Good school lawyers respect the missions and cultures of schools and value the same things a good school values, like collegiality and devotion to the best interests of students and the institution. They are good listeners and wise problem-solvers and communicators. They also understand and respect the distinctions between management and governance, and they skillfully support the head's ability to lead and manage and the board's ability to govern. Sometimes schools are lucky enough to have a trustee or parent or alum attorney who fits the bill. Sometimes they are even lucky enough to receive pro bono legal services from that person. But when the stars are not perfectly aligned, it is important to seek and hire the right lawyer.

Good independent school lawyers understand their clients' fee sensitivity and the need for efficiency. Calling a lawyer before a rift or crisis can save significant time and expense compared with litigation. A long-term relationship with a school lawyer is important even if, occasionally, the school accepts assistance from a generous parent or trustee willing to handle a particular legal matter. You need to know that an experienced lawyer is available to help quickly, regardless of changes in the parent body and the board over the years.

Some schools have counsel who is respected and consulted by both the head and the board, and that's great. If the attorney is the school's attorney, however, he or she cannot represent the head in a matter that might pose an actual or potential conflict of interest. One situation where a potential conflict of interest might arise is in the negotiation of a transaction between the head and the school, such as an employment contract or separation agreement. Another potential conflict situation might arise when both the head and the school are defendants in a lawsuit. In some situations, where the interests of the head and the school appear to be aligned and no actual conflict of interest is perceived, an attorney might be able to seek written permission and a conflict waiver allowing representation of both the head and the school. But sometimes the school and the head prefer — or should have — separate representation.

When should I call a lawyer?

Heads and boards sometimes wait too long to consult counsel about the head's employment agreement. It is a good idea for both parties to seek counsel early, whether for a first-time contract or a renewal. One key way to avoid ill will and awkward departures is for the parties to negotiate a good contract that both feel provides necessary protections and fairness. Even well-meaning boards sometimes underestimate the impact of contract delays on a head's morale and sense of security. A lawyer with independent school experience can provide important negotiating assistance, advocating for the head in a manner that the board respects and trusts. As that trust develops over time, often the negotiations are "friendly," and counsel is trusted by both negotiating parties. But good counsel will make clear whom he or she represents and when a party should consider seeking independent advice.

Heads should seek legal advice very early when dealing with sensitive personnel or student/family issues. The "practice" of law is aptly named — experienced independent school lawyers or lawyers for heads have seen and solved many problems commonly faced by schools and heads. They can help you strategize, document, and deal with challenges in ways that protect you and the school. They will also help you understand and protect attorney-client privilege and evidence, which can be critical in the event litigation is unavoidable. They may suggest independent investigation of certain allegations (such as sexual harassment). They can help you tender a threatened claim or lawsuit to insurance carriers to try to obtain reimbursement or payment of legal fees and any settlement or verdict. If you consult counsel early, he or she may be able to help you find ways to "manage out" a difficult employee or family without ill will or the threat of a lawsuit. Good independent school lawyers understand the laws that apply to schools and can help you structure your approach in compliance with those laws. They also have practical, common-sense experience in human relations and documentation techniques that prevent lawsuits or, at least, bolster your defense.

If you are sensing that your performance or continued employment is in question in the board's mind, you should seek counsel immediately. A lawyer with employment law and independent school experience is a critical resource for a head at such a time. Calm, objective advice from a good lawyer will help guide you through a very stressful time. The earlier you seek advice, the better the chance you can turn the situation around or protect your reputation and financial position. And remember, one of the best ways to protect yourself against a damaging personnel action is by consulting with counsel before you negotiate and sign your contract. Counsel can help you build in fair contractual protections before problems arise, when your relationship with the board is strong. It is also important to seek counsel immediately in the event you face any accusation of misconduct, so counsel can help you determine whether you need counsel of your own.

There are wonderful lawyers out there devoted to doing good work for schools and heads. Find one before you need one, and call one before disaster strikes. That way you can maximize the value wise counsel can bring to any search for solutions. ■

propriate levels, given the cost of living in your area and the scope of the responsibilities of your employees. You should also go above and beyond in your background checks of those you employ. Always end your interview of a former employer with the question, "Would you hire this employee again?" As in all important decisions, you will rely heavily on the advice of your core group of administrators charged with managing the functional areas of school operations, but never forget that you are ultimately responsible for all personnel issues. It will only take one employment lawsuit to bring that lesson home.

You will be expected to be able to articulate your ideas in your writing and public speaking, but the significant challenge you face is encouraging all who work at your school to share in the ownership of community values. Heads of school should remind all school employees that all adults in schools teach children by their everyday actions. Heads of school will quickly find out that it is not just the children who are watching — everybody is watching the head of school.

As the Katrina experience demonstrated, nobody can do the head of school job alone. You will depend on your faculty and staff, and they will depend on you. Your faculty needs to know that what they do every day is vital to the success of a school: If things are broken in the classroom, the school is broken. You have a responsibility to hire and support the best teachers you can and to hold them to high standards of care and consistency. Some of your toughest decisions will have to do with your faculty. How do you balance the long-term service of a popular teacher with an impulsive act of irresponsibility? How do you tell a person who lives to teach and is failing in health that it is time to step down from the classroom? How do you move a mediocre teacher on? How do you share those decisions with the wider community? You do so with the well-being of your students and the mission of your school in mind — and with compassion.

Your relationship to your senior staff is critical. Find the best people and give them enough room to do their jobs. Trust but verify. Heads must know enough about every aspect of school operations to be able to decide who is most effectively using his or her resources and who needs help in accomplishing his or her mission. Be clear in your expectations. Set personal goals, and ask primary staff to do the same and to explain to you how they are going to help you accomplish your goals. Heads have to balance individual staff needs with the overall school requirements. If you have three divisions in your school, you must encourage individual leadership and responsibility within each division without sacrificing the overall school vision.

The demand on a head of school is to find the right balance between supervision and intervention, competition, and collaboration. Encourage collective responsibility for the overall success of the school. Communication is critical. Don't be afraid of meetings, but be clear in the purpose and expectations of those meetings. Require full participation and mine for conflict — face the tough topics head on. Instill in your senior staff the importance of honesty; seek out bad news but use such information to solve problems, not to assess blame. Your most critical leadership task is to establish trust while not encouraging complacency.

DEMANDS OF FUND-RAISING

A head of school's ultimate success will be measured in available resources needed to accomplish the mission. Although all your relationships with primary staff deserve your attention, you will find that your association with your development/advancement office will be one of the most demanding. More often than not, you will find yourself the point person in asking for the gifts needed to endow your school's operations. Many new heads are intimidated by the prospect of asking for money for the school; however, it should be one of the easiest demands you face. You know best what your school needs to succeed, and you can best articulate those needs.

By virtue of your position, you embody the school and thus command a great deal of respect from your older alumni who have fond memories of their experiences. If you have an alumni constituency who did not have a good experience or if your school has experienced events that have alienated your giving base, you have the obligation to lead your institution in a direction that will encourage those with financial resources to support your plans for the future.

One head of a very successful southern school brags that he has never asked for a dime. His job is to run the best possible school, and his board and his development office take care of the fund-raising. Most heads are not as fortunate. Most will find themselves spending a great deal of time cultivating and stewarding those who have the means and inclination to support independent education. Don't ever forget that no one knows as much about your school's product as you do and that you are the best salesperson for that product. Your fund-raising enthusiasm directly translates to most prospective donors as enthusiasm for your job. It is what you were hired to do.

Raising money among current parents can be a delicate issue. It is difficult for a parent who has made a significant contribution not to expect your attention once the gift has been processed, and your obligation to all the children in your care and to the long-term health of your school may be in conflict with a wealthy donor's specific expectations. It is a difficult situation every head of school will face, and it requires courage to explain why you are taking actions the donor does not agree with. Be prepared to be unpopular for some of your decisions. Be consistent in your standards so that you can build trust in your decision-making. Never think that all of your decisions will be widely accepted or supported. You simply have too many constituents, each with a different set of priorities, to make everyone happy. Heads of school face unique sets of demands from every direction, so it is imperative to communicate clearly what you stand for and to live according to the fundamental values of the school you lead.

THE HEAD'S FAMILY

Not only is everybody watching the head of school, but his or her family and partner are also constantly under scrutiny. It is not easy being the child of a head of school especially if that child attends the school, nor is it easy to be the mostly silent partner of a head of school. Those who share their lives with a head of school may find it a lonely existence as they are usually defined by their relationship to the head and are expected to play a supporting role in school events. If a partner has his or her own career, school commitments may make it difficult to fully pursue that work. Even if a partner has the time to devote to school affairs, he or she will never fully share in the recognition or sense of accomplishment that a head of school feels. The demands on the partners of heads are more difficult to meet since the first lady or first gentleman of the school usually has only limited staff support and often faces those challenges alone.

The demands on heads are many and, if allowed to be, can be totally consuming. You have obligations to your family that you need to balance, and you need to set priorities that honor the significance of your responsibilities to them. Most heads err on the side of being workaholics, and if they are not physically present in the office or at the many events that go on at our schools, they are there mentally during most of their waking hours. You must make the time to be a good parent and partner, to appreciate what your partner or family gives up to support you, and to thank them. Set priorities that include consideration of those who share in the demands of your challenging profession before you tackle the trials of leading an independent school.

TAKING CARE OF YOURSELF

You also have an obligation to yourself. You have been hired to lead, and you cannot lead effectively if you are not well or are a prisoner of the stress that goes along with your responsibilities. Reflect honestly on your state of mind, make some time in your day for what you love, exercise regularly, take time off — not only those scheduled school closings but also the vacation time you have accrued. Make sure you have regular health checkups, and don't delay getting treatment on those medical issues that interfere with your effectiveness as a leader. Don't be afraid to have an honest conversation with your board chair about those school-related issues that keep you up at night. Most heads feel fully responsible for all of a school's employees and its students, not to mention the extended alumni families of our institutions and past and present parents. This is a potentially overwhelming demand for caretaking that one person simply cannot meet. To do your job effectively, you have to be at your peak performance, both mentally and physically. Caring for others begins with caring for yourself. You will not meet the many demands of being a head of school if you fail to honestly assess and meet your individual needs.

A sterling administrator feeling momentarily overwhelmed by the demands of her own assignment once asked her head of school, "Do you ever feel that your job is just too hard for you?" The candid answer was, "Yes, I

continued on page 146

PERSPECTIVE

CONFLICT WITH THE COMMUNITY

Ellen Moceri, Head of School
Ransom Everglades School
MIAMI, FLORIDA

Zoning

In my graduate courses in educational administration at Teachers College of Columbia University and in the several courses I took at the Klingenstein Institute, I never heard anyone mention zoning. In my second year as the head of Ransom Everglades School, however, as we tried to renovate our middle school and bring it into the 21st century — while, at the same time, complying with recommendations from the Southern Association of Colleges and Schools — we ran into a hornets' nest of neighborhood activism over zoning. We hadn't realized that our neighbors were already up in arms because a piece of property near our school, located in the midst of a well-to-do neighborhood, had been zoned for high-rise condominium construction. Our desire to build a gymnasium that was 25 feet high (thus requiring a zoning variance) seemed to represent the same kind of threat. The game was on, and the learning curve was steep.

I hadn't expected that anyone would object to our project, which would provide more playing fields, more green space, and a gymnasium/ community center for middle school children. Eight years before we began our zoning odyssey, we had acquired a piece of land adjacent to the school — perfect for a regulation soccer, lacrosse, and football field. At the time we began our project, an abandoned house was in the middle of the land; it had a nonfunctional (and dangerous) empty swimming pool, invaded by dying Banyan trees. Surrounding this scene of dilapidation was our dilapidated middle school built in the slapdash 1950s Florida architecture of concrete and exposed pipes. Our need was great: a completely renovated middle school, a gymnasium, and a playing field. The threat we posed was minimal — or so we thought.

The Opposition

The first group comprised three friends and professional colleagues, who had bought three houses in a cul-de-sac adjacent to the land we hoped to make into a playing field. So what was the problem? These folks felt that if we turned the vacant lot into a playing field, we would create something akin to the Orange Bowl stadium with lights, blaring noise, and thousands of fans. (They had obviously never attended a middle school soccer game.)

The neighborhood association was a broader group, and they were no happier with our plans. Their goal was to stop any growth that would have an impact on traffic and thus on their neighborhood. My meetings with various representatives of this group were perhaps the most contentious. They thought we would be destroying Banyan trees and old oak trees when, in fact, we would be ridding ourselves of a dead Banyan tree and moving, successfully, three oak trees while creating our three-story gymnasium.

I found myself in the position of defending the importance of our school as a significant part of a healthy neighborhood. I invited members of this group to visit the school, oversee the plans, and make suggestions about the future development. I also tried to point out to them how much we lived the mission of the school — to give more to the community than we took from it. I extolled our many community contributions, especially the fact that our Breakthrough Program, a summer enrichment program for at-risk public school students, took place on our middle school campus. But they were not persuaded.

The last group of neighbors we dealt with was the most important because they had the most to gain from our proposed changes. These neighbors lived on a narrow lane across from the entrance to the school. Every morning, our parents lined up as far as the eye could see to wait their turn to enter the school. And every evening, they repeated that activity. Needless to say, we blocked the street for a good portion of the day and made it very difficult for our neighbors to come and go at will. When we told them that our new construction plans would change the entrance to the school from their lane to a much broader street on another side of the school, they were thrilled. Because they were the closest neighbors to the construction site, we worked with them to add the landscaping that would improve the view from their homes.

So the stage was set for our first hearing at the city commissioners' meeting where we hoped to get the variance in zoning that would accommodate the height, in a residential area, of our proposed gym and the use of our vacant lot for an athletic field. Since I was no expert on zoning law, I depended greatly on the advice of our lawyers. However, halfway through our attorney's complicated presentation to the city commissioners, I knew we were going to lose this round. We had not only neglected to do our political homework, but we had also failed to create the emotional buy-in necessary to counter the impassioned presentations of our neighbors.

All major controversies are, in their essence, political ones. And all politics is local. I asked the vice president of our board of trustees, a member of a respected Cuban family in Miami, to arrange meetings with the Cuban city commissioners so that we could present our needs and the positive impact of our project on the City of Miami. The head of our Breakthrough Program met with the African-American city commissioner to explain how beneficial the changes in our middle school campus would be for the African-American, Haitian, and Hispanic students who were part of our program. Finally, one of our board members, who was a friend of the city commissioner for Coconut Grove, arranged a meeting at the school so that we could present the advantages for Coconut Grove in improving our school. I also met with 67 different groups of neighbors in an intensive "charm offensive."

The Outcome

In a wonderful compromise, spearheaded by the commissioner from Coconut Grove, everyone, including the most aggrieved neighbors, agreed to a variance to allow the building of the gym and the creation of a playing field. And we agreed, by contract, that if the school ceased to exist, the land would revert to residential zoning.

Every time I step onto our middle school campus, I am reminded that no matter what area of expertise we heads of school need to master — be it zoning regulations, fund-raising, or personnel law — that mastery serves one great purpose that we need to keep in the forefront of all of our efforts: to provide the resources necessary to develop the full potential of our students so that they may use their talents to serve and improve their communities. ■

feel that often, but it's just a little bit too hard. The truth is that constant challenge is one of my favorite features of the job. I have to grow." No other position in independent schools requires so much, calls for such a variety of skills, or confers such trust on an individual human being as the headship; but it is also true that no other position affords such magnificent, invigorating growth opportunities and such deep satisfactions. We commend headship to you, in all weathers.

PART V

PEOPLE, CONSTITUENCIES, RELATIONSHIPS

PARENTS

Reveta Bowers

IN THE BEGINNING

Several times each year, we fill our school's community center with prospective applicant families ready and eager to learn more about The Center for Early Education. At every gathering, I stand before the audience looking at their faces and wondering which of them will join our school community. After talking several minutes about the history of the school and how it has impacted and shaped our programs, I tell them what they came to hear: how our education will impact their children. They sit forward eagerly to learn about our mission, our curriculum, our facilities, our goals and objectives, and how they have all been developed to provide a wonderful education for their children. But then I take a turn that most are not expecting: I talk about *their* relationship to our school and how joining our school community as parents commits them to an education for themselves as well. I speak about the kind of trusting and open relationship we need with parents and how, as their children learn to be good students, they will need to learn the skills to parent those students. In some ways, it is the most important message of the morning.

At all times, our work as head of school requires that we keep in mind what is in the best interests of our students. Our mission statements, philosophies, and core values are stated in terms of what we hope to achieve with the children and adolescents we serve. As I stand before these parent audiences, I am struck by how I have talked more and more over the years about their role in our school and our educational objectives for them. Recognizing the important role parents can play in helping us fulfill our mission, I am convinced that we will never be successful in providing an exemplary education for our students unless we also forge strong working relationships with and provide a comprehensive education for parents as well. The relationships that we have worked to establish with parents during my 38 years at The Center for Early Education have been some of the most productive and rewarding and, at times, challenging aspects of my career as a school head.

This important work begins the moment prospective parents search our websites or call our schools for applications or to make inquiries. The subtle and not-so-subtle messages of respect, engagement, commitment, and expectations are communicated, affecting what the public understands about our schools. I have often told prospective parents, as well as faculty and staff, that if we can work together to create supportive, nurturing, and respectful places for adults, we will have gone a long way in creating a healthy and thriving community for our students. The hopes, dreams, and aspirations of our parents for their children can be better realized if there is, from the outset, a clear, purposeful, and vibrant relationship with parents.

Therefore, we must be careful about the promises and warranties people assume we make during the admissions process and how that sets the tone for everything that follows. Parents come to our schools with high expectations. For some, this will be their first experience with an independent school. For others, it is the continuation of what they experienced as children, and they seek admission for their children to a school that will further that experience or be a sharp contrast to it. Nonetheless, all parents hope that they are initiating a relationship that will be worth the sacrifices they will make for their children to be able to attend. No matter the socioeconomic background of the family, every family will be expected to devote their time, energy, and personal resources to provide this education for their child. Many of our families make tremendous sacrifices to access our schools for themselves and their children. Some drive considerable distances, while others must reprioritize their lifestyles. Whatever their ability to pay our fees and tuitions, all parents who gain entrance to our schools are going to be making conscious decisions about how much they can do and at what cost.

OUR MISSION WITH PARENTS

Although very few of our mission statements reflect our relationships with parents, implicit in those statements is our need to have a partnership with parents in working with their children. Unless parents have "bought into" our mission, they will challenge our goals and objectives throughout the education of their children. Thus, we need to be clear with parents about their explicit and implicit role in that education and how much we value that partnership. Some school heads say that they would rather not have parents as partners because this would lead to shared decision-making in all aspects of their child's education and beyond to broader operations of the school. But I would say that a strong, candid, and consistent partnership can further the mission of the school, help us honor our core values, and make for lasting and committed relationships even after the children graduate.

Schools are now beginning to add language to their contracts about their expectations for parents. Many forward-thinking schools have taken the time to develop parent covenants that express the school's desire for parent involvement and behavior. It is difficult in any institution to play by the rules if the rules are not articulated. For schools with no such document, engaging parents in developing a covenant can be a great way to begin.

Parents who are already experienced in your school have thoughts about what makes a "good and respectful" community member. Whether it is following the rules of the carpool line, honoring volunteer commitments, or attending school events and functions, the majority of parents in our schools recognize when others have violated the norms of the community, and they have strong feelings about those instances. Parents are watching to see how we deal with those infractions and whether the rules apply to everyone consistently and in ways that are transparent and fair. Community members are better behaved when there are explicit rules and norms for their behavior and when the school calls people on their missteps. If we want parents to support the mission and vision of the school, then they need to understand their role in helping the school realize that mission and that vision. On page 153 is the covenant that parents sign and return to our school at the beginning of every school year:

We have found the language in this covenant to be straightforward, clear, and concise enough to be remembered easily. You might spend some time thinking about what kinds of language would be important to put into a covenant for your parents. To be clear, it is not just parents whom we expect to sign and adhere to a covenant. All constituent groups in our school, including trustees, faculty and staff, and students, sign similar covenants.

THE COMMITMENT OF TIME

We rely on parents in so many ways to make our schools places of excellence. We begin every school year asking them to participate in our annual fund campaigns. We solicit their volunteerism on projects, school events, field trips, and all manner of committees. We ask that they come to meetings, "Back to School Night," "Applying for College," parent education programs, class potlucks, parties, receptions, and picnics. If we are well-organized, we send out a calendar each summer that lists the school-day, evening, and weekend activities of the school. Making sure that parents have timely and adequate notice of school events is a good way to ensure their attendance and gain their lasting appreciation. Nothing is more irksome to a parent than finding out about an event with short notice or, even worse, no notice at all! Making sure that classrooms are notifying parents of activities in a timely manner ensures that our busy parents, grandparents, and friends will make the time to attend and to participate fully in the school life of their children. One of our alum parents once told me that she and her husband had never fully appreciated how important these communications were until they joined a secondary school community that did not place the same value on timely notifications and expectations.

PARENT COVENANT

I understand that all members of the school community must behave in a way that supports the Mission and Core Values of the school. Thus, while a parent of a child enrolled at The Center for Early Education:

1. I will abide by school rules and policies and will support the mission of CEE through actions such as encouraging inclusion and embracing diversity.
2. I will actively communicate with other members of the school community openly, directly, promptly, and constructively without resorting to gossip and rumor.
3. I will model appropriate ethical behavior for my children and others and will exemplify Caring, Respect, Inclusion, and Honesty.
4. I will honor my financial commitments to CEE whether they are required or voluntary.
5. I will fulfill my volunteer obligations and will be an active participant in educational opportunities for parents.
6. I will commit to reading and responding to oral and written communication from the school, including school publications such as the Friday Bulletin, Parent Handbook, and website postings.
7. I will support the security procedures of the school at all times.

I understand that my signature below indicates that I will adhere to the items listed in this Covenant, in the Parent Handbook, and in the Reenrollment Contract.

Please Print Parent Name Clearly	Please Print Parent Name Clearly
Signature	Signature
Date	Date

Schools also need to be clear about families' financial obligations in addition to tuition, as well as expectations for their time and energy. And when they have made that effort, we need to thank them graciously and promptly. It is important to give parents choices about how they spend their time and share their expertise with the school so that they can also manage their other commitments. Developing resource databases that list the special talents, skills, and connections of people in your school community can enrich not only the school experience but the school curriculum as well. Bringing parents in to discuss their specializations with students, teach units on their area of expertise, or work on a committee that utilizes their talent is a wonderful use of their time. And parents can often provide internships or field-trip experiences that broaden and deepen the education of students and teachers.

THE OPTIMAL MATCH

During the admissions process, all schools work to choose students and parents who will be a good "match" for their schools. We look for families who believe in our mission and support our core values. Families who are good matches are articulate and passionate about the reasons they would like to see their children in the school.

Because at The Center for Early Education we admit very young children into our toddler programs, we are often interviewing parents of 15- or 16-month-olds. Although they have just begun to know who their children are, they often tell us that they are *very* sure that our school is the *perfect* match for their family. For the most part, these parents are bright, well-educated, and skilled in their arguments. They "give good interviews," and thus we can be fooled into thinking that they *are* perfect for our school even if the match is far from perfect. Sometimes we take some reassurance from the recommendations of current or former families who know the applicant family, but much of the time we have to rely on our first impressions and our instincts. The most important questions to ask of ourselves are "Do we want to spend the next six, eight, or 12 years with these people as our partners in the education of their children?" and "Do we want them to become members of our school community?" If the answers are yes, then we've found a good match for our school. But don't be fooled into believing that what you see is what you'll get! Just as our students grow and change, so do their parents. Be prepared to understand the developmental changes in parents just as you adjust to and accommodate those in your students. As parents change, so does their relationship with our schools.

Given the current economic downturn, some families experience unprecedented changes in their lives. While many will weather these changes philosophically and practically, others will be thrown into unknown waters. The presence of the school in the lives of their children becomes of paramount importance. The constancy, reliability, and support of the school can help families navigate these unexpected shifts. Major changes in the lives of our families almost always are experienced by the school in some way. Our ability as institutions to be supportive, resilient, and flexible in dealing with parents who are going through turbulent times will help us continue to be vital and sustainable communities. The promise schools make to parents is similar to the vow we take in a marriage: to be there in good times and in bad. As learning communities, this becomes especially important for us to model, whether we are talking about a sudden learning challenge that arises, a disciplinary situation, a death in the family, or a financial setback. All require us to step up and assist the family to the best of our ability.

There is no such thing as a perfect match of a family to a school. At some point in almost every enrollment, there will be an issue, a "speed bump," a disagreement, or a change in commitment that challenges us to be responsive. What we seek is to achieve to the best of our knowledge and ability an optimal match from everything we've come to learn about those parents and that child during the admissions process. Together, our hard work, cooperation, communication, and trust can support the development of a positive relationship and a "good enough" match.

THE DIVERSITY OF PARENTS

Just as our schools are striving to become places of diversity for the children we serve, we must be mindful of the multicultural characteristics and diverse needs of our parents as well. Whether we're speaking of diversity in terms of race, culture, religion, socioeconomic status, sexual orientation, age, marital status, geography, or school affiliation or educational background, our schools need to be welcoming, safe places for parents as well as for students. This means that at all times we have to be conscious of what we say and do and put in writing. We must be sensitive to how our salutations on letters, our bulletins and forms, our events, our school calendar, as well as the visual displays on our campuses, will be perceived by the adults and students in our communities.

If we are to fully engage parents in the life of the school and its activities, we need to ask the important questions below as we go about the business of delivering a high-quality education and building a thriving community:

- Have we written our school calendar in ways that can accommodate the different work schedules and abilities of our parents to attend events?
- Do our school communications help the families in our community feel recognized, understood, and included?
- Do our parent education programs speak to different segments of the parent body, or do we seem to only acknowledge them as one group?
- Have we thought to provide special services or opportunities for different groups of parents? Affinity groups? Events? Receptions? Parent education opportunities?
- Do the artwork, visual displays, collections in our libraries, and website structure make all families feel that they are important members of our school community?
- How are parents and guests greeted when they come onto our campus? Have we created an ethos and a school culture that make parents feel welcomed and acknowledged?
- Have we reminded and educated faculty and staff about greeting everyone and sometimes going out of our way to make a potentially underrepresented group feel good about being in our hallways, classrooms, and offices?
- Do we speak about the value of diversity and the important contribution *all* parents make to the ethos of the school so that all families understand their cultural contributions and relevance to our institutions?
- Do we find ways to help faculty and staff parents integrate into the

parent body in important and visible ways? Have we made clear to them their role as parents as distinct from their roles as employees?

The adjustment that many of our new parents make to our schools can be even more difficult than the adjustments their children make. Socioeconomic, language, and even geographic differences can impact these transitions and make walking onto our campuses challenging and stressful. Anticipating those possibilities can prevent embarrassing situations and smooth the way for more positive and productive relationships with parents.

THE EDUCATION OF PARENTS

Parent education is probably one of the most challenging but beneficial initiatives a school must undertake. So often in our mission statements, we refer to the lofty goal of "lifelong" education. Many schools have worked diligently to fund and sustain comprehensive professional development programs for faculty and staff, but few have put the same kind of thought into providing an educational program to help parents develop their parenting skills.

A well-executed parent education program can advance the mission of the school, enhance the relationship between teachers and parents, and provide support for parents in raising healthier and more competent children. The curricular and learning goals and objectives that we articulate for students are equally important in planning a parent education program. A design that is rooted in helping parents better understand what is developmentally appropriate at various ages and stages makes for better parent partners and more appropriate support systems for their children. "What is normal and expectable at certain grades and ages?" "Along the broad spectrum of normal development, when should parents be concerned that their children appear to be missing important milestones?" These issues need to be put into a context that parents can understand in order for them to deal with their children in supportive ways.

Schools have an imperative to develop programs that will support the school and parents in expanding their parenting skill base and increasing their understanding of what the school can and cannot do and should and should not be responsible for. But we need to keep in mind that just as our students have different ways of learning, so, too, do their parents. We must strive to provide opportunities for learning that differ in approach, breadth, timing, scope, and ambition. Good teaching and learning for adults in our schools must be mindful of different work schedules, commutes, and accessibility, as well as the depth of the topic. Consider the following suggestions for parent education:

- Morning coffee talks or chat groups for non-working parents or parents with flexibility in their daytime schedules and who may not have childcare in the evening
- Early morning one-hour commuter breakfasts on topics of interest
- Book clubs or groups for parents that allow them to explore and discuss a book, article, or research paper on a topic of interest
- Parent education evenings with other schools that combine resources and budgets to bring in well-known speakers
- Panel discussions that include faculty, administrators, experts, and even parents on topics of interest or concern
- Grade-level or age-level meetings each year that allow for in-depth discussions and presentations on both curriculum and developmental readiness
- Focus groups that encourage parents to bring up topics that are timely and current in their own lives

Being mindful of the competitive educational marketplace and the choices parents have to seek an education for their children should inspire all of us to think about becoming the "go to" place for parents in terms of their own education and development.

PARENT AS TRUSTEE OR BOARD LEADER

One of the most delicate relationships to negotiate as a parent in a school is that of the parent trustee or board chair. Given the high profile of board members in many of our schools, often these wonderful volunteers are seen as having exalted status within the parent body or special privileges that don't extend to other parents. This is a widespread misperception. It is critical during the nomination process to articulate the role of current parents on the board so that expectations for behavior, conflict of interest, and stature are clearly understood. A discussion of board culture is also important. Consider the following questions.

- Do parents on your board leave their parent issues outside the boardroom?

PERSPECTIVE

BATTLING SATAN IN THE SUBURBS

Bruce L. Dennis, Head of School
The Packer Collegiate Institute
BROOKLYN, NEW YORK

When I became head of school at Packer Collegiate Institute, an extraordinary pre-K to 12 independent school in the Brooklyn Heights section of New York City, I had just completed a 35-year career in public education in New York, the last 16 years of which were spent as a public school superintendent. From 1992 to 2004, I was superintendent of schools in Bedford, New York. This community served a student body of close to 4,000 children spread out over nearly 58 square miles in five neighborhood elementary schools, a middle school, and a high school in the affluent Westchester County communities of Bedford, Pound Ridge, and Mount Kisco. Three years into my superintendency, I was confronted with what was surely the most unusual and vexing experience of my educational career: the allegation by three parents that the Bedford Central Schools were promoting satanism and violating the First and Fourteenth Amendment rights of their children.

The first signs of the problem can be traced to a trading card game called "Magic, The Gathering." The goal of this game is to cast spells in order to reduce the opponent's "life total" to zero or less. Designed by a Ph.D. in mathematics, the game was marketed to preteen boys (including my own nine-year-old son, who had become captivated by its complexity and visually engaging imagery). The game even developed a professional playing circuit where participants could earn considerable cash prizes. "Magic" was being played in an afterschool club at our middle school and in a before-school activity at one of our five elementary schools, where a parent volunteer oversaw the children who participated.

Initially, two parents came to me with objections about the game, contending that its images posed a danger to young children and that the activity was not safe for their mental health. Skeptical but wanting to be open and receptive to all our families, I invited these parents to meet with two board members and me, and I also invited the parent who was overseeing the elementary school club.

While I remained unconvinced that the game was dangerous, I decided to send it to three independent mental health professionals, none of whom was connected to our school system. I also imposed a 30-day moratorium on the game. This later turned out to be an especially wise decision even though it caused an initial uproar in our socially progressive community where our more liberal families felt that I was bowing to pressure from the religious right or, less kindly, selling out to those who would censor and control creative expression and seek to damage our schools. My response was simple: I

continued on next page

- How would a trustee who is also a current parent handle a potential issue or conflict in your school? Through the same channels as other parents?
- How willing and able is the board chair to have difficult conversations about parent trustees who step over the line?

BATTLING SATAN IN THE SUBURBS

believed the game to be safe, but if someone had alleged that the water in our school was impure, I wouldn't simply sample it and see whether it tasted all right. I would bring in bottled water, close off the taps and drinking fountains, and have our water tested to see whether it was safe to drink.

Nineteen days later, having received written reports from the psychologists and psychiatrists that the game posed no harm to students, I asked the board at a public meeting to restore the "Magic" game. At that same meeting, one of the originally complaining parents, Bible in hand, poked me in the chest with her finger and threatened, "I'm going to bring you down as the superintendent who promoted satanism in his schools." No stranger to being threatened, I smiled and told her to "give it her best shot." Little did I imagine that she and a small coterie of like-minded individuals would embark on a five-year vendetta against our public schools that included bringing legal action, first in the U.S. District Court alleging 113 separate violations of their children's First and Fourteenth Amendment rights, and finally in the U.S. Court of Appeals on the final three charges.

What quickly became clear was that, for these families, the issue was never just the game. Instead, they formed a small but virulent "Association Against the Seduction of Children" and sought to directly influence and alter an instructional curriculum they contended had offended their religious beliefs. Their curricular targets were wide-ranging and bizarre: They included the Yale Decision-Making Program, developed by Yale University's Department of Psychiatry "to equip young adolescents with the skills to make good personal choices"; the DARE Program (Drug and Alcohol Resistance Education), part of our fifth-grade curriculum to comply with our state's required policy of drug and alcohol education; the study of owl pellets, a research-based science activity that is endorsed by science teaching organizations around the world; and a raft of children's and young adult literature, including books like *Bridge to Terabithia*, a Newbery Medal-winning children's novel that was recognized as a "notable children's book" by the American Library Association and a "best book" by the School Library Journal, and *My Side of the Mountain*, a Newbery Honor Book and winner of the Hans Christian Andersen Award.

For a good portion of the first year of the legal battle, I spent about 70 percent of my time dealing with the court case or its residual impact. Much of my focus was on supporting our talented faculty, who saw themselves at the nexus of this attack on our community, which was being covered by the *New York Times*, the *New York Daily News*, all of the major New York television networks, and even The 700 Club and Court TV. I was also busy fielding phone calls, interacting with our attorneys, and keeping our very supportive Board of Education informed. To

- Are parent trustees aware of their increased visibility in the school community? That of their spouse or partner?

A Governance Committee that is clear about the answers to these questions can screen potential candidates through these important lenses and avoid

the enduring credit of our board and community, they refused to back down although they were ultimately forced to spend almost half a million dollars defending our school system. Eventually, all of the litigation was concluded, and our district was fully vindicated with all charges dismissed in the courts.[1]

What were the major takeaways from this ordeal? First, no matter how informed, intelligent, or enlightened a particular community may be, a few resolute individuals with national support (in this instance from the religious right) were able to turn our town and school system upside down. Second, a small handful of parents cannot be permitted to derail the curriculum of an entire school district by leveling specious and irresponsible allegations about instructional practices simply because they have determined that certain aspects of curriculum or pedagogy do not meet with their approval. Third, at its core, leadership in schools is still all about teaching.

In addition to representing our schools to the media, time and time again I was called on to educate our board, instruct our community, and, most important, be there for our students and their teachers. The first calls I returned were not to NBC or CBS but to the Fox Lane High School newspaper. I also spent quite a bit of time visiting our middle and high school social studies classes, answering students' questions about a controversy in which they, themselves, were actually involved. Frighteningly, some of our most outstanding teachers had begun to question the successful instructional practices that had served them and their students well for many years, and they were understandably feeling gun-shy as they became the focus of intense media scrutiny that questioned those very methods. Our teachers needed their superintendent to tell them that he trusted them and that they should continue to exercise the good judgment that had characterized their work in the past.

The media coverage of which I was most proud came in the form of an editorial in the now defunct weekly newspaper, *The Patent Trader*, which carried this message in its final paragraph: "The sterling reputation of the Bedford School District was being blackened by silliness. Dr. Dennis and his board did the only thing you can do when there's a monster under the bed; they shined a flashlight on it. More than one speaker asked, 'Why are we spending such time and energy on this nonsense?' The answer is, we do not invite our afflictions. Two lost moms with Satan on their minds could have happened anywhere. They happened to have happened in Pound Ridge. Dr. Dennis and his Board, by exposing the Devil to the light of reason, made Him shiver and flee. May he stay away long." ■

[1] For more information, see *Altman v. Bedford Central School District*, 245 F.3d 49 (2d Cir. 2001).

uncomfortable situations in the future. Teachers need to know that a parent trustee has no more rights than any other parent and is sitting in the parent conference with his or her parent hat on and not in the role of trustee.

Trustees who continue on the board after their children have graduated will often comment on how liberating it is to be seen as "just a trustee" in the school community. Issues of confidentiality, addressed most effectively during new board member orientation and with trustee covenants and open conversations within the boardroom, can clarify the role of trustees as well as that of trustee leaders who also function as parents in the school.

WHEN EMPLOYEES ARE PARENTS

Often some of the most sensitive relationships in our schools are those with faculty/staff whose children attend our schools. Many independent schools encourage employees to bring their children to our institutions for their education. After all, what better endorsement than to have our faculty and staff enroll their own children in our schools? But we need to remember that just as our faculty and staff are on display each day, so are their children. The fishbowl effect is never more in evidence than when dealing with faculty/staff as parents. As much as we would like to believe that our employees can be objective and reasonable in the work setting, often that is put to the test when there is a problem in the school with one of their own children. We know from our own experience as parents that objectivity and professionalism can at times fly right out the window in the face of a learning hurdle or a disciplinary issue. When our children are hurting, we are hurting. Just as we cannot expect detachment and logic from our parent body around emotionally loaded issues or problems that arise, neither can we expect that from our co-workers who have children in our school. Appropriate boundaries, professionalism, and objectivity are laudable but difficult goals in these situations.

Schools need to think about how they can create some guidelines or protocols so our employees can function most effectively as parents on our campuses. It might be appropriate to develop a list of suggestions for employees to consider *before* they enroll their children in our institutions, such as the following:

- Will you or your spouse/partner be the primary contact when the school needs to communicate about your child?
- How will you feel about seeing members of the school community and your colleagues on your weekends and in your free time? Will you feel as though your free time has been eroded if you have to spend time with families of your child's friends or classmates?
- What kind of conversation and agreements have you as an employee made with your children, especially older children, about your own work and your professional space while you are both on campus?
- Should this not work out for your child personally or educationally, how will that impact your continued employment with the school?
- Can you expect to have honest and forthright conversations with your colleagues who are teaching and working with your child, and will those conversations adversely impact your professional relationships if things don't go well?
- Is this school the best match for your child and not just simply more convenient for you and your family?

Some of the most painful professional and personal conversations schools have are with employees who are disappointed with or embarrassed by events in the education of their children in our schools. When things go well, it can be a terrific opportunity to take advantage of the same excellent education being offered to the families in our schools. When something goes amiss, it can be distressing for the teachers or staff members who feel that they and their children are more visible or under greater scrutiny in the community of the school. However, the educational opportunity for children of employees to attend our schools can also serve as a wonderful attraction and retention tool, particularly in a competitive market!

THE QUIET STORM

One of our parents once told me that our school was a good place for his child when everything went well, but it was a GREAT place when his child hit a speed bump or experienced a setback! I was enormously pleased that this parent felt that was true of our school, and it has proved over the years to be an important goal to sustain. However, things don't always go well year after year for the kids we serve. It is in those times that a school is severely tested. We need to operate on the assumption that for every good day we are having with a student or a family, we are making a "deposit" into an account of goodwill and trust, but we also have to remember that parents may need to make a withdrawal from that balance of goodwill from time to time.

There are so many ways in which our relationships with parents can go off the tracks. Most often, parents become anxious, worried, fractious, or demanding when their children are having difficulty in school. The age of the student makes no difference, nor does it seem to matter whether the difficulty is academic, physical, emotional, or social. Parents want their children to do well in school. In all ways and at all times, parents deserve to feel that the school is making good faith efforts to operate in the best interest of their children. When a parent starts to feel that this trust is misplaced, that the school has not been as honest, candid, or helpful as it should, then the relationship between school and parent is likely to become strained or even damaged.

Having clear policies for communications, interactions, conferences, grades, administrative contact, and parent behavior is essential to maintaining good relationships with parents. Schools are moving toward publishing clear and explicit student and parent handbooks, contracts, and covenants for behavioral expectations. Just as we have clear ideas for employee and student conduct, so should we have them for parent conduct. Parents may have no idea that they have stepped over the line if no one ever pointed out where the line was! When concerns surface, do we have clear expectations about the expected protocols and sequence for parental interactions with the school? Are parents expected to go to the teacher first with their concern? Is there a system of deans or advisors that parents are expected to contact before coming to see the head? Do administrators check with parents to make sure they have followed those protocols before scheduling a conference and helping them bypass a well-known series of first steps? How can we build trust with our faculty and staff if not by sharing with them information we are hearing from parents and by having clear and candid conversations about the next course of action?

In today's educational climate, stifling the voices of parents is not only unwise, it is impractical. We hear increasingly in the public sector that parents are asking for and being given greater and greater authority and responsibility for decision-making in schools, particularly those schools in crisis. Having wise, trusting, well-educated parents increases our chances that when a problem arises, we can expect to have open and constructive conversations about solutions, alternatives, and possibilities. It is in situations where we can meet as adults to calmly explore possibilities that some of the most appropriate interventions, solutions, compromises, and opportunities emerge for our students and our schools. Clear channels of communication are the building blocks for creating communities of trust and transparency in our schools.

Parent surveys and questionnaires, focus and discussion groups, an annual State of the School meeting, and well-prepared and regularly scheduled parent conferences and grade reports are useful vehicles in understanding how parents' perceptions are shaped and where you need to put your school's communication resources and energy.

THE JOYS AND TRIUMPHS OF WORKING WITH PARENTS

Even though the primary mission of our schools is educating our students, good schools understand that the effectiveness of our institutions can also be measured in the satisfaction of parents. Parents today are more insecure and uncertain about their children's futures. In the face of rising financial crises, increasing unemployment and workforce globalization, overburdened and challenged public school systems, and uncertain standards, they look at our schools, our curriculum, and our programs and are often astounded at how quickly the educational landscape has changed and how different their own education was from what their children experience. We cannot take their support, patronage, or continued retention for granted.

Helping parents understand and appreciate the work we do and, in turn, realize how important they are in the educational outcomes and objectives we strive for is essential to the building of effective and excellent schools. The opportunity to work with parents who are appreciated and appreciative in return is rewarding for all of us who work in schools. To see parents graduate with their children and return to our institutions to apply for their grandchildren is paramount to the furtherance of our mission. Working collaboratively and cooperatively with parents should be one of the goals for school sustainability now and in the future, for it is those parents who value our education and our programs who will support our schools with their time, their energy, their talent, and their personal resources today and tomorrow.

FACULTY

Bodie Brizendine

WHEN I WAS HEAD of school at Marin Academy (CA), Anna Heidinger, then admission director, had a wonderful way to talk about making choices. She used to say, "You can do a lot of things at Marin Academy; you can't do them all, and you can't do them at the same time." I think this mantra travels well into the land of headship: You can't do it all, and you can't do the many things you have to do all at the same time. This call is particularly applicable to a new head's work with faculty, especially in that the vast majority of new heads come from the academic or teaching sector of school life. It's what they know best and it's what they have done well: all the more dangerous! The inclination to "do it all" in the academic life of the school is more than tempting, no matter the size of the institution. Unless you are leading a school in which you are the only teacher, this is a challenge you will face whether you have one dean, 12 deans, or none.

And here's the rub. You are indeed responsible for the academic program.

With the traditional moniker of "head," you are the head teacher, the teacher of teachers, and the whole school is now your classroom. It's complicated, it's dicey, and it's very important to find the right stance and the right balance. Peter Esty, long-time head of several schools, once defined this dance as "standing forward and stepping back." It is this sense of being-there-but-not-doing-it-all that defines the challenge of working with faculty.

THE HOW'S

Overall, there are some frameworks that will guide, in a larger way, your work with faculty as you enter a new school. I call these the "how's" of the job — the way in which you figuratively and literally walk through the halls — and these frameworks shape your engagement with the adults for whom you are responsible and upon whom you deeply rely to further the mission of your school:

1. **Recognize that you are part of a continuum.** In most cases, the school was there before you and will be there when you leave. Let the faculty know that you recognize that you are involved with something larger than yourself, and let them know that you respect that greatly. Honor the past with an authentic voice, and make yourself a bridge rather than a break.
2. **Articulate the difference between "growth" and "change."** Although these words are often cut from the same cloth, they suggest two very different approaches and can work far beyond semantics. You're always building on something, which may, indeed, mean change, but it is always building on *something*. Honor that something.
3. **Never confuse responsibility with ownership.** The faculty is not "your" faculty, and to suggest so is to infantilize adults. This distinction holds true for all aspects of the school: *my* school, *my* students, *my* board of trustees.
4. **Understand power and never pretend that most of the bucks don't, indeed, stop with you.** No matter how democratic your community, you do have certain decision-making power that faculty do not, and that makes a very large difference. You get to set the tone, and you are responsible for it.

5. **Understand the difference between "legislative" and "executive" decision-making and always try to be as clear as possible in distinguishing between the two.** Design and articulate the decision-making process as often as you can, respecting the adage that information in itself is power. And when you can't be completely visible in your decision-making for whatever legitimate reason, tell the faculty that you cannot. Trust them to trust you, even if as head you are asked (and you will be!) to prove yourself trustworthy over and over again.

I used to keep on my bulletin board two words Robert Evans, a clinical and organizational psychologist, offers for the "how" one should lead: with *conduct* and *purpose*. I can think of no better words to guide heads in their work with faculty, no better words to summarize the five points listed above. It's really about respect, about self-awareness, about having a purpose larger than self. Lead, always, with "conduct and purpose" in mind.

THE WHAT

And then there's the "what" of the work with faculty. What will you actually be doing in concert with faculty, and how do you lead them into furthering the mission of the school? In keeping the larger frameworks in mind, how do you affect that Esty stance of "standing forward and stepping back"? And how do you position your work away from the management and into the leadership realm? In metaphoric words, how do you move from deciding when exams occur to leading conversations about their value? There are four distinct arenas to consider.

First and foremost, it is your charge to articulate the values and set the standards. Your key work with faculty is at this level: setting and maintaining the tone for the school. The more voices of leadership, the stronger the institution. I call this "echo-making" or "purposeful redundancy," and when it goes into effect, your own words come back to you from others. In the best of worlds, both you and the faculty are saying, "These are the things that matter most here."

Naming what matters most means framing priorities and challenging assumptions: no small thing. This is where strategic work becomes your best

continued on page 171

PERSPECTIVE

HANDLING A CRISIS ON YOUR CAMPUS

Jayne Geiger, Head of School
Far Hills Country Day School
FAR HILLS, NEW JERSEY

We found child pornography on the laptop of a teacher!

This was not a message I wanted to receive while sitting in the dentist's chair, about to start a root canal.

I made three phone calls on the way back to school: to my board chair, the school attorney, and a crisis management consultant whose workshop I had attended at NAIS, Jane Hulbert. I did then, and still do, carry her card in my wallet and keep her number on my cell phone. Within hours, we had a legally sensitive communications plan in place to ensure that the following happened:

- The proper authorities were immediately alerted. Pending the result of the police investigation, appropriate action would take place with the teacher in question. The associate head and I would meet with the teacher together and escort the teacher off campus if warranted.
- We would remain in constant contact with the authorities. As head, I would be the only person to speak to the inevitable press/media. Faculty and staff would be informed first thing in the morning with an appropriate amount of information. The board chair and I would call each trustee at 6:00 am.
- Parents would receive the news via an initial email (we alerted them to look for it through the Info Exchange phone service we used at that time) with the assurance of follow-ups as more information became available.

Via telephone, Jane coached my responses to the press. I took their calls on speakerphone with the associate head and board chair present to assist me from the sidelines, ensuring that I stuck to the message.

The key: Seek help from experts. Not only was Jane an expert in crisis communication, she kept me steady and calm. Inform your board chair and trustees appropriately. Communicate frequently to constituents, even if the message is that there is no news.

- **Write down** what you are going to say.
- **Reassure** parents that their children are safe.
- **Anticipate questions**, and be ready to answer them.
- **Stick to the script** — do not go out of bounds. (Do not "vamp" when responding.)
- **Recognize a leading question** from the press or a busybody. Don't take the bait.
- **Practice "closing" the conversation.** A reporter will push. You can take charge by saying, "Thank you. I need to end the conversation now." Be clear and firm.

Be confident, knowing you have sought help and that crises do have a resolution and sometimes even a silver lining. Our communications plan produced trust among all constituencies for the short- and long-term. The authorities did their job well, and our students and school remained safe. ■

friend, and no matter the model used (and there are plenty of options and opinions on these), it is your job to name the questions, face the challenges, and advance the conversation. To do so, you need to demand that the faculty be open to professional growth. And if they don't have experience in this, you need to give it to them. If, for example, one of your challenges is enhancing a multicultural perspective, then you have to make sure that the faculty are ready, in the words of Cornel West, "to enter the conversation and be willing to be changed by it." Your task is to keep faculty exploring and learning, and your job is to make clear that this is an expectation.

This means making sure that you hire faculty who can be both learners and teachers. There are many ways for heads to be involved in the hiring and firing of faculty, and much of this is determined by the size and demands of the school you lead, but making sure that you have the right faculty to do the work of your school is arguably one of the most important things you do. Whether you are involved at the very beginning with reading resumés as some heads do, or whether you interview after some significant, earlier vetting as other heads do, make sure that all involved know what your non-negotiables are for every adult joining the institution. Name the values you want echoed, and hire with those values in mind.

And perhaps the most delicate of all balances called for by your leadership with faculty will be the one between individual and institutional needs. Who is not meeting the standards of the school? Who among several receives the internal appointment for advancement? What happens when an excellent teacher is not a good citizen of the school? Above all else, it is your responsibility to name what is best for the school and to keep that foremost in decision-making around all matters and especially in personnel concerns. Here the "answers" are not always so clear, and you will find yourself in situations of complicated judgments needing much weighing and vetting. Schools, for better and for worse, often position themselves within the metaphor of "family," giving each decision about faculty an emotional accounting not often matched in other CEO experiences. Again, the call for great care is coupled with the call for great clarity, and I go back to the words of Robert Evans: conduct and purpose. Don't confuse the two, but employ them both.

The second arena regarding the "what" of your leadership with faculty is to find or create ways in which to honor their good work. Mike Riera, head of Redwood Day School, has a wonderful phrase about working with adolescents: "Catch them being good." Children are not the only ones who desire to know that they are doing good work, and faculty, the lifeblood of any school, also deserve this witnessing. Creating meaningful rituals and ceremonies around faculty work makes for important institutional acknowledgment, and it is your job to make sure these exist. The most important way to acknowledge faculty is to make sure that you recognize the importance of its voice. More often than not, the faculty are the loyal members of the community and some of the best keepers of the school's mission. Include them in the work of the school in significant ways and always expect the best of them. Let them know that you not only desire their input, you need it.

A third consideration in your work with faculty is your role as inspirational leader and provider of resources. You need to make sure, either through your own work or through the work of the administrative team if you have one, that faculty members have all the up-to-date resources they need to be those ongoing learners you desire. Keep faculty professional development near the top of your list. Ask yourself, what are the structures for adult learning at this school, and how do I support them? How are faculty made aware of the current policies and best practices regarding school life? And finally, and perhaps most important, ask yourself how you are serving as one of those resources. Are you doing enough for yourself so that you can be inspirational? What are you reading? What are you learning? What professional development are you involved in and how are you sharing that with the faculty? Remember, you are called "head teacher" for a reason.

Finally with all faculty member engagement, there is the call to know them, know yourself, and, as much as possible, know the facts. This is especially true in challenging times of hard decision-making or interpersonal conflict, where you are often put in that difficult role of judge. Experience tells us that few are the times in which you can't take something home and sleep on it. In other words, speed is rarely a value and often a detriment. Take some time, do all the fact-finding you can, understand the players, and acknowledge your own biases. When appropriate, seek the advice of others, especially fellow heads who can best understand your challenges and who possess a distance you do not, allowing for a perspective you can't have. All of this takes a considerable amount of emotional resilience and a steady hand on the tiller. There's not a lot of room for the need to be loved and there's plenty of room for a healthy skepticism about those professing love.

In the good day-to-day life of working with faculty, what is needed are three things: respect, trust, and presence. Consistent and careful candor helps faculty members understand your trustworthiness, and it is this that develops their trust in you. And showing up means everything. Witnessing good work, walking the hallways, seeing the games and the performances — these make all the difference. Teachers want you to see them at work, and they want you to understand their commitment to the school you share. This, above all else, builds the rapport with them that is so critical for your daily work.

Leading faculty presents a tremendous opportunity to set tone, further the mission, and make a difference to the school and to the students within it. As agents of transformation, heads of school inspire faculty and, in turn, faculty inspire heads of school with great teaching and good work. Together, they move a school forward, holding the school's mission as their guide. In the best of worlds, the relationship is one of a fine partnership in the spirit of collaboration and shared purpose.

STUDENTS

Jack Creeden

MOST OF THE HEADS of school I know decided to work in education because they enjoyed interacting with students. It seems logical, therefore, that someone who has spent the early part of his or her career as a teacher, department head, divisional director, or other administrative staff would find that communicating with students as the head of school would come naturally. The behaviors you employed in those previous positions while working with students should produce the same results in your new role of head of school, right? Perhaps not!

I remember speaking at an All School Assembly during my first year as head. The easy bantering, gentle teasing, and repartee that I used as part of my teaching and advising style early in my career felt pretty comfortable to me, and I believed most students enjoyed this approach as I was getting to know them in my new school. So there I was in front of the entire school, making an announcement about an upcoming event and encouraging students to attend.

I added that I hoped students would also visit the student-operated snack bar where one of my favorite seniors, Matt, would cook up one of his special burgers for them. I then proceeded to describe how Matt would sing and dance his way through the cooking and presentation of the burgers, which he did on a nightly basis. Everybody in the assembly giggled, but Matt turned beet red, embarrassed that the head of school had singled him out in front of the whole school to make fun of him. Boy, did I blow that one! Adolescent Psychology 101 taught us that very few teenagers like attention to be focused on them in front of their peers. It took me weeks to restore Matt's confidence in himself and convince him that the head of school would not "pick on him" again in front of the student body.

The task of communicating and interacting with students as head of school can be daunting. It's clear that what the head of school has to say is critically important, but there are new and different levels of significance attached to your oral and written behaviors that you must pay attention to in order to avoid a mistake like the one I made. What you say will now be interpreted in multiple ways: I guarantee it!

"BUT THE HEAD OF SCHOOL SAID IT WAS OK!"

When you are head of school, the problems and students who end up in your office won't be the easy ones. Quite the contrary. Instead, it's the complicated and messy situations with student behaviors, activities, and programs that will appear. Although you dealt with hundreds of students earlier in your career, what you say now and the decisions you make will have a larger and more powerful impact.

The head of school's decisions set the direction and tone for the school and affirm the school's priorities. Therefore, your decision-making process and communications need to be careful and intentional. You need to know the school's history and core values in reference to the issues with which you are dealing. It's a good operating principle to ask how the school's mission statement is supported or contradicted by the issue under review.

Clever students will attempt to subvert the chain of command as they search for a supportive answer at the highest level of authority (the new head's office). You are absolutely certain that you were hired to solve problems for the school, but you must resist that Type A impulse to "fix it" if the student request or issue is properly handled in another administrative office or in the classroom. There is nothing more powerful, in the mind of a student, than to believe that "the head of school supports my point of view!" Often it is best to admit, "I don't know," and direct the student elsewhere.

NEVER SURPRISE THE BOSS

Everything you have read about the centrality of the relationship between the head of school and the chair of the board is true. A good relationship is absolutely essential to your effective functioning as a school leader. And such a relationship requires that the chair of the board know when there are potentially disruptive student issues before you.

There's no formula that you can apply to determine whether the issue is too insignificant for the chair's review. The board chair/head of school partnership requires sharing information to create the balance between governance and management responsibilities. It's appropriate in your regularly scheduled communication with the board chair to preface your comments by saying, "I don't think this is something you need to do anything about, but I just wanted you to know that it's an issue I'm dealing with right now." It's easier to mutually conclude that a student problem happily went away or was quietly resolved than it is to apologize to the chair for belatedly advising him or her of a troublesome student matter. When in doubt, inform.

WHAT HAPPENS OFF-CAMPUS AFFECTS THE CAMPUS

Independent schools wrestle with how to respond to off-campus student behaviors that contradict the school's values. When these incidents occur, you need to know how the school has responded previously. Does the school have a policy, rooted in the mission statement, of responding to off-campus behaviors? Has this policy been challenged by litigation? Does the policy differentiate in any way if there are municipal, county, or state laws involved? Have there been incidents in the past where the administration, parents of involved students, and other members of the community successfully worked together to implement the policy? What provisions are there for making sure that the appropriate school officials speak with the students involved?

In the absence of a written policy, it's tempting for a new head to create a policy "on the fly." Sometimes there is neither time nor opportunity to organize the right group of faulty and staff to formulate policy. Time can be of the essence, and decisive leadership calls for immediate action to send a clear message to the community. But in the aftermath of the disruption, the head of school can use the incident to convene the right groups of people to create a policy based on a discussion of the institution's core values and mission statement. Never miss an opportunity, in a less volatile environment, to use a recent student incident off-campus to discuss what values are important to the school in responding to student behaviors.

AND BABY MAKES TWO

When there is a pregnant student in school, the first concern must be for the health of the mother and child. But once that is ensured, opinions may diverge on the best policy to follow. Obviously, this is a time when the head of school needs to make sure that the board chair receives early and accurate communication, while assiduously honoring the partnership balance of governance and management.

In addition to referencing the mission statement, the head of school must deeply understand the social, emotional, cultural, and perhaps religious or political context in which the school finds itself. Preserving the integrity and confidentiality of the student (or students) is of utmost concern, as is controlling, where possible, the range and nature of parental or other student behaviors in response to the pregnant student's continued presence in school.

The head needs to clearly define for the community the nature and extent of support the school intends to provide for the student while enrolled. The decision should derive from the mission statement and have full board endorsement. The school may also need to respond to those who object to her continued enrollment.

A TRANSPARENT DISCIPLINARY PROCESS

No issue generates more discussion and armchair second-guessing than the disciplinary process at a school. Everybody is an expert on how the process should operate, and most parents find the policies acceptable until one of their children or a close acquaintance is involved. Then it gets interesting.

I have a good friend who says, "If the process is faulty, then the parties involved never get to focus on the behaviors that were the reasons why the student was in trouble in the first place." I think she is right.

The best and most transparent disciplinary systems have clear and concise policies that are fair, uniformly applied, and open to scrutiny. Students have the greatest confidence and trust in a system that is predictable and consistent. Achieving that level of trust and consistency is critical.

Perhaps the greatest challenge in administering a transparent disciplinary system is in collecting information from students in a just and responsible manner. Reminding students of the importance of telling the truth seems to be the best way to begin a discussion about possible offenses. Referring to those sections of the mission statement or core values that speak to honesty in school interactions grounds the process for students, parents, and the community. In today's litigious society, schools often make sure that at least two faculty members are present when students are being questioned.

It is easy to remind ourselves that we must operate on fact and not rumor, but, in reality, differentiating the facts from "what I think happened" or "what I suspect happened" is no easy task. Once the fact base has been established, it is essential to honor the precedents that have been established, and to have all decision-makers support the sanctions to be applied. There's nothing worse than a faculty member of the Honor Council publicly announcing that he or she does not agree with the council's findings.

In today's highly connected world, those responsible for a disciplinary system must be aware of the cyberspace rumor mill, the new equivalent of carpool gossip for students. What is said on Facebook or elsewhere in cyberspace should not determine an outcome, but it should be in your worldview as you try to control what is going on, both within and outside your own disciplinary process.

I've yet to be involved in a disciplinary case where at least some portion of the faculty did not feel that they were the last to know what was happening. Timing is critical in highly volatile cases, and those responsible for the system and the head of school must work diligently to keep the faculty, on a need-to-know basis, abreast of developments. However, one must acknowledge that Facebook and Twitter communication among students will always

PERSPECTIVE

HANDLING A CRISIS ON YOUR CAMPUS

Linda Johnson, Director
Co-Chair, Education Law Group
McLane, Graf, Raulerson & Middleton P.A.
WITH OFFICES IN NEW HAMPSHIRE AND MASSACHUSETTS

It can happen at any school at any time.

The phone rings. A clearly distraught parent tells you that her daughter has been sexually assaulted by an older male student at your school. What do you do? Do you call the police? Do you call the boy's parents? Is it reportable abuse? Whom do you call first?

The head's primary consideration is to take care of the immediate safety and well-being of the students involved. Is the female student still at the school? Is she in distress? Has she received appropriate medical care? When did this occur? Are other students involved or impacted? The head should evaluate whether it is necessary or beneficial to provide emotional counseling or other support to the students. The head of school, together with members of the response team, can help the parents evaluate whether someone at the school can provide the counseling assistance needed. If outside help is needed, they can help find an appropriate outside provider.

How a head of school handles a crisis can mean the difference between a possible lawsuit with the concurrent media nightmare and a potentially high-risk situation that is managed in a calm and deliberate manner that appropriately addresses the interests of everyone involved, including your greater school community.

Properly responding to a crisis involving student misconduct, possible criminal acts, and reporting obligations begins long before any individual situation actually occurs. The school should already have in place a crisis response or reporting compliance team trained and ready to help evaluate, among other things, mandatory reporting obligations. A reporting compliance team often comprises the head of school, assistant head, dean of students, dean of faculty, and the school counselor. Most states have abuse reporting statutes that require immediate reporting to a government authority such as Child and Family Services. In addition, there may be other state mandatory reporting laws such as those regarding hazing, hate crimes, or criminal acts in safe school zones. The head of school should already have on hand a listing of any mandatory reporting laws that apply in the state in which the school is located.

One of the initial questions to be asked in a crisis such as the hypothetical one described above is, "What are the ages of the students?" The answer to this question will help determine whether mandatory reporting is necessary. However, even when the answer to the question indicates that no law mandatorily requires the school to report be faster than any formal mode of communication between the faculty and administration. Patience, a whole lot of understanding, and trust among the faculty about the legitimacy of the disciplinary process are essential.

Opinions vary about how and when to involve the parents of the students under review. I've always tried to approach this from the perspective

to authorities (e.g., both students are over the age of 18), the head should still evaluate whether the school should report. Consideration should be given to what "should" be reported as well as what "must" be reported.

Early in the response, the head should consider contacting legal counsel and the board chair. High-risk situations can be emotionally charged and stressful. Involving the outside, objective viewpoint of legal counsel can be extremely helpful. Likewise, informing the chair of the board and the executive committee can provide the head with helpful information such as how the school has handled other crises in the past. It also serves to keep the board chair apprised of developments. Usually, it is best not to report to the full board until the matter has reached conclusion, and even then it's important to maintain the privacy of the students involved. The head might provide only enough information — without naming the people involved — to enable the board members to fulfill their fiduciary duties, which include staying informed about the school.

Once the head of school has taken care of the immediate safety and well-being concerns, he or she should conduct such investigation as necessary to find out what happened and determine how the school should respond. He or she should develop a plan of investigation that includes a review of the school's handbook and policies, including the school's disciplinary process. It will be helpful if the disciplinary policy provides the head with discretionary authority to deviate from the normal process if necessary. In our hypothetical, for example, the school will want to keep notice of the sexual assault as confidential as possible to protect the student from further emotional trauma. In addition, when a student's actions violate school policies and may also be criminal, before the head of school speaks to the student, he or she should have a conversation with the student's parents and suggest that they might want to seek legal counsel to help them decide whether — or when — they will allow the head to speak with their child. It is quite possible that statements taken by the school from the student could be requested or subpoenaed by the police in the course of a criminal investigation.

The head should also consider whether to proactively develop a media response, identify a media spokesperson, and advise appropriate individuals to refer all contacts to the spokesperson. Often someone from the media will call, and there is no time to prepare a response.

Throughout the process, the head will need to evaluate all communication and notification plans. Beyond the police, state authorities,

continued on next page

of a parent, believing that if a senior administrator was spending significant time questioning my child about a serious offense, I'd like to know about it in advance. I believe that we owe that early notification to parents and that it promotes trust in the system. However, there are some who believe that once parents are notified, they will advise their child to refuse to answer any ques-

HANDLING A CRISIS ON YOUR CAMPUS

and parties involved, are there any others who need to know something about the situation? This might include the students' dorm parents, advisors, or teachers who may need to be told at least a limited version of the situation to ensure that the students' needs are being met. On a case-by-case basis, the head should evaluate who needs to know what, balancing the privacy and other interests of all involved. Very often, regular meetings with the response team members and with the families can be helpful in managing a crisis situation. In addition, the head should evaluate whether any notice is required pursuant to the school's liability insurance coverage.

Once the head understands the facts involved, he or she should determine what disciplinary or other response the school should take. Have any school policies been violated? What disciplinary action should be invoked? Are there other supportive or responsive actions that need to be taken to assist the target, the perpetrator, or the overall student body, such as counseling, an all-school meeting, follow-up training, etc.? Appropriate records should be maintained about the handling of this matter with the understanding that in the event of a lawsuit, all documents with the exception of attorney-client privileged documents may need to be disclosed.

A school has not completed its response to this crisis when the head of school metes out a disciplinary action. There may also need to be ongoing follow-up with the students and their parents to ensure that there is no negative aftermath that the school should respond to. Finally, once the matter has been fully investigated and responded to, the head would be wise to hold a debriefing session of the reporting compliance team, appropriate school administrators, and legal counsel to discuss how the matter was handled. Involving legal counsel can help cloak the debriefing and self-evaluation meeting with attorney-client privilege so that it cannot be used later against the school.

Each crisis will bring new variables that a head of school will have to assess and respond to. Above all, the head should remain calm, be objective, and be a leader. The students and their parents, as well as the response team and school administrators, will be relying on the head of school to be in control at all times. Careful handling of a crisis response by a head of school can help manage the crisis at hand and further instill confidence in the school's overall policies, procedures, culture, and mission. ■

Recommended Books

Deskbook Encyclopedia of American School Law 2010, published annually.

Preventive Law for Schools and Colleges: A Practical Guide for Administrators, Risk Managers, and Legal Counsel, 2004.

tions until they are present. I know that happens occasionally, but I would rather develop a more open model and deal with possible obstructionist parents when they appear.

Finally, the head will need to determine the best way to talk about the transgressions with the student community to help everyone learn from the incident. Some schools have traditionally discussed the incidents at All School Assemblies with rather full disclosure. Others elect to mention the behaviors but to leave out the names of the individuals involved. Whichever approach is used, it is important to the community's development that some discussion of rules, policies, and sanctions occur, preferably in small advisee groups so students have a chance to voice their opinions about behavioral expectations and have a responsible adult respond. This can be a powerful teaching opportunity to promote healthy social and emotional development.

TELL ME IT'S NOT THE BOARD CHAIR'S SON

It is never easy to expel the boss's child, but it seems to happen to everybody at least once in his or her career. Sometimes, the board chair fully understands and embraces both the spirit and letter of the school's policies, and then the process is easier. But usually it's not that simple!

In one school, a board chair's son helped organize an off-campus party and was responsible for delivering most of the alcohol that was consumed before students came to the Homecoming Dance. Decoding the reports from more than a dozen students, all of whom were seniors, and determining appropriate sanctions was the first challenge. Then the parents of the involved students split into two groups, one that worked with the school and the other that challenged policy, process, and appropriateness of sanctions. The issue was further complicated by the fact that the party occurred at the board chair's house when he and his wife were away for the weekend.

The incident was resolved fairly because the head of school and fellow administrators planned everything they did before they actually spoke to students or parents. And they reconvened as a group every day to pool the knowledge they had collected. It was essential that the school already had a clear policy that had been carefully reviewed by the school attorney about its intention to respond to off-campus behaviors that affected the reputation of the school. And although it consumed most of a week for the head of school and other administrators, the head met on multiple occasions with the students and parents to keep the lines of communication open. The board chair, by the way, was in the group of parents supporting the school. Sometimes you get lucky!

HOW TO STAY INVOLVED WITH STUDENTS

One of the great joys of becoming a head of school is that you have the opportunity to interact with students from all grade levels in a variety of settings. That's also one of the challenges, given the multiple demands on your time. Some heads stay connected by teaching a course. Others find that they can team-teach or serve as a guest presenter on topics of special interest in their field.

If classroom teaching does not seem possible, then find something that fits with who you are and puts you in a context that is not artificially created. I know of a head who spends every Friday morning visiting classes. At first, the faculty thought she was "checking up" on them, but the head described it as an opportunity to learn firsthand what the faculty and students were doing so she could share it with the board, prospective families, and others. I enjoy showing up unannounced at rehearsals for the winter musical or athletic team practices. I just stand by, quietly watching. The students know I am there and appreciate the fact that I took the time to observe them outside of a game or public presentation.

Some heads like to find a place on campus early in the morning where they can greet students as they arrive. This is different from working the carpool line, where the focus is often on the parents. Showing up to say "good morning" as students pass by may seem like a minor effort, but it means a lot to the students. And the kids will notice if you are present in good *and* bad weather (literally and figuratively) because this indicates that it means a great deal to you also.

It's impossible to accept every invitation to every special event, but the more of those you are able to make, the greater the opportunity to interact with students, even if for a short period of time. Carving out time to participate in class trips, which involves more time, is helpful but must be carefully monitored.

"THESE KIDS ARE OUT OF CONTROL"

It's no secret that the most effective student organizations are those that are clear about their objectives, receive excellent faculty advising, and promote strong leadership among the ranks of its members.

I know of a service organization at an independent school that has a very specific mission statement and guidelines about how students are to be involved. There's also a clearly delineated series of increasingly responsible leadership positions so that the organization is always in the process of grooming its next leaders. And it is not surprising that there's a strong set of expectations for commitments that must be fulfilled if membership is to be maintained. One of the most popular teachers in the school is the club's advisor, and it is his job, when necessary, to tell a student that if certain tasks are not completed, his or her membership in the organization will be revoked. It takes an incredible amount of faculty time, but the results are unmistakable.

On the other hand, I once worked with a student organization that was publishing material some in the school community found to be of poor quality and sometimes offensive. The students spoke of it as "their publication," whereas I considered it a community resource that represented faculty, alumni, parents, staff, and current students, all of whom read the publication. It's always challenging to talk with young, bright, and creative students about freedom of the press, but I balanced those conversations with the core values of the community that spanned generations. I also enlisted the support of the faculty advisors to produce specific guidelines about what was acceptable to print or photograph, based on the school's mission statement. It provided us with an opportunity to teach important lessons in a non-classroom setting.

THE REQUEST FROM THE CONTROVERSIAL STUDENT ORGANIZATION

Schools often struggle with a student request to organize a club around a particular religious preference or sexual identity, especially if there has been a history of avoiding any mention or presence of that topic throughout the school. Once again, the starting point for all schools must be the mission statement and core values. In addition, one hopes that the Office of the Dean of Students has published criteria that must be met for any student group to be formed and that the criteria are linked to principles described in the mission statement.

Each student group should have a mission statement that outlines its goals and potential contributions to the community. That document must be in sync with the school's mission statement; otherwise the club's existence can be challenged as a passing fad or a particular interest that has no place in the school's curriculum (i.e., all the school does with intention). In most cases, the Office of the Dean of Students and the student governing association are responsible for making sure that the proposed club meets all criteria for membership.

If the presence of the club on campus is seen as possibly disruptive, then the head of school should advise the board of trustees of the organization, its mission, and the degree to which the group meets the established criteria for clubs and organizations. It's not the responsibility of the board to approve student clubs, but the board should be clear about how the proposed club is in line with the mission statement of the school and has met all criteria for approved clubs. The board may also need to be educated about how other independent schools have dealt with the same or similar groups so they can respond to complaints or concerns with factual information and not innuendo or rumor.

It goes without saying that the faculty advisor is a critical participant in this process, assisting with the development of a mission statement, framing the student discussions to keep a focus on the cogent issues, and not allowing students to be distracted by the sometimes emotional or nonessential matters.

Because the approval of some groups can be controversial, the head of school must remain closely involved with all of this activity, and he or she must be prepared to respond to questions from faculty and staff, parents, alumni, and other members of the larger community who may not understand the club's mission or why the school is considering the organization.

CONCLUSION

Although we always say that the faculty are the heart of all good schools, it is the students who make the place come alive. Staying connected to them keeps heads of school vibrant, up-to-date, and mindful of why we got into teaching in the first place.

Remember these operating principles as a new head of school, and you'll continue to enjoy working with students:

- When you are the head of school, your words are heard differently across the student body than they were when you were a classroom teacher or divisional director. Craft your messages with different kinds of students in mind. You have to communicate with everybody!
- Students believe that the head of school has the final say on all issues, so even a slight note of interest can be seen as full approval. Proceed cautiously.
- When in doubt about a complicated student matter, formulate your decisions on the centrality of the matter based on your school's mission statement.
- There's no substitute for a precisely worded, balanced policy statement about student behaviors. Proceed without one at your own risk.
- Never hesitate to tell the chair of the board when you are working on a volatile student issue. Remind him or her that you are not asking the board to get involved, just to be aware.
- Everybody is an expert on the disciplinary system, but only you and the dean of students have to implement it. Be deliberate, decisive, and inclusive as you collect information and apply sanctions.
- Revise student behavioral policies as needed by consulting with comparable schools to make use of best practices. No need to reinvent the wheel.
- Students love having the head of school show an interest in their classes and activities. Get out of the office, wander around, and be visible.
- The best student organizations have the most active and astute advi-

sors. Be intentional about matching the right faculty to the student organization.

- Proposed student groups that may cause unrest in the school must be viewed through the lens of the mission statement. Apply it in all circumstances when responding to emotional or loud denunciations from critics. Being in sync with the mission statement levels the playing field.

THE BOARD OF TRUSTEES — FRIEND, FOE, BOSS, OR PARTNER?

Norman Colb

THIS CHAPTER IS ABOUT forging a strong relationship between the head of school and the governing board, a topic of considerable importance for prospective school leaders. I have been studying this relationship for most of my career, both during the 25 years I spent in public school administration and the almost 20 years I have served as the head of an independent school. I've been privileged to have worked in some of America's best schools and school districts, and, whether public or independent, the schools were staffed with serious professional educators; and their governance groups — whether school committees or boards of trustees — were filled with well-intentioned volunteers who cared deeply about getting education right.

Early in my career, I thought that the governing board was largely ornamental. As my responsibilities increased and I gained a closer look at the board and a deeper understanding of its workings, it became ever more obvious that the board was an essential partner in the running of the school or district. If the board worked smoothly and effectively, the school or system almost certainly did as well. And the reverse was also true: A snarling, dysfunctional board was almost always associated with an institution that was just as dysfunctional as its board. It also became clear that one of the single most important relationships in the school (or system) was that between the head of school (or superintendent) and the governing group. This has not been theoretical for me: I have watched myself both succeed and fail in attempting to build a relationship that could energize schools to stretch for real excellence.

In short, I've been there, and I offer the insights that follow, more as hard-won lessons learned than as research-based findings. I am not a scholar of the subject — such scholars certainly are worth the attention of anyone aspiring to be a head of school — but what I have gleaned about board-head relations is certainly true for me and may be of use to those who wish to try their hand at headship.

Creating an effective relationship with the board is not a casual matter, nor can such a relationship simply be assumed. Because working well with the board is so central to the success of both the head and the school, building a solid relationship is worth every bit of the attention and thoughtfulness it takes. The head has other essential responsibilities such as, most obviously, ensuring that students are receiving a first-class education. Budget management, staffing, fund-raising, and public relations also require the head's attention. But building a working relationship with the board is one of the most essential of the long list of heads' responsibilities, and, again, getting this right takes work.

And I am not talking solely or even primarily about what it takes to secure your tenure. A good board can serve as a vast pool of expertise for the head and ultimately for the school. There is a very strong possibility that you are not well-versed in all of the domains involved in running a dynamic school. If it is to thrive, the school needs ready access to expertise in matters ranging from debt financing to facilities planning and management, from marketing to public relations, and more. Schools are complex organizations that must cope with the challenges of a rapidly changing environment. The best heads know enough to know the limitations of their backgrounds. More, they are confident enough about themselves to be open to receiving help from their trustees.

THE IMPORTANCE OF THE BOARD

The board's significance may surprise a prospective head because, in many schools, the board does most of its work out of public view; indeed, members of a school community may first become aware that the board even exists at ceremonial occasions such as graduation. What does the board of trustees actually do? Ask teachers, parents, and students, and their answer may well be some variant of a shrug. But in the life of a head, the board is every bit as important as students or the teachers and coaches whose efforts are so obvious to everyone in the school. Unfortunately, the board's importance may first become apparent when things are not going right. When there is dissension among trustees or when the board has lost confidence in the head, the school community may first discover the board. More than discover, members of the community can do little but watch as many of the functions that normally proceed smoothly grind to a halt. Be assured that in the life of a head, the board is every bit as influential during good times, although it may do almost all of its work behind closed doors.

Experienced school heads understand the board's importance. If you were to eavesdrop on the conversations heads have when they huddle together over dinner at a professional conference, you might well hear a great deal of talk about the board. Teacher morale, fund-raising, and all the rest get their due, but it is the board that often receives the most attention, especially over the second glass of wine when inhibitions begin to dissolve.

So here you are, newly installed as head of school by the board that selected you, a board that is eager to help you succeed. You are now in the legendary honeymoon period, a period you want to last as long as possible, although — be assured — it will not. You have foibles, idiosyncrasies, and gaps in your skills that are sure to make themselves known within months if not days, and the honeymoon simply will not — cannot — last for the length of your tenure. In fact, trying to make the honeymoon last almost certainly guarantees your eventual disillusionment and possibly even your early departure.

FORGING THE BEST RELATIONSHIP WITH YOUR BOARD

The question that deserves your attention is this: How can you forge the best possible relationship with your board? I offer the following suggestions with the hope that they will serve you as well as they have served me.

1. Become involved in selecting new trustees.

In the healthiest schools I know, a prospective trustee is invited to join the board because she or he is committed to the school and has demonstrated a desire to move the school ahead toward realizing its aspirations. (Someone who is fundamentally at odds with the school or the direction it is pursuing should not be asked to join the board and, when such an individual does join, the results can be quite dire.) As the head, you likely know many potential trustee candidates and no doubt have insights to share about them with your board. And you should. While you do not want trustees who rubber-stamp your every idea, you certainly do not want anyone on your board who is out to remake the school.

In the world of independent schools, trustees who are selected to serve on the board should have two essential attributes. They should have demonstrated a fundamental appreciation for the school and the major goals it has set for itself, and they should have expertise in the areas the school will need during the next chapter of its development. Good trustees should not be expected to approve everything the head wants to do. Indeed, effective boards ask tough questions and add value to the school by doing so. The point here is that trustees on independent school boards should be committed to supporting the school, not changing it. The best trustees keep score about the value they have added by answering this question: How have I helped move the school closer to realizing its aspirations?

2. Help your board focus on the future.

You definitely do not want your board to spend its time informing you of the latest missteps of your most marginal teacher or familiarizing you with parking-lot complaints. It is simply not useful or healthy for your board to sweat the small stuff even though — and this is important — the small stuff can exert enormous gravitational pull on trustees' attention, especially if your trustees are also parents of children in your school and they hear all the problems.

Not only do they hear them, but other parents burden your trustees with complaints and then inform them that their job is to make the situation better. How difficult to be a trustee in this situation! Imagine how vexing it is to explain over and over again that you, as a trustee, are focused on the future and are working on the school's most important strategic initiatives. This is a very tough case for a trustee to make, and you should sympathize with this dilemma, one that is a predictable part of each of your trustees' experience. (One of the best trustees I've ever worked with felt she had to stop going to athletic contests because disgruntled parents would almost literally line up to complain: The coach wasn't playing their child often enough, or the school wasn't recruiting enough athletically talented students, or it had been weeks since the head had shown up at a game. For several months, maintaining her enthusiasm for the athletics program almost required her to stay away from the games she truly wanted to attend.)

Again, in any school, and especially in day schools, the parent community exerts considerable pressure on your trustees and especially on trustees who have children in your school. You, on the other hand, want your trustees to focus on the big picture, not the sludge. To this end, it is perfectly appropriate to make your expectations clear to trustees, and one of the most effective times to do so is when new trustees are going through an orientation process. (I want to underscore this point: All new trustees should go through an orientation process; they should not even attend their first meeting without understanding what their responsibilities are and that chief among these is taking the long view.)

But how, then, is a trustee to respond to a disgruntled parent? One answer is that trustees should encourage the disgruntled parent to follow the school's communication protocol, usually by speaking first with the faculty or staff person with whom the parent has a complaint. It is also helpful for you to let your trustees know that you want to hear what they are hearing. I suggest you tell members of your board that you welcome their phone calls about any issue that matters to them. Offering trustees such unlimited access will keep you informed about potentially significant issues, and it also communicates the message that trustees do not need to bring these issues with them into board meetings.

PERSPECTIVE

TEN THINGS I LEARNED ALONG THE WAY

Jean G. Lamont, Partner
Educators' Collaborative
HAMDEN, CONNECTICUT

1. **Cultivate strong relationships with board members** — especially the key players. This should include not only having individual meetings to discuss school matters but also hosting social gatherings to enable board members to get to know you on a more personal basis.

2. **Never go into a board meeting when a crucial or controversial issue will be addressed without alerting key opinion-makers on your board and ascertaining that you have their support.** Being political is a skill well worth developing if it doesn't come naturally.

3. **Make your board chair/president a key ally.** To the best of your ability, have a say about who is selected to be board chair/president. Agree on a mutually convenient and effective way to stay in close touch with him or her.

4. **Secure legal counsel who will be readily accessible,** who understands the culture of schools, and who gives advice that is reasonable. Use this resource whenever there is the potential of legal complications.

5. **Identify ways to get to know your faculty on a personal as well as a professional basis** as well as mechanisms to let them get to know you. Include a question or comment about their personal lives in many if not most of your individual conversations with them.

6. **Do not assume that the lack of negative feedback means everything is hunky-dory.** Work hard to find out how things are *really* going, and find a wise member of the community or an outside mentor to help address problems. In other words, do *not* dig a hole for yourself that becomes too deep to climb out of!

7. **Take every vacation day coming to you.** It is important to pace yourself and renew your energy, but you are also an influential role model — and a school full of workaholics is *not* a good thing.

8. **Build into your calendar time to visit classes and interact with students.** If it's possible to carve out time to teach, do so. The time you spend with kids is usually the most fun you'll have on the job, and time spent "in the trenches" helps you keep your finger on the pulse of school life and builds credibility.

9. **Don't neglect your important personal relationships.** It is very easy for a significant other or members of your family or friends to feel taken for granted. No job is worth jeopardizing this part of your life.

10. **Finally, and maybe most important, know what values, issues, and concerns are non-negotiable for you** — in other words, what you'll go out on a limb for. Be wise in garnering support for these ideals, and make use of the important position you have to achieve something you believe in. ■

In short, help your board move away from the details and focus on those broad issues that can shape the school's future, such as responding to changes in the school's geographic region, developing strategies for attracting and retaining outstanding faculty, creating new programs that respond to student interests, and planning and funding new facilities. Challenge yourself to think about what your school needs to do if it is to be vital five years from now, and board-level issues will flow. Not only will they flow, but getting ahead of them will require the best thinking possible, and your board should be doing a great deal of that thinking. Many trustees have real expertise, and when they donate their time to the school, they should be asked real questions that require serious thought and sophisticated analysis.

3. Encourage trustees to stay current about educational issues.

Trustees should be expected to attend educational conferences and read selected journal articles (a second topic for the trustee orientation program). Trustees need this background if they are to thoughtfully address the issues you put before them. As a rule of thumb, your board agendas should devote most of the time to issues and problems for which there are no easy answers. Some of these issues and problems are practical. (Should the school take on debt to complete the capital campaign? And, if so, should the interest be charged to the capital campaign or to the operating budget?) Other questions are more abstract and value-laden. (Is the degree of competition in our school appropriate or unhealthy? How much should concern about college placement shape the curriculum? Do performance-based assessments or conventional examinations promote more genuine learning?) These are complex questions, and answering them requires that trustees be well-informed.

4. Use your trustees' expertise.

I do not agree with the conventional wisdom that a sharp line should separate what the board should do (policy setting and stewardship) and what the head is supposed to do (administration). In my experience, insisting on such a division of duties is neither practical nor helpful. In practice, both the board and the head have important responsibilities in policy-setting as well as in administration. Not only do quite a few issues include both dimensions, but successful heads know that trustees can often see issues in new ways if they are welcomed into the school's administrative decision-making process. Trustees can bring a fresh perspective, and many of them have real expertise and can serve the school exceptionally well as volunteer consultants.

Admittedly, blurring the distinction between policy setting and administration can occasionally lead to serious problems. That said, on balance I have found that my decisions end up being significantly better when I have listened to the insights of trustees and taken advantage of their expertise.

5. Encourage the board to develop a strong and purposeful committee structure.

Much of the board's work should be done in committee. Effective boards have strong committees, each of which has a clear mandate. Given strong, fo-

PERSPECTIVE

ADVICE TO SOMEONE WHO HAS BEEN FIRED AS HEAD OF SCHOOL

Agnes (Aggie) Underwood, Vice President, Managing Associate
Carney, Sandoe & Associates
BOSTON, MASSACHUSETTS

Often in a school, a head who has been fired will stay until the end of the year, even though he or she might have received the notice of termination long before that. *How you leave an organization is just as important as how you begin.* No one likes to be fired, but there are ways to cope and rebound — and learn from your experience. Here's some advice:

- **Even though you may be angry and upset, be gracious.** Say to yourself that this is a teaching and learning opportunity for you and those around you, especially if students, parents, and your colleagues might know. You do not have to talk with colleagues about any details — in fact, you should not — but if you leave graciously, that will be remembered by your current employer and colleagues and will be passed on in references. The universe of schools is a very small one.

- **Make sure in parting that you find several people who will be references for you.** In today's world, referencing is usually done by telephone, so a written reference is fine, but there will definitely be a follow-up call. Be honest in your next job search about why you were fired or riffed. Transparency is valued highly in job searches. Today, more information than anyone cares to know can be obtained on just about anyone, so it pays to be forthright with potential employers at the appropriate time.

- **Always remember to be honorable and behave with dignity and equanimity.** There is almost no one who some time in their lives will not face a similar situation. ■

cused committees, only a small amount of the full board meeting need be devoted to reviewing — and then almost invariably approving — the work that has been done in committee. For example, the Finance Committee should do the heavy lifting involved in monitoring the current budget and shaping the one for the coming year. Then, at the meeting of the full board, the committee should present its recommendation along with the recommendation's underlying rationale. Similarly, the board should have a Development Committee that defines philanthropic opportunities, identifies appropriate fund-raising strategies and prospects, and, again, goes on to make specific recommendations to the full board for what ideally will be the board's efficient review and approval.

6. Always be straight, clear, and forthcoming with your board.

If one of your aspirations is to have a successful, long tenure in your new position, then this is the one suggestion you will want to remember when all else fades: no surprises and no sugarcoating. If you are about to expel a student, inform your board. If a teacher has violated a school policy in a serious way, tell your board. If admissions activity is not living up to your expectation, tell your board.

You may be tempted to engage in a certain degree of happy talk when communicating with the board. After all, you want the board to be pleased with your work and delighted with their own. Be assured that you will have occasions to explain just how strong the school is and how much it is accomplishing. But a school is a complex social organism, and not everything always goes just right. Tell your board what is keeping you up at night.

One of the advantages of being transparent and open is that your board will come to believe — without your making the point explicitly — that you do not inhabit an ivory tower. On the contrary, you are aware of the dark side of things, and, even more important, you are doing what it takes to set things right. As you assure your board that you are invested in working on problems, you will help convince trustees that they can focus their attention on the school's long-term needs. If, on the other hand, you keep problems from your board, don't be surprised when a trustee uses the board meeting to alert you to the school's dysfunctions. You do not want to spend precious board meeting time responding to the newest crisis trustees have unearthed.

As important as it is to be straight about problems, communicating about them need not necessarily occupy the full board. Serious problems can well be agenda items for your periodic meetings with the chair of the board or the board's executive committee or both. If you make a practice of meeting regularly with your board chair and the executive committee, and if you use this time to review worrisome issues, then your full board should know that you are doing so. Many trustees are happy to know that you are paying attention to problems in your school. They do not necessarily want to know the details.

7. Find your board chair's favored "radio frequency."

What does your board chair want to know? Is she or he most comfortable talking about educational philosophy? Or does she or he want to know in detail all the problems with which you are grappling? In my current position, I have had the privilege of working with five outstanding board chairs. While all shared a number of traits — for example, all cared deeply about the school — there were differences, too. One chair wanted to focus almost exclusively on strategic, long-term issues. He was happy to schedule monthly hour-long conversations with me and was even happier when these meetings ended early. And when a serious problem knocked on my door, he was satisfied with knowing only the barest outline. But another chair was not particularly interested in strategic discussions. He wanted much more detail about specific problems facing the school and signaled clearly that he wanted to know them almost as soon as they presented themselves. He wanted me to call him whenever the need arose. And I did.

The point is that it is the head's responsibility to determine the content and the frequency of the communications that satisfy the board's chair. I learned early on to ask the question directly. You do not want to be the head who rambles on and on with details to a board chair who is uninterested. Nor do you want to wax philosophical with a chair who is hungry for the day-to-day issues that are occupying your time.

8. Help the board evaluate you in a meaningful way.

Early in my tenure, I thought that the board's effort to formally evaluate the head was largely an empty exercise that was not worth the effort. I remember brazenly saying to my board that I was working as hard as I could and that I was more than ready to accept the board's judgment about whether to retain me. I went even further, assuring my trustees that when I was no longer serving the school, they could simply not renew my contract, and I would require of them neither justification nor a severance package. I have grown less brazen with the passing of time, although I remain somewhat skeptical about the worth of most approaches to evaluating the head of school. But over the years, my board and I have developed an approach to evaluation that, at least for me, is worth the effort it takes. I offer it not to suggest that this is the best system for you but simply to prompt you to think about helping your board develop a system that will best serve your needs.

Briefly, several years ago, the board and I developed a strategic vision for the school, a vision that includes priorities ranging from the quality of the instructional program to the school's financial sustainability. The specific elements of this strategic plan do not matter here. What does matter is that the board and I have a clear set of priorities, that we agree about them, that we publicize them, and that we are excited about them. I take this strategic vision seriously and use it as a template to shape most of the half dozen or so preliminary goals I establish for myself early each year. I share a draft of these proposed goals with the leadership of the board who, after reviewing this list for a week or so, either accept my priorities or modify them as they see the need to do so. These goals in turn help structure my year. Then, at the end of the year, I write a reflection about how well I have done in achieving each of them. The evaluation process culminates when the board uses my self-reflection as the basis for its own evaluation of my work. At this point, the board is, of course, entitled to add any additional observations that do not relate directly to my goals. (Such observations typically relate to matters of style rather than substance.)

I like this approach to evaluation for three reasons. First, it helps me focus my attention on important issues. Second, it helps the board understand how I spend my work day, which, when you think about it, is far from obvious to anyone who is not there with you day by day as you carry out your responsibilities. And third, this system helps remind trustees that they, too, have responsibilities for achieving the school's overarching goals. Indeed, in the best of all possible worlds, my goals serve as something of a model for the board's own self-evaluation, which, in turn, can be quite influential in shaping the board's approach to its responsibilities and how it keeps score about its own effectiveness.

CONCLUSION

I began this treatise by noting that I was writing as a practitioner rather than as a scholar, and I want to end in roughly the same place. I count myself one of the most fortunate people I know in that I can look back over a work life with genuine pleasure. So many people of my vintage look forward to the end of their careers with a sense of relief and the promise that they will find rewards in retirement that have eluded them in their careers. For me, however, as I move toward the end of my career, I feel blessed to have found a profession that is so inherently interesting and rewarding. If I have any regrets, it is that in a matter of only a few years I will be moving on to the much reduced rewards of copious free time punctuated by the occasional fishing trip.

I mention this because too much talk about serving as a head of school is tinged with stories of friction, dyspeptic constituents, and edgy and contentious boards of trustees. My reality has been quite different. When a head has achieved a solid working relationship with the board of trustees, school leadership can be far more a joy than a burden. Cultivating such a relationship requires thoughtfulness and effort, but once that relationship is established, the work can be enormously rewarding.

Serving as an effective head is more art than science, and so it is inevitable that you will find your own way, a path that may well reveal truths and practices that work for you and differ significantly from those I have discussed here. In the end, the single most important point I can offer is that a solid working relationship between the head and the board is essential to the head's success and is worth careful cultivation.

I wish you every success and a career filled with the deep pleasure of helping your school be the best it can be.

THE LEADERSHIP CIRCLE

THE ADMINISTRATIVE TEAM

Jim Power

SO AFTER GOING THROUGH a number of interviews and two mind-numbing days of courting every possible constituency (who knew the world would give seventh-grade boys so much clout?), you finally land your first headship. Congratulations! As you open your new desk in your new office in your new school, you remember the two words of advice that that $10 K/day consultant gave you at the seminar: "It depends." There are no hard and fast rules, just general principles, values, and intuitions to help you make it through this grand adventure.

This chapter focuses on your new team and what you can do to make it work as well as possible. Being a new head is a bit like walking into the middle of a movie. The action doesn't stop. You can't call a "time out" to catch up. And nobody's whispering wisdom to you as you buy your popcorn and watch Tom Hanks. Perhaps the first thing you'll want to do is deepen your understanding of the school's context and where it stands in its history. It's important to remember that — unless you are starting a school — you aren't the only head; you're just the most recent flavor. (An angry alumnus may someday remind you that "You are simply a temporary steward of this institution!" And he'll be right!)

Like it or not, much of what you'll do, especially during your first few years, will be seen through a lens that has your immediate predecessor's fingerprints all over it. This is not meant to scare you, but it's a sobering realization. A friend took a headship in a school where the previous head actually returned to the school's math department. "It was a bit like living with my wife's first husband. Every time I wanted to move the furniture, I'd have someone come in and say, 'But Bill really liked the divan next to the window.'"

By the way, one task trustees should do for you is to help you, especially if your predecessor had a less than wonderful exit. Most former heads are extraordinarily gracious and are deeply invested in the school and in your success. After all, a real sign of successful headship is how an institution fares after a leader has left. Occasionally, though, a head leaves under less than ideal circumstances, and if that's the case for you, the board should try to help you deal with this — whether it's setting up a few "get-to-know-you meetings" or giving the predecessor clear guidelines about what is needed and expected from him or her in terms of an ongoing relationship with the school.

What's more pressing than dealing with your predecessor, though, is the relationship with your new teammates. Again, you are walking into the middle of the movie, and you're not quite sure who the good guys are. Lots of folks will want and need your time, so count on plenty of one-on-one sessions. (You might look at that first August as a "month of a thousand conversations," conversations during which, by the way, you may do very little talking.) Each conversation will give you another angle through which you can glimpse the reality of your new school. No one's "take" will be perfect, but after a while, your gut will give you an overall sense of where things stand, especially if you've taken the time to review seminal documents such as the latest accreditation report, budget, and strategic plan. You might want to read through the last year's board meeting minutes while you are at it.

Be wary of individuals who seem especially needy or exasperated. Some folks who have been on the outs with the previous head may see the first month of your term as their golden opportunity to rectify the past. Feel free to end a number of these sessions without making any decisions or offering any specific advice. "I'll need to think about that" should be your mantra, and if someone compares your walking onto campus with Nelson Mandela's walking out of jail, smile and give that colleague plenty of leeway!

WORKING WITH THE NEW TEAM

While you are new, the team is not. They have a history. In all likelihood, they know and accept one another's quirks and idiosyncrasies. If you have an executive committee of a half dozen people, odds are that one or two of them may have applied for the chair you now occupy. There's also a good chance that other committee members are aware of this fact, and this may be difficult, not just for your new teammate who may feel justifiably disappointed in the outcome of last year's search but also for his or her sympathetic colleagues on the committee.

A suggestion: One way of getting a head start on understanding your team's dynamic — do not chair the first few administrative meetings. Run through a cycle for six weeks or so where each member of the team serves in this function. This will give you a chance to sit back and observe how they work together. It may feel a bit artificial during the first few minutes, but soon, the meetings will return to their customary flow. Doing this may also give your new teammates a sense of your shared leadership approach, and it will send all the right signals about how you want to listen and get to know them.

You will have to earn your team's trust. You may have been a revered and beloved figure back at your old school, but here you are just the stranger the trustees preferred for some still undetermined reason. No one's calling you "Chips" behind your back just yet. To earn that trust, you'll need to model

continued on page 206

PERSPECTIVE

SEVEN STEPS TO A GOOD MENTORING RELATIONSHIP

Joan G. Ogilvy Holden, Head of School
St. Stephen's & St. Agnes School
ALEXANDRIA, VA

In my 26 years as head of school, I have always viewed mentoring as one of my key roles. It has been rewarding, not only in the relationships that I have formed but also as a way to strengthen our field and contribute to effective leadership. My own models have been strong ones, and I am grateful to have had the good fortune to be mentored by such individuals as Bill Polk (Groton School) and Earl Harrison (Sidwell Friends School), to name only two of the many who have advised, coached, and supported me throughout my tenure as a head of school. I have also been mentored by many individuals for whom I was nominally serving as mentor. I strongly believe that I have learned as much, if not more, from them as they have learned from me.

For many years, I have been honored to be a mentor in the NAIS Fellowship for Aspiring School Heads professional development program. I have worked one-on-one with individuals in the Washington, DC, metropolitan area and across the country. As I explain to my board of governors at the beginning of each school year, these relationships are among the most rewarding and gratifying I have ever experienced. One particular relationship comes to mind, and I'd like to share what I feel were the essentials in building that relationship.

1. **Be a good listener.** In any strong relationship, being able to listen is key. The person I was mentoring was working through both professional and personal goals, and she needed someone to hear what these were. I also sensed that she needed to think out loud, to "test" various ideas with me, whether they regarded specific roles she anticipated at her next school or areas of school life for which she felt she would not be suited.

2. **Be patient.** Patience is certainly not one of my virtues. Naively I expected, upon embarking on this relationship, that my mentee would take my sage advice and run with it. This was not the case, and I learned that I needed to develop the ability to respect my colleague for her position and be willing to wait for her to get to the place where she felt fully ready to take the next step. At times, I could feel myself becoming impatient with this process, yet upon reflection I understand the real importance of each person's own timing and readiness to seek another administrative position. At one point, I thought I had really convinced her to step out and apply for other positions, but at the 11th hour, she said she was not ready and wanted to stay at her school for another year. This was the right thing for her to do. Yet at the time, I admit, it took great patience on my part to understand this. Being constantly supportive and positive is essential to a mentoring relationship. I knew that was what I needed to do when she decided to wait another year.

3. **Be willing to push the individual.** In spite of what I have just written about being patient, I also feel that there is a time when a mentor needs to push. Done correctly, this can give the mentee the confidence to move forward. It is very difficult when one has been well-placed and supported within an institution to take the step of looking outside that

nurturing and comfortable situation. It can be frightening to think about moving away from a school that has treated you well and where you are loved and highly valued. That was certainly the case with my colleague. Therefore, I recognized the need to push her at times.

4. **Meet with the person you are mentoring in his or her own environment.** I found that spending half a day with my colleague helped me see her strengths firsthand. I think it also meant a great deal to her that her mentor was willing to spend the time and make the effort to visit her in her own school. She was clearly beloved at her school. Seeing this helped me understand her difficulty in taking the step to seek other positions as nothing else could have done. At her K-12 school, I understood her strong sense of community and her ability to work with students of all ages, as well as her ability to work with all faculty members. She was able to move through the hallways with ease and grace and wisdom. My visit also allowed me to get a glimpse of another school. As head of school I seldom get the opportunity to do this. I learned a great deal during my visit to her school, not only about her but about the many areas in which her school excelled.

5. **Check in periodically and at unexpected moments.** I believe that it is extremely important to demonstrate ongoing care for the person you are mentoring. This happens when you pick up the telephone or send a quick email just to touch base and see how things are going. This unexpected connection can mean so much.

6. **Think outside the box.** There are moments when it is highly valuable to brainstorm with the person you are mentoring to explore different options, tracks, and possibilities. Seldom in our careers do we have the time to think creatively about our own strengths and how they can transfer to different positions and situations within the independent school community. We may get locked into certain career tracks or paths that can prevent us from pursuing a variety of possibilities and becoming all that we can be. My colleague was moving toward pursuing a middle school position, but we were able to discuss the possibility of a lower school or upper school position as well. Having seen her at her own school, I was convinced that she could be extremely effective at any level.

7. **Finally, make it a long-term relationship.** My most meaningful relationships as a mentee have been with those mentors who still check in with me and are quietly behind the scenes supporting me. I have learned from them the importance of keeping up a long-term relationship with those I have had the privilege to mentor. It is very rewarding when I get to the point with such a person, who may now be a fellow head of school, that I can say, "I look forward to coming to work for *you* someday!"

It has truly been one of the highlights of my tenure as head of school to be able to establish these rich, lifelong relationships. ■

integrity in everything you do. You'll need to actively listen as if each member of the school is the board chair's best friend, and you'll want to affirm all the good you see in meaningful ways. Don't forget, too, how important it will be for you to model the same kind of warmth toward staff workers that you do toward benefactors. With a new boss around, even the most sensible adult can experience a dose of the Holden Caulfields in perceiving, rightly or wrongly, "phonies."

One of the things you may discover early on is that the leadership group is a "committee" but not necessarily a "team." You may find some members of the group saying things to you privately after a meeting — things you wish they'd said *during* the meeting. Don't be afraid to say, "You raise a great point, Biff. And that's *exactly* the issue I'd like you to bring up at next week's meeting. Is there a way I can help you do this?" When the committee becomes a team, its members will be willing to sacrifice their own particular initiatives for the greater good. They will be comfortable being direct with each other. They will be able to challenge one another and disagree without being disagreeable.

You may find that there is a split between the Academic/Student Life Division heads and the Advancement/Business Office folks. Because you've been in the academic world most of your professional life and may not know as much about philanthropy or spreadsheets as you do about the Boer War or photosynthesis, you'll find you need to lean more heavily on colleagues who are in charge of areas where you lack expertise. This makes perfect sense. At the same time, your need to spend more time with the advancement director and business manager can exacerbate tensions that already exist.

By the way, especially if you are new to the world of philanthropy, you may spend more time than you ever anticipated working with Advancement. Some schools arrange to have the new head, the previous head, and the advancement director spend time meeting with as many top benefactors as possible — before the new head even starts at the school. This allows for a seamless transition in the eyes of donors who have the ability to make transformational gifts. It used to be said that schools followed the 80/20 rule, with 20 percent of the donors creating 80 percent of the gifts. Now it seems that some schools are observing a 90/10 rule, and this makes it more important than ever to make sure you don't lose a would-be donor during transitions.

You might spend some time, perhaps at your first team retreat (make sure you schedule at least one of these per year, preferably at an off-site location), with a facilitator who helps the group focus on teamwork. Part of this may involve an assessment of some sort, the results of which can guide further discussion. Understand that you are *not* going to change every member of the group into a warm and fuzzy. (If everyone wore a Fred Rogers' sweater, that would be bad for the leadership team!) Your goal is to allow everyone to feel comfortable enough to share his or her talents as fully and as effectively as possible. To do this, you have to create a culture that promotes risk-taking. This will take more than just one retreat with one facilitator, no matter how good he or she is. This is the kind of long-term goal that you should focus on with the group each term. Be sure to build in time at the start or end of each semester to ask "How are we doing as a team?" If that question is greeted by stony silence, you might want to hold such retreats more often.

It's important to remember, too, that, as talented in interpersonal relationships as you may be, you aren't a miracle worker, and you can't expect to change anyone's personality. Popeye was onto something when he observed, "I am what I am!" Remember the difference between problems and dilemmas. (Problems have solutions.) So, as much as you may long for that group hug at the end of the retreat, consider it a win if the anonymous survey you administer at the end of the day says something like "not a total waste of time." That may be your first big win.

CONCLUSION

Here are some suggestions on how to work with your administrative team.

1. **There are no blueprints for successful headships.** There are situational challenges that require you to read, adjust, and communicate on the fly. Often, "It depends." Alas!
2. **Deliberately cultivate honesty and open communication with all colleagues, but especially with your leadership team.** You don't want a bunch of "yes" men (or women) in your inner circle. You need people who can speak truth to power, who can be direct with you, who are free enough to challenge you when you need challenging.

3. **Don't ever assume that you are the smartest person in the room.** If you are lucky, you're not. Your goal is to tap into, develop, and get maximum value out of the collective wisdom of your leadership team. Yes, you are often the final decision-maker, but you aren't Lord of the Manor.
4. **History didn't begin the day you graced the campus with your presence.** Understand the past, particularly the immediate past. Do your homework. Try to figure out what's important, especially with veteran administrators and senior faculty who often feel very strongly about issues that may seem less significant to you. Having a good connection with senior colleagues may help you avoid some embarrassing land mines.
5. **Listen. Listen. Listen** — even if you've heard the story before. Some members of your team have a need to tell you their story. They need the quiet affirmation of your attentive listening. So listen even if you think you know how the story ends. This is what it means to be part of a team.
6. **Work with your administrative assistant and be proactive in figuring out how you can work well together.**
7. **Even though you are keen to understand the school's history, nobody wants to hear about your last school, especially if it in any way casts your present one in a negative light.** If you rewrote Eton College's English curriculum, or if every student you've ever taught got a 45 on the IB, or if you were Tom Brady's quarterback coach, that's great. But keep it to yourself. Nobody — but nobody — wants to hear about it.
8. **Affirm in as many meaningful ways as possible all the good that your team members are doing.**
9. **Understand that nobody can do everything in that job description you agreed to, so don't beat yourself up.** You know what your flat sides are. Try to compensate for them. So if you've never asked a donor for a million dollars, spend some extra time with the advancement director who has. That's what your team is for, after all!
10. **Time is precious, so save it whenever you can.** Rather than play phone tag with a parent or alumnus, ask your administrative assistant to book your phone appointments. This may feel a bit artificial at first, but it will

save time for both you and your contact. (Just make sure you do your own dialing. You don't want your assistant announcing on the intercom, "This is a call from the head.")

11. **Work with each of your direct reports to set annual goals.** Most of these should be "reasonable" goals, but build in a few "stretch" goals, too. Get these goals on paper, and use them as an agenda to review progress in November and March and at the end of the year. During your first year or two, you might want to make these as conversational as possible, and be sure to build in plans for professional development, too.
12. **Almost all those who come to see you have a problem.** See that particular problem as a ball they hold in their hands as they enter your office. Your goal should be to make sure that, unless it's an emergency, they leave the office still cradling that ball. Yes, you want to listen and brainstorm and strategize. But you are not the Shell Answer Man. Your job is to help your teammates and colleagues develop their own problem-solving skills. An instinctive response to take on the problems of others can create a massive work/life imbalance for you. (Folks who see themselves as "people pleasers" or those who have grown up in families where there was alcoholism or substance abuse need to be particularly vigilant in this area!)
13. **Remember that you don't work for NASA.** In schools, life and death don't revolve around "o-rings." Thank God! You are in a people business. Your goal is to develop trust with students and adults, to work together, to forge or reinforce a vision, and to do your very best with those people to make that vision a reality. You will come up short from time to time, and schools are messy places. Know that in advance, and enjoy the laughs that come your way. Your sense of humor may be your most important and most lasting gift to the school!

THE HEAD OF SCHOOL AND HIS OR HER EXECUTIVE ASSISTANT

Bruce B. Stewart and Abigail P. Browning

THERE IS LITTLE DOUBT that one of the core members of any head of school's management team is his or her top executive (or administrative) assistant. In a unique professional appointment that encompasses virtually all the operations of a school, this individual serves, among other things, as the personal ambassador, scheduler, office manager, writer/editor, and confidant to the head. Several factors drive a successful relationship between the two:

- The ability to jointly build relationships with people throughout and beyond the school community
- The capacity to maintain unyielding trust and support between and for one another
- The willingness of the head to delegate responsibilities effectively and with ease and confidence
- The ability to candidly and comprehensively communicate with each other about nearly every major action each person undertakes
- The aptitude to serve as a mutual sounding board for all (or most) of the ideas, projects, and personnel matters passing through the head's office

Competency, efficiency, integrity, and affability are vital and fundamental attributes of the successful executive assistant. The executive assistant is often the person whose engaging face and voice warmly welcome all the increasingly complex constituencies to the institution and successfully set the tone for matters that follow. The executive assistant, in step with the head, must be a school ambassador who is both adept and genuine in relating to students, faculty, staff, administration, trustees, parents, alumni, major donors, and other key institutional supporters as well as the neighboring community.

Additionally, he or she must connect well with persons in the broader region, such as representatives of religious organizations (especially when the school is affiliated with a community of faith); police and fire security; those who deal with issues like construction permits and enrollment caps; other local, state, and federal bodies; and a wide range of peer institutions and regional and national professional associations.

The assistant must also work closely with the development office in relating to the school's key supporters, including foundations, corporations, alumni, parents, and others who are major volunteers or donors. Indeed, these relationships are vital to the long-term strength and viability of any independent school, and they rely heavily on clear and consistent communication between assistant and head. A successful executive assistant must be able to make people feel welcomed, heard, and respected. He or she must be able to capture detailed information about concerns and inquiries that is accurate and reflects — insofar as possible — the issues to which the head will be asked to respond.

Truly, a great strength in this position is the skill to hear not only what is said but what is implied and then to discreetly convey that information in a way that will help prepare the head for upcoming meetings, telephone calls, or emails. Alerting him or her to issues that will almost inevitably be cropping up in the community is crucial. The concern of one person may well portend the concern of many. In this capacity, intelligence enhanced by both emotional and moral depth is of expansive value, and the head's commitment to meeting regularly with the assistant is vital.

For many of the people who contact a head of school's office, the fundamental concern is being thoughtfully, sensitively, and caringly heard, especially if it is a first encounter. Further, they frequently need a prompt and substantive response. Consequently, the head needs to know precisely what the issue is that is waiting to be addressed. In initial follow-up, an executive assistant can be very helpful in gathering data and information from faculty, staff, and other key administrators such as a principal or dean, business manager, development or athletic director, diversity coordinator, or admissions or financial aid officer. Sometimes, too, the assistant can refer visitors or callers to an office where they can be better and more promptly assisted — saving

continued on page 215

PERSPECTIVE

TEN THINGS I LEARNED ALONG THE WAY

Arnold E. Holtberg, Headmaster
St. Mark's School of Texas
DALLAS, TEXAS

My career as head of school has encompassed innumerable experiences, including successes and failures, sound ideas and initiatives, and well-meaning trials that went nowhere. But there are a number of accomplishments, programs, and actions that I am most glad for. Along the way, I have learned a great deal. The 10 things listed below are those I consider the most important.

1. **Before making any decision, ask this one fundamental question: How will this decision affect our students and their learning?** At St. Mark's, we truly believe that it is all about the boys. Our purpose is to educate them to become good, contributing men. To that end, focus on mission, mission, mission. Being market-sensitive is, of course, only common sense; however, the mission of our school and our commitment to our boys must come first.

2. **Employ the right teachers, coaches, and advisors.** This is vital if a school is to be successful. At St. Mark's, we established an Office of Faculty Recruitment to seek, identify, and hire professional staff members who will best suit our needs while finding fulfillment at the school. To ensure that new faculty members are successful from the start, we have established a sound orientation program. Our commitment to professional development is also very strong, and, over the years, we have sought funding and have made no compromises in providing resources for our teachers to grow as professionals and persons. We define professional development rather broadly, supporting not only the pursuit of advanced degrees and attendance at workshops and seminars but also research and development in one's field. Our evaluation system mandates that teachers and their supervisors establish mutual goals and teachers receive substantial feedback during the course of the year to ensure mission congruence and top performance. Freedom, autonomy, support, and accountability are central to the growth and supervision of our faculty.

3. **Make a commitment to diversity in enrollment and hiring.** This is one of the most important things we have done during my tenure. The richness of every conversation is enhanced when different voices are brought to bear. Moreover, deliberations become richer and encompass many more dimensions when adults and students of different races, ethnicities, religions, and nationalities express their opinions about any matter. Since 1993, the percentage of persons of color in our student body has grown from approximately 17 percent to just more than 37 percent. Our faculty's diversity has grown considerably during the same period. In the early '90s, fewer than 10 percent of our faculty and administration were persons of color; today, that percentage has risen to 18. In independent schools, we acknowledge and understand the need to be representative of the broader population for evident educational reasons. To achieve this result while sustaining the school's commitment to its historic principles requires clear thinking and hard work. And, while we have made

great strides at St. Mark's in this respect, we know that our work in this area will never be done and that there is greater need to be intentional in how we live out our diversity.

4. **Prepare students for leadership and responsibility.** The school's "Statement of Purpose" includes this sentence: "St. Mark's aims to prepare young men for assuming leadership and responsibility in a competitive and changing world." While we have taken the concept of developing leaders seriously throughout our history, we took a new and intentional step in this direction in 2005 by establishing a Leadership and Ethics Program based on Gus Lee's book, *Courage: The Backbone of Leadership*. All members of the faculty and staff receive education about leadership principles, and every boy in grades 1 through 12 is exposed to training in respectful behavior and "courageous decision-making." Along the way, St. Mark's has developed a formal relationship with the University of Richmond's Jepson School of Leadership Studies so that we can stay abreast of current thinking in the field and take advantage of the expertise of the Jepson School faculty.

5. **Respect the privacy of members of the school community.** I am fervent about ensuring that we adhere to our principles first and foremost. One of these principles is that we respect the privacy of members of our community and do not share certain information with others. Years ago, one of our students was involved in a disciplinary matter that became public. A local magazine investigated and reported on the incident, publishing a conclusion that was erroneous. The magazine called me and inquired about our disciplinary proceedings. Per policy, I declined to comment. Nonetheless, the publication ran a story that impugned my integrity and cast a negative light on the school. While I was tempted to clear my name, I refused to divulge specifics of the case, merely telling representatives of the magazine that they had printed a damaging story without the facts.

6. **Encourage all students to share their talents.** Early in my time at St. Mark's, I concluded that our boys needed to have an additional opportunity to make their own particular voices known. Each of them has talents, abilities, and inclinations; however, I was concerned that some of them did not have the chance to share their passions with others. In 1994-95, we established the Senior Exhibition program whereby each member of the senior class makes a presentation in a rather formal manner, either on his own or with a partner, to a segment of the student body about a talent, commitment, or interest. As one senior boy said during the early years of the program, "The Senior Exhibition has quickly become one of the richest traditions at St. Mark's." Through the program, we have learned so much more about our senior boys and have given them the opportunity to make public presentations that have grown their confidence and solidified their place as individuals in our school community.

7. **Make the school affordable for middle-income families.** In the mid-1990s, we realized that the standard formula for

continued on next page

TEN THINGS I LEARNED ALONG THE WAY

calculating financial aid was insufficient to meet the financial need of families who truly could not afford our tuition and fees. Thus, we began to explore the issue of middle-income financial aid. We analyzed our own financial aid applicants' files and came to the conclusion that something needed to be done. We spent approximately one year creating and testing an extended formula in order to better serve middle-income families in a systematic, organized, and objective manner. We approached prospective donors whom we knew were sympathetic to the notion of making our educational opportunities available to families caught in the middle, and St. Mark's Middle Income Financial Aid Program became a sustainable reality.

8. **Don't back down if you believe you have made the right decision** — even if it's controversial with those in power. During my first month at St. Mark's, I confronted a difficult disciplinary matter. After consulting with the appropriate individuals, I concluded that the students involved must be expelled. In this case, the always painful process of expelling students was complicated by my desire to establish myself at a new school and the fact that the parent of one of the boys in question had significant ties to members of our board of trustees. Angry and emotional conversations ensued, yet I held to the original decision. Years later, the two trustees who were most critical of my actions were named to a significant honorary position at St. Mark's, that of Life Trustee. Both men have since become close friends and individuals whom I trust and whose advice I seek. They, in return, have sought my assistance from time to time. The lesson learned is that if one does the right thing, good things follow.

9. **Establish an endowment fund to support the repair and replacement of campus facilities.** In the early 1980s, St. Mark's set just such an objective. However, it wasn't until the 1990s that we committed ourselves to raising the funds necessary to achieve our goal. We were fortunate to have donors who understood the need to sustain the school's physical plant and keep the school from falling into the deferred maintenance trap. In recent years, our funding has allowed us to address virtually all facility needs. Fulfilling this historic commitment has allowed us to weather downturns in the economy successfully while keeping our plant in good shape and not mortgaging our future.

10. **Resist defining yourself by your job or position.** I have found this one to be very important. I realize at school and in the broader Dallas community, I am headmaster of St. Mark's School of Texas. However, it is vital for me to simply be myself, to engage in activities that bring me pleasure and fulfillment. Also, it is very important for me to maintain balance in my life by attending to my family, friends, and church. I love my work and am proud of my accomplishments, but I do not measure myself by these alone. Every now and then, I ask myself the question, "How would I feel about myself if I walked away from my current position?" I certainly hope the answer will always be "Just fine." ■

the head valuable time while even more aptly serving the inquirers.

Faculty, staff, administrative colleagues, and currently enrolled students and their parents should always get priority attention, as should trustees and other major supporters of the school. One must always remember that it is the child or employee who feels unseen or unheard who can become a danger to self and the community. In today's tension-filled climate, heads must make every effort to be promptly and thoughtfully responsive, and executive assistants can be of tremendous help in tuning into the pulse of the school and the more immediate needs of faculty, students, and other core constituents.

Time is a primary asset to any head of school, and anything that an executive assistant can do to conserve time is of profound importance. Can emails and letters be redirected to another office or responded to by the head's assistant? Can there be a gentle knock on a conference door to help conclude a meeting in a timely manner? Can scheduling of individual appointments or group meetings be done more efficiently? For example, can the head go to part rather than all of a particular event or meeting (at the beginning or end), both to conserve time and to enhance impact?

An assistant can handle travel arrangements (cabs, planes, trains, rental cars, hotel and meal reservations, and the like). He or she can prepare individual meeting folders with an agenda, succinct background information on each participant, essential written materials, and detailed time and location information. He or she can prepare notes reminding the head of someone's birthday, anniversary, giving profile, or special circumstances like a child's academic performance or involvement in various school or community activities. When a head is well-informed about a person he or she is seeing — and, most important, about that person's children, other family members, and personal and professional activities — it can add greatly to effectiveness. Who among us isn't happy to know that we are well and accurately remembered and that our work, family, services, and contributions are prized and valued? An assistant who routinely gets that type of background information for a busy and engaged head significantly improves the efficacy of the head of school's office. Such context and background are of major value for all meetings, but they are particularly helpful when travel is involved and when supportive assistance can't be close at hand.

It is also a major contribution when the assistant has a good relationship with the head of school's spouse. Keeping the head's family informed about activities they may be asked to attend or events they will be expected to host is key. A good assistant regularly coordinates the head's personal calendar with his or her professional one and helps make certain that the head's schedule allows appropriate time for family, reading, and exercise, as well as for fun, rest, and relaxation. The most effective heads balance their schedules, and executive assistants are fundamental to that process. Assistants can often juggle calendars and change or defer appointments in the event of unforeseen circumstances or emergencies or simply to allow for important personal time. When an executive assistant has successfully cultivated strong community respect, he or she can facilitate a change in the head's schedule with minimum negative impact. Today, the intensity and fullness of the workload of a head virtually cry out for this kind of internal diplomacy and managerial support, and it should be a point of focus for any successful assistant.

Handling a head of school's expense statements, setting up meeting times and places, responding to requests for information, and coordinating catering needs, etc., are all primarily unseen but important services of an executive assistant. Similarly, coordinating the head's calendar with the school's master calendar and arranging various trustee meetings and events are fundamental duties of an assistant. Board chairs, committee chairs, and trustees are busy and involved people. They need to receive prompt and sensitive attention from the head's assistant, this time acting in his or her key role as the head's office manager. The assistant must know when to interrupt the head to accept a telephone call or visit from a trustee, parent, or major donor. Some issues simply can't wait, and the best executive assistant will recognize that. Indeed, the executive assistant ought to have the capacity to independently exercise that same kind of good judgment with all constituencies. Family crises, serious illness, accidents, security threats, and similar events demand great skill and discernment from a head's assistant. His or her equanimity and calmness in a time of challenge can set an important tone for everyone, and it can help keep a head focused and in control in periods of crisis. Mutual trust in these unforeseeable moments is a powerful asset, and well-established closeness between a head and his or her assistant proffers invaluable support.

Developing that interconnectedness takes time, openness, and thoughtful attention on an ongoing basis. Both must take the time to communicate regularly and with complete candor, and it must be bedrock certain that strict confidentiality is always maintained. A good assistant is a constant source of significant information for a head but must never violate the confidences that a head shares with him or her (and vice versa). This principle of confidentiality for an assistant should apply to all school constituencies, including board chairs, trustees, employees, parents, students, alumni, and the like. Being a true confidant where a head may speak his or her mind without becoming vulnerable to a breach of trust is perhaps the most valuable contribution an executive assistant can make.

Today, technological competencies are an increasingly important dimension in an executive assistant's repertoire. It is not uncommon for a head of school to get literally hundreds of email messages in a very short period of time. Skill and judgment in sorting these and promptly responding to some, delegating others to supporting offices, and selecting those that the head must see immediately or take home for evening reading are an increasingly important asset in an executive assistant. Many heads still seek to handle much or most of their electronic traffic directly, but more and more heads are delegating this function in the interest of efficiency. Further, scanning websites, googling or bing-ing, searching for needed information, downloading documents, completing surveys, and adeptly accessing the constantly growing possibilities of technology are all of tremendous value to a head of school's office.

In some areas, critical weather, health, and crisis data have become a concern, and up-to-date information is best obtained electronically. An executive assistant can play a central role here as the first source of vital security information. He or she must be able to reach the head of school immediately when necessary, and there must be a written list and system for informing the head and other central contacts of major concerns. Timely action in today's school world can be the difference between safety and tragedy. Often this kind of responsibility means contact after normal working hours, on weekends, during vacation days, or while traveling. A good executive assistant cannot be a clock-watcher but must be willing to be on the job even at off times or at some distance from the school. Witness, for example, 9/11, Hurricane Katrina, and the increasingly random violence that has invaded many of our academic institutions. Safety and security for all are a head's first responsibility, and he or she needs unwavering support from his or her executive assistant in this highly volatile area.

A veritable cornerstone for an executive assistant's work is the planning and coordination of the meetings — and their related details — of the head of school's senior management team. Many heads refer to this body as the school's Administrative Council (AC), and it usually meets weekly, often over lunch to provide some relaxed social time at the beginning of the meeting. Members of the AC usually include all the direct reports to the head such as associate and assistant heads, development and chief financial officers, athletic and admissions/financial aid directors, principals, and diversity coordinators. The executive assistant can be of major support to the head in reserving meeting space, providing for refreshments, and sending out a timely agenda prepared in collaboration with the head. Additionally, compiling appropriate data, reports, and other materials and sending them, in a timely manner, to all AC members well before a scheduled session is crucial. The head's executive assistant should be certain that all necessary electronic support systems for any meeting are in place and ready to function (computers, etc.). He or she should be prepared to take detailed minutes and then to distribute and file them (and all other pertinent materials) as a basis for both current action and future reference.

Many AC decisions become the basis for school policies or inform plans of action (designating the persons involved and pressing issues, times, dates, deadlines, and places) for matters that the council has decided to address. Hence, this group's activity is central to the efficient and effective functioning of a school, and it must be well-supported and carefully monitored. Probably no one is more suited for this complex support coordination than the head's executive assistant. He or she has the head's immediate attention as well as ready access to all other senior administrative personnel and trustees.

Also, the board and its committees have requirements and follow-up needs similar to those of the AC. Trustee committee chairs, often as many as 10 or 12, generally require significant help in arranging meetings, setting agendas, and ensuring that good minutes are taken and filed. It is often the executive assistant who is the contact point for the head of school with the administrative representatives to the various board committees. The executive assistant can provide major support similar to the assistance he or she provides to the AC. This liaison work is of profound importance to the head, as both the AC and the board are key to the institution's healthy operation. This arena of management is one of fundamental significance, and it requires ready and continuous communication between the head and the executive assistant and often includes considerable board chair involvement as well. Sound governance at the highest level of operations is vital to institutional stability and orderly operation, and it deserves the closest possible attention from the head, executive assistant, and board chair. The assistant must give this responsibility primary focus, keep the head fully and promptly informed, and openly seek guidance when it is needed. Here it is wise to remember that the only bad question is the one left unasked.

In sum, virtually no head of school can handle his or her work effectively without a competent, organized, and socially adept person in the position of executive assistant. The professional relationship needs to always be one of trust and mutual respect, and confidentiality must be an absolute given. Further, humor and grace go a long way in making the pressures of leadership manageable. Having an executive assistant with emotional and moral intelligence — as well as intellectual acuity, personal loyalty, and true people and communication skills — is a management asset of indisputable importance. Heads must be certain to regularly nurture and express appreciation to their assistants, to support them fully, and to provide fair and competitive compensation. Assistants must be consistently aware of the intense pressures that all school heads face and their understandable need for reinforcement and support. Open and honest discourse about all school-related issues — while managing a demanding and well-ordered schedule that has an appropriate measure of downtime — is essential to a head's success in institutional leadership and in living a balanced and informed life. There may be no better investment to make in ensuring one's success as the leader of an independent school than fostering a strong professional relationship with the executive assistant.

ABOUT THE EDITORS

Gene Batiste is vice president, Leadership Education and Diversity, at NAIS. He holds a B.S. in the social sciences, summa cum laude, from Wiley College (a historically Black college/ university) and an M.Ed., Phi Delta Kappa, in urban education and public school administration from North Texas State University. He is currently in the Mid-Career Doctorate in Educational Leadership Program at the University of Pennsylvania. He came to NAIS in 2000 after serving as assistant head of school and Upper School director at Crossroads School (MO). At St. Mark's School of Texas, Gene taught psychology, sociology, and Modern World; served as sophomore, junior, and senior dean; directed the Robert E. Dennard Visiting Scholars program; and directed the school's diversity efforts as director of intercultural affairs from 1990 through 1999. Gene comes from a military family, having lived in Japan, Hawaii, Washington, DC, and San Antonio, Texas. Gene and his partner, Scott Honeychurch, live in Washington, DC, with their Soft-coated Wheaten Terrier, Toby.

Jay Riven is currently head of Middle School at Parish Episcopal School in Dallas, Texas. A graduate of Montgomery Bell Academy in Nashville and Northwestern University, Jay earned a master's in social work, specializing in addiction treatment and mental health. After five years of working in correctional facilities and hospitals in Texas and the Northeast, he had his first independent school job at Pace Academy in Atlanta, Georgia, in 1999. He served as a counselor and academic dean, ultimately creating Pace's Middle School in 2004 with Dr. Paul Oberman. Jay then became head of Middle School at Valwood School in Valdosta, Georgia, where he continued to teach English and coach. He is married to Jennifer and has two children, Hailey and Zach, both just beginning school themselves. Jay continues to be in awe not only of his own heads of school past and present but also of those who contributed to this book, their experiences, their contributions to their field, and their willingness to share their stories.

ABOUT THE AUTHORS

Richard Barbieri has been active in the independent school world for nearly 40 years, as a teacher-administrator at Milton Academy, executive director of the Association of Independent Schools in New England, and interim head of eight schools, from Maine to New Mexico. He has been writing for *Independent School* and other general and educational publications for over 30 years and has led numerous workshops for trustees, administrators, new and experienced teachers, aspiring heads, and others. He is currently busy writing and doing pro bono work between interim positions.

Reveta Bowers is serving her 39th year as the head of school at The Center for Early Education, an urban preschool through sixth grade independent school in Los Angeles with 539 students. Devoted to children and education, Reveta has served on a number of boards and is currently board chair of the California Community Foundation, past president and now secretary of The Educational Records Bureau, and a member of the Advisory Board to the Klingenstein Center at Teachers College. She served on the board of the Walt Disney Company for 10 years, on many school boards, and on those of the Council for Spiritual and Ethical Education and the National Association of Principals of Schools for Girls. She served as a trustee and treasurer of the NAIS Board of Trustees and as past president of the California Association of Independent Schools. For the past 10 years, she has also been on the faculty of the NAIS Institute for New Heads. She has had a long and rewarding career in independent schools and finds her work with parents and young children to be continually satisfying.

Bodie Brizendine has served in independent schools all of her professional career and in 2007 became the 14th head of school at The Spence School, an all-girls K-12 school in New York City. She was head of school at Marin Academy from 1995 to 2007. Before that, she held senior administrative positions at San Francisco University High School and The Bryn Mawr School for Girls in Baltimore.

Throughout her 31 years in education, she has taught English. Bodie holds a B.S. from Towson State University and a master of liberal arts from The Johns Hopkins University.

Abigail P. Browning, a graduate of Summit School, the first independent school in Winston-Salem, North Carolina, has always had a keen interest in education. After receiving her B.A. from Vanderbilt University, she owned a business and taught dance in Nashville, Tennessee, for two years before moving to Washington, DC. In the nation's capital, she worked as the executive assistant to the head of school and facilities coordinator at Sidwell Friends School for two years under co-writer and former head Bruce Stewart and interim head Stephen Barker. In addition to her administrative duties at Sidwell Friends, she was active as a soccer coach and summer program dance teacher and in community programs.

Carolyn Chandler, now serving her fifth year as head of school at Metairie Park Country Day School in New Orleans, was assistant head of school and then associate head of school at Country Day in the three years prior to her post-Katrina appointment as head. For 19 years, she taught mathematics and did administrative work as director of studies at Girls Preparatory School in Chattanooga, Tennessee. Carolyn taught English and French in a public school in Chattanooga before entering the independent school world. The mother of two grown sons, she now joyfully dotes on her small grandsons, Orrin Heath Chandler and Paul Quentin Chandler.

Norman Colb has served as head of Menlo School in Atherton, California, since 1993. He began his career in the Brookline (MA) public schools, first as a teacher of English and then as the district's director of English and language arts. From 1978 to 1983, he served in the Newton (MA) public schools as the assistant superintendent for curriculum and instruction. For the 10 years before coming to Menlo, he was the superintendent of schools in the Mamaroneck (NY) public schools. Norm received a B.A. from Brandeis University in 1964 and an M.A.T. from Harvard University in 1965.

Joseph Cox, headmaster of The Haverford School, Haverford, PA, since 1998, is president of the Pennsylvania Association of Independent Schools and secretary of the International Boys' School Coalition. An adjunct professor in the University of Pennsylvania Graduate School of Education, he holds an M.A. and Ph.D. from the University of North Carolina at Chapel Hill. With degrees in 19th Century American Literature and Southern Literature, he is the author of several books. He has also taught English and writing at the U.S. Military Academy and the Dwight D. Eisenhower Graduate Studies in Leader Development.

Jack Creeden was a head of school for 15 years, first at Fountain Valley School of Colorado and recently at Providence Day School in Charlotte, North Carolina. He is vice president of the Board of Trustees of NAIS and serves as a member of the National Commission on Accreditation.

Katherine Dinh is the head of Prospect Sierra School, a K-8 school in El Cerrito, California. She has spent 13 years in independent schools, working as an English teacher, department chair, division head, and head. She was co-founder and teacher at The Academy of the Pacific Rim School, a premier charter school in a suburb of Boston, which opened in 1997. Just prior to becoming head of Prospect Sierra, she was principal of Middle and Upper Schools at Metairie Park Country Day School in Louisiana, which was significantly impacted by Hurricane Katrina. Living in Houston temporarily in the aftermath of Katrina, Katherine founded and directed the New Orleans Academy of Houston (NOAH), a pre-K-8 school for students displaced by Hurricanes Katrina and Rita. Katherine holds a bachelor's degree in English from the University of Virginia and a master's in international education from Harvard University. She serves on a number of boards, including the NAIS board. She lives in Marin County with her husband Woody Price, head of The Branson School, and their son Henry. She enjoys food that she doesn't cook and is a novice triathlete.

Vincent W. Durnan, Jr., is director of the University School of Nashville in Nashville, Tennessee, a K-12 school with 1,025 students. Vince worked as a teacher, coach, and administrator at schools in California, Connecticut, and Hawaii before coming to University School of Nashville in 2000. During the past 10 years, his responsibilities have included leading by example 14 administrators (who wear different hats) covering all phases of school operation. He is also continuing work on his dissertation to complete a doctorate in leadership, policy, and organization at Peabody College of Vanderbilt University.

Ilana Kaufman, head of Windrush School in El Cerrito, California, is a longtime leader and teacher in progressive Bay Area independent schools. Ilana has served as an accreditation visiting team member and chair for the California Association of Independent Schools/Western Association of Schools and Colleges. She has attended the Harvard Graduate School of Education, Programs in Professional Education, and is a founding and longtime faculty member of the National Association of Independent Schools/California Association of Independent Schools Developing and Mentoring Leaders of Color seminars. She serves on the board of the California Association of Independent Schools and has specific expertise in organizational and leadership development, multicultural and global education, organizational finance, strategic planning, and environmental stewardship and sustainable design.

Mike Murphy is headmaster at Shorecrest Preparatory School in St. Petersburg, Florida. Mike is married to Robin Murphy, an Arbonne consultant who is also organizing a book on table settings and menus for entertaining. Mike and Robin have reached the empty-nest stage of life. Mike's oldest son, Matt, is a bartender in Georgetown (Washington, DC) and is seeking a career in nonprofit environmental law. Robin's oldest son, Ryan, will complete a master's in mechanical engineering at the University of Central Florida in May. Andy, the youngest of the boys, is a computer graphics major at Valencia Junior College. When not at school, Mike is an avid sports fan. Kayaking, biking, running, birding, and reading continue to be his favorite pastimes. "Pathways to Headship" in Chapter 4 is his professional biography.

Jim Power is in his seventh year as head (principal) at Upper Canada College, a K-12 boys school in Toronto. Before moving to Canada, Jim served as head at Georgetown Prep for 11 years. A former English teacher, Jim earned an Ed.D. in educational leadership with a focus on character development. He and his wife, Mary, have five children.

Fran Norris Scoble has spent over 40 years in education as both teacher and administrator. She has been an independent school administrator for over 30 years, and she was head of Westridge School in Pasadena, California, for 18 years. She has served on national boards, including that of NAIS, and has led numerous workshops for teachers and administrators. Following her retirement as head of Westridge in 2008, Fran has continued her commitment to effective leadership in schools as a leadership coach and consultant to boards of trustees. She finds her new life as coach and consultant deeply satisfying and looks back on her retirement from heading Westridge as a well-timed completion of an exhilarating and rewarding life chapter.

Marcia Prewitt Spiller is in her 21st year as head of The Children's School in Atlanta, Georgia. Currently, Marcia serves as chair of the board of NAIS. She is also on the board of directors of the Southern Association of Independent Schools (SAIS) and the Elementary School Heads Association (ESHA). Marcia conducts seminars and workshops on diversity, multicultural curriculum, and teacher training. She also works with the Southern Association of Colleges and Schools (SACS) and SAIS to accredit independent schools in the southern region and Latin America.

Bruce B. Stewart served as head of school at Sidwell Friends School, Washington, DC, from 1998 until his retirement in June 2009. He received an A.B. in economics from Guilford College and an Ed.M. from the University of North Carolina at Chapel Hill. He served as dean of student affairs at North Carolina School for the Arts; director of admissions, director of the Honors Program, assistant to the president, acting academic dean, acting president, and provost of Guilford College in Greensboro, and was head of Abington Friends School in Pennsylvania for 14 years. Currently retired, he is married to Andra Jurist and has three daughters and three grandsons. He serves on the boards of School Year Abroad, NAIS, and the Leon H. Sullivan Foundation.

Amada Torres is the director of academic research at NAIS. In this capacity, she conducts original research and produces reports on national studies of interest to NAIS schools. Prior to joining the NAIS staff in February 2005, Amada was senior manager for the Latin American and Iberian Peninsula Group of the Corporate Executive Board, a membership-based provider of best practices research and analysis. From 1993 to 1998, she worked as an economic consultant in the Office of External Debt with the Ministry of Economy and Finance of Peru. Amada holds a bachelor's degree in economics from the Universidad del Pacífico in Lima, Peru. She was awarded the prestigious Chevening Scholarship to pursue a master's degree in finance and business economics at the University of Essex in the United Kingdom, where she graduated with highest honors.

Andrew T. Watson is completing his 10th year as head of school at Albuquerque Academy after starting his independent school career at Fountain Valley School in Colorado Springs and then serving as upper school head of Potomac School in McLean, Virginia. A native of Ohio, he completed undergraduate work at the Ohio State University before earning his master's degree at Yale University. He states that his fascination with and enjoyment of the head of school's role is due to the caring, creative, and open atmosphere of Albuquerque Academy and to the outstanding colleagues and board members he has worked with throughout independent education, particularly the dear friends in each of his refreshingly different, but similarly life-changing, schools.

D. Scott Wiggins is currently in his eighth year as head of school at Lawrence Academy in Groton, Massachusetts. Scott's career has included service in five different independent schools as a teacher, coach, and administrator, punctuated by law school and a five-year term as a criminal prosecutor along the way. Scott's biography is covered in detail in "Nontraditional Paths to Headship" in Chapter 4.